Praise for *Connecting to Change the World: Harnessing the Power of Networks for Social Impact*

Provides the frameworks, practical advice, case studies, and expert knowledge needed to build better performing social-impact networks.

HARNESSING THE POWER OF
NETWORKS FOR SOCIAL IMPACT

CONNECTING
TO CHANGE THE
WORLD

PETER PLASTRIK
MADELEINE TAYLOR
JOHN CLEVELAND

"Provides social entrepreneurs with a powerful new tool for organizing change—the creation of generating networks that empower and unleash the complementary energies of large numbers of independent and interdependent actors."

—**Bob Friedman**, *Founder, Prosperity Now*

"A thoughtful and practical work that can help anyone looking to harness the power of networks in service of social change. The book sheds light on fundamental questions one must ask when trying to understand how and when a network might help you achieve your goals."

— **Faizal Karmali**, *former Associate Director, Innovation & Networks, The Rockefeller Foundation*

"Offers inspiration and hands-on know-how to changemakers looking to further their impact by building networks for action. Whether you're a social entrepreneur, a nonprofit executive, a funder, or a grassroots activist, you'll find strategies, tools, and cases that you can use to power your vision as well as your everyday work."

— **Kathy Reich**, *former director of organizational effectiveness grantmaking, Packard Foundation*

"Chock full of advice and hard-won lessons from the frontiers of today's net-centric innovations. This is required reading for social change makers who are coming to understand that there is an art, a science and a discipline essential to design, develop, maintain, sustain and grow powerful networks."

— **Sterling Speirn**, *former President and CEO, W. K. Kellogg Foundation*

Available at https://islandpress.org/books/connecting-change-world (for discount, enter Plastrik) or at Amazon.com

D1523680

Praise for *Life After Carbon: The Next Global Transformation of Cities*

24 Cities. Hundreds of Climate-Change Innovation. Urban Transformation. Four big new ideas are replacing the failing concepts that built the modern city. Cities leading on climate innovation are converting climate disaster into urban opportunity and shaping a worldwide transformation that affects billions of people.

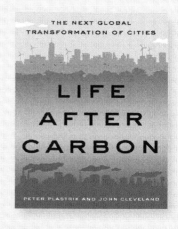

"*Life After Carbon* presents an inspiring account of actual urban change that could not have been written just 10 years ago; there simply wasn't enough going on then. It is compelling reading for local government leaders everywhere...If your council is considering declaring a climate emergency and getting in on this action, I urge you to pick up a copy of this book to see what other cities are doing and how they're doing it."

— **Sadhu Aufochs Johnston**, *former city manager, Vancouver*

"*Life After Carbon* is a vivid and multifaceted look at the cities leading the global transition to a post-carbon world. Drawing insight from and connections among the communities at the forefront of urban climate innovation, Plastrik and Cleveland chart much-needed and promising pathways into the future."

— **Edward Mazria**, *Architecture 2030*

"Plastrik and Cleveland give readers nothing less than a new and compelling vision for what cities could be: carbon-free, climate adaptive, biophilic and nature-rich, with restorative closed-loop metabolisms, and, of course, wonderful places in which to live. Together these stories, ideas, and emerging practices chart an optimistic urban future. Life After Carbon is an essential resource for planners, mayors, and citizens (all of us) with a vested interest in accelerating this future."

— **Timothy Beatley**, *Teresa Heinz Professor of Sustainable Communities at the School of Architecture at the University of Virginia*

Available at https://islandpress.org/books/connecting-change-world (for discount, enter Plastrik) or at Amazon.com

In Harm's Way: How Communities Are Addressing Key Challenges of Building Climate Resilience

In Harm's Way builds on reports by the Innovation Network for Communities, with new chapters and updates about increasing climate resilience at the local level. Contents include:

- Essential Capacities for Urban Climate Adaptation
- Playbook 1.0: How Cities Are Paying for Climate Resilience
- How State Governments Can Help Communities Invest In Climate Resilience
- Can It Happen Here? Improving the Prospects for Managed Retreat by US Cities

"John Cleveland and Peter Plastrik bring a unique outside-inside perspective to all their work—looking across multiple cities and systems to understand how to build the practice of resilience, the challenges of changing governance models, and the funding cycles and mechanisms which all work adheres to—whether we realize it or not. In Harm's Way was born as a guide for governments and practitioners to gain the clearest understanding of how to plan and finance climate adaptation projects in ways that are equitable and implementable."

— **Amy Chester**, *Rebuild By Design*

Available at Amazon.com

Welcome to the Edge of Chaos: Where Change is a Way of Life

We spent two years immersing ourselves in complex adaptive systems theory in the hope that Mother Nature's rules for evolution could teach us something useful about how to help organizations take advantage of turbulence to evolve and take themselves to the next level of innovation and impact. The insights of complexity theory turn out to be an excellent guide to the transformative re-design of human institutions like organizations and communities.

"We are moving quickly to the edge of chaos in many profound and critical ways. Some would say we are already tumbling over the precipice, taking so much precious life, and so many life support systems, with us. But *Welcome to the Edge of Chaos* presents a counter-analysis that says the edge should be welcomed, indeed embraced as a time that can and will unleash extraordinary creativity and innovation in the ways we live and work. . . . The authors posit that, at times of disequilibrium, there are always individuals in a 'spiral dance' at the edge—one foot in the old, one in the new, experimenting and creating emergent patterns of productive, tangible, and successful work."

— **Spencer Beebe**, *Salmon Nation*

Available at Amazon.com

Visit us online at www.networkimpact.org and www.in4c.net

Book design by Carol Maglitta, One Visual Mind

CONNECT > INNOVATE > SCALE UP

How Networks Create
Systems Change

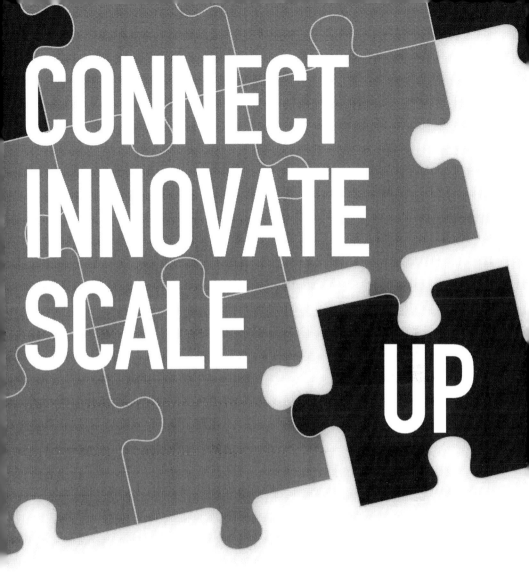

CONNECT INNOVATE SCALE UP

How Networks Create Systems Change

Peter Plastrik
Madeleine Taylor
John Cleveland

FROM THE
AUTHORS OF
*CONNECTING
TO CHANGE
THE WORLD*

Table of Contents

Dramatis Personae   8

Introduction   11

1: Networks Seeking Large-Scale Impact   **23**

Water Equity   25

Tuition-Free College   32

Talent Supply Management   36

Newsroom Communities   41

A Maze of Choices   45

Networks & Seeking Scale   49

2: Targeting Systems for Change   **53**

Leveraging Systems   54

The Power of Mindset Change   57

Wading Into a System   58

Approaches to System Change   61

The Adversarial Approach   64

The Alternative Approach   65

The Authority Approach   68

Understanding Systems   70

Lived Experience   73

Networks & Systems Change   78

3: Developing Social Innovations   **83**

Types of Social Innovations   85

Key Features of System-Changing Innovations   88

Stages of Innovation Development   90

Concept Stage: Making an Innovation Hypothesis   93

Prototyping Stage: Designing and Testing   100

Operations Stage: Managing and Implementing   104

Scaling Stage: Pathways to Scale   109

Networks & Social Innovation Development   111

4: Taking Pathways to Scale   **115**

Green Buildings   116

Scales and Levels   119

Jumping Scales   125

Pathways to Scale   126

Taking New Products and Services to Markets   128

Growing New Practices in Fields   134

Persuading Governments to Adopt Policies   143

Innovation Adoption   146

Morphing Networks   149

Network & Pathways to Scale   151

5: Designing Networks of Networks   **155**

Networks of Networks   157

Network Structures   166

Strategic Hubs   168

Distributed Control   172

Toward An Ecosystem   176

Networks & Structural Design   178

6: Leading Social Innovation Networks   **183**

Innovation Broker   186

Network Weaver   188

Trusted Strategist   191

Story Teller   196

Leaders as Learners   199

Networks & Balanced Leadership   200

CODA: The Long Arc of Systems Change   **205**

Gratitude   209

Notes   213

Resources   229

Appendices   235

About the Authors   241

Index   243

For Alvaro, Chinwe, Janet, Juan, Keith, Margaret, and Richard—
sharing our dreams and work, inspiring and generous in your guidance

—

For Anne and Amanda—friends and comrades
on the network path

The world doesn't change one person at a time. It changes as networks of relationships form among people who discover they share a common cause and vision of what's possible.

— Margaret J. Wheatley

Relationships move at the speed of trust, and social change moves at the speed of relationships.

— Rev. Jennifer Bailey
(Faith Matters Network)

History tells us that innovation is an outcome of a massive collective effort—not just from a narrow group of young white men in California.

— Mariana Mazzucato

Dramatis Personae

Leaders/funders of social innovation networks appearing in
Connect > Innovate > Scale Up

Spencer B. Beebe
Salmon Nation

Scott Bernstein
Center for
Neighborhood
Technology
(formerly)

Dana Bourland
The JPB Foundation

Gary Cohen
Health Care
Without Harm

Jennie Curtis
Garfield Foundation
(formerly)

Radhika Fox
US Water Alliance
(formerly)

Bob Friedman
Individual
Development
Accounts

Bill Guest
Talent Innovation
Network of
West Michigan

Mami Hara
US Water Alliance

Chrystie Hill
Gates Foundation

Asima Jansveld
High Line Network

**Sandhya
Kambhampati**
OpenNews

Sarah Klaus
Open Society
Foundations
(formerly)

Katy Lackey
US Water Alliance

Luis Lugo
Doug and Maria
DeVos Foundation

Oluwole A. (OJ) McFoy
Buffalo Sewer Authority

Lisa Mensah
Opportunity Finance
Network

Mauricio Lim Miller
Community
Independence
Initiative

Anne Mosle
Ascend at the
Aspen Institute

Shweta Narayan
Health Care
Without Harm

Erika Owens
OpenNews

Johanna Partin
Carbon Neutral
Cities Alliance
(formerly)

Olivia Roanhorse
Roanhorse
Consulting

Doug Ross
Campaign for Free
College Tuition

Emily Simonson
US Water Alliance

Marjorie Sims
Ascend at the
Aspen Institute

Jennifer Tescher
Financial Health
Network

Maggie Ullman
Network building
consultant

Sisi Wei
OpenNews

Karen Weigert
US Green Building
Council

Ben Welsh
Los Angeles Times

Morley Winograd
Campaign for Free
College Tuition

Jeff Yost
Nebraska Community
Foundation

Introduction

The story in which you believe shapes the society that you create.
Yuval Noah Harari

This book tells many stories about people who are changing the world for the better. Dozens of stories about social innovation networks, shared by the founders, managers, members, and funders doing the nitty-gritty work. Stories about connecting, innovating, and scaling up innovations to transform the innumerable systems that are failing us at home, nationally, and globally. Stories of collaborations that play out over decades, requiring endless adaption by their practitioners.

It also tells a story of know-how—the growing body of practical knowledge and skills that network-building innovators have learned by doing. We, your coauthors, have created this story as a set of frameworks filled with how-to insights and lessons. We synthesized these understandings from across dozens of cases and our own experiences in network building and social innovation development, as well as many other sources of expertise. The frameworks illuminate choices, problems, and opportunities that innovation networks typically face, especially how to take innovations to scale. They provide ways of thinking and advice that you can use and customize to your own situation.

Your story is here, too. It's the story of the future you—someone who we hope gets even better and more resilient, goes even faster and further, at making a big difference. Whether you're starting an innovation-making network, or in mid passage with one, or taking your second, third, or umpteenth shot at social innovation—you will find inspiration and guidance in the pages that follow. You may also find a sense of camaraderie, of belonging, with the dozens of social innovation network entrepreneurs you meet here.

Ultimately, though, this book contains just one overarching story: the world must be changed and a powerful and proven way to change it is through connecting, innovating, and scaling up.

Eight years ago, we published *Connecting to Change the World: Harnessing the Power of Networks for Social Impact*, showing how people the world over were forming networks, instead of organizations, to foster social change. We call these *generative social-impact networks*—groups of individuals or organizations seeking to solve a difficult problem in society by working together, adapting over time, and generating a sustained flow of activities and impacts. The networks' members forge powerful, enduring personal relationships based on trust and reciprocity; they link to form a unique and renewable capacity—a network—that can have large-scale impact.

Connect > Innovate > Scale Up has a different focus. We step into the particular terrain of networks designed and managed to achieve system change by developing and scaling up social innovations. This is remarkably fertile soil, a global seedbed for growing transformative change. But it is also an uneven and mostly uncharted landscape; one's footing can be shaky and direction can be uncertain. What does this important, but tricky, work look like, how is it done?

We have lived and worked in this territory for several decades, and visited with and learned from many of the pioneers who are in these pages. Reflecting on these experiences led us to develop explanatory frameworks about the five topics at the core of this book. (Each topic is the subject of a single chapter.)

- **Systems change.** What approaches can social innovators take? What are the most powerful levers they can use?

- **Social innovation development.** What types of scalable social innovations can innovators develop, and which innovation-development processes do they use?

- **Scaling pathways.** What types of scale can social innovators target and what are the pathways they can follow to scale?

- **Social innovation network design.** What network models can social innovators design, implement, and evolve to ensure their innovations gain traction and scale?

- **Network leadership.** What unique roles must social innovators play to most effectively guide social innovation networks?

Our insights are grounded in the practical experiences of dozens of social innovation networks with which we have consulted and partnered closely in the past few years. These collaborations have targeted a range of systems for radical change: affordable housing, college financing, community development, energy supply, financial services, health care, higher education, human services, the journalism profession, water management, workforce development, and more. Most have been operating for many years, even decades—a typical timespan for reaching significant scale. The great majority are focused on systems in the US, but several operate internationally.

Networks Rule

Social innovation is the key to making big, intentional, and equitable social, economic, and environmental changes in our troubled world. This transformational role is not new. "In the long story of human history," explains social innovator Michael Sherraden, a sociologist who directs the Center for Social Development at Washington University, "massive social innovations have created conditions that make technological and economic advancements possible. Not the other way around." Today, much of the attention on innovation is on technological and business innovation, especially digital products and services. These have social impacts, of course, but they are mostly driven by profit-seeking motives and rarely have systemic social impacts.

Social innovations reach for a higher bar. They must be, as the *Stanford Social Innovation Review* spells out, "more effective, efficient, sustainable or just than existing solutions." The value they create must accrue "primarily to society as a whole rather than private individuals." They seek social impact by targeting human needs, not just consumer desires. They use financial returns to achieve social impact, not private profit. And they dramatically affect the performance of big systems.

Networks are the way that social innovation happens. This is not widely recognized. Instead, we are usually told that "lone genius" inventors supply innovations to the rest of us. Look closely, though, and you'll see that behind successful innovations there are networks, not single individuals. That's what Andrew Hargadon, a professor of innovation and entrepreneurship, discovered when he studied numerous well-known innovations. He uses the example of Thomas Edison, developer of the electric light bulb, phonograph, and other devices, to illustrate this. Edison "did more than perhaps anyone else to fix in our minds the notion that innovation is the province of the creative genius and his or her inventions," Hargadon says in his book *How Breakthroughs Happen: The Surprising Truth About How Companies Innovate*. But, he continues, Edison "was neither that heroic, that imaginative, nor that alone." He "didn't invent the electric light, but he brought together previously disparate people, ideas, and objects from his network of past wanderings in a way that launched a revolution."

It's not just Edison who didn't innovate alone. Successful innovations, Hargadon concludes, are usually accomplished by networks of people: "In contrast to lone inventors, communities draw other actors, objects and ideas together into tight knit networks, where people's roles become clear and interdependent . . . where ideas become shared organizing principles."

Another study of innovation also uncovered its communal nature. Innovators seeking new ideas depend on engaging with other people, report the authors of *The Innovator's DNA: Mastering the Five Skills of Disruptive Innovators*, a fascinating study of business entrepreneurs based on surveys and interviews. "Innovators gain a radically different perspective when they devote time and energy to finding and testing ideas through a network of diverse individuals."

Network building is also a defining characteristic of the many social entrepreneurs who are widely celebrated as change-making leaders. "The world's leading social entrepreneurs are not innovators working in isolation," says Anamaria Schindler, former global co-president for Ashoka, which has elevated and supported leadership by social entrepreneurs for four decades. "Their success depends on creating roles for other people to step up and lead change and further spread solutions."

Although social innovation is a collective activity, it's not the same thing as a mass movement. Movements are the demand side of social innovation. They can be a necessary condition for inspiring deep-seated changes in some systems. Black Lives Matter, #MeToo, the Navalny-sparked protests across Russia, the global climate emergency, LGBTQ rights: these and other movements surge into existence demanding vital changes and commanding public attention and the streets. A movement's ideals, such as racial justice, can inspire, inform, and activate millions of people. "Social movements challenge existing power relations, cultural beliefs, and practice through sustained public activism and demonstrations," notes a Frameworks Institute analysis. They "can provoke a more serious reconsideration of an existing way of thinking about the world."

But movements alone are usually insufficient for making fundamental, wide-spread change happen. They need networks of people to develop detailed changes—innovative policies, practices, services, and the like—and ensure that they are widely incorporated into systems.

It turns out that networks are essential for the creation of large-scale social change. They convert the impatient aspirations of movements into a flow of promising social innovations. And they are used by leading change advocates—network entrepreneurs—to assemble and harness the combinations of skills, perspectives, and resources needed to make large-scale impact. The true superpower of most social innovators is their ability to mobilize networks of people and organizations to create and implement novel and potent solutions to social problems.

Drivers of Collaboration

Social innovation networks are everywhere now. People are starting networks to develop, implement, and spread innumerable innovations. "Social innovation has moved from an emergent field to become a global phenomenon," note Kriss Deiglmeier, former head of Stanford University's Center for Social Innovation, and Amanda Greco. Although these networks operate openly, most are off the radar screens of the media and established institutions. They have proliferated, but no one knows how many of them there are, and few people are involved in more than a handful of them. There is no inventory of the array of social innovations they are producing.

Social innovation networks play out an inspiring drama: courageous changemakers with modest resources band together to take on large, seemingly unmovable systems. "There has been a shift in the previous two decades which were more focused on the role of individuals (social entrepreneurs) and organizations," Leslie Crutchfield and Heather McLeod Grant report in *Forces for Good: The Six Practices of High-Impact Nonprofits*. "Now the focus is on larger networks, ecosystems, and collective impact." There are several reasons for this shift.

Focus on systems change. The ambition to instigate change of entire systems—the world's health care systems, for example, not just a single hospital, or a nation's water system, not just a single city's water utility—leads to the recognition that it takes many people and organizations, aligned in purpose and methods, to leverage change at that scale. This awareness is growing in the government, nonprofit, and philanthropic sectors.

"Leaders who will succeed in the coming years will recognize that some problems are too big to solve alone," says Diana Aviv, CEO of Partnership for American Democracy. "They will participate in meaningful collaborations that maximize the assets of multiple organizations, deepen the group's collective knowledge, and move together in ways that also fulfill individual missions."

The challenge of instigating systemic change is driving the growth of collaborations, say leaders of The Bridgespan Group, a global nonprofit that advises change leaders: "Funders and nonprofits increasingly recognize that no single organization or strategy, regardless of how large or successful it may be, can solve a complex social challenge at scale." Barbara Picower, president and chair of the board of one of the largest philanthropies in the US, highlights the importance of this reason for investing in networks: "It has become clear to us at The JPB Foundation that complex social issues like poverty cannot be solved by single grantees working alone. Instead, we have found that we can help them proceed faster and further in their missions when we take a 'hub and network' approach to funding."

The push to change systems is further boosted by growing efforts to address inequities produced by social and economic systems. "There are inequities at every level of systems change that must be recognized and addressed," observe John Kania and Mark Kramer, developers of the collective impact approach, and Peter Senge, a prominent systems scientist, in "The Water of Systems Change." Addressing inequities calls for deep, all-encompassing system transformation that embraces people and ideas that have been kept outside of the mainstream for generations. As Edgar Villanueva writes in *Decolonizing Wealth: Indigenous Wisdom to Heal Divides and Restore Balance*, "All of us who have been forced to the margins are the very ones who harbor the best solutions for healing, progress, and peace, by virtue of our outsider perspectives and resilience. When we reclaim our share of resources, when we recover our places at the table and the drawing board, we can design our healing."

Emergence of digital power. The rise of digital technologies—including smart software, big data, cloud computing, social media, and mobile apps—enables long-distance, distributed, instant connectivity among people and provides them with new tools for collaborating to address social problems. It's much easier now for people to connect and stay connected with lots of other people and to collaborate across great distances. "For the first time in history it is possible, without ever leaving your home, to use technology to find a network of hundreds of thousands of workers who wake up every day and ask themselves the same questions you ask," says Sara Horowitz, founder of the Freelancers Union, in *Mutualism: Building the Next Economy from the Ground Up*. It's not just ideas that are supported by these digital technologies; services are also being redesigned to take advantage of them. In the United Kingdom an app called Good SAM alerts more than 25,000 volunteers—off-duty doctors, nurses, paramedics, and first responders—when someone nearby has a life-threatening medical crisis. The proliferation of mobile financial services is increasing access to capital for people with low incomes. Social-media platforms and other digital tools are transforming political campaigns and civic activism, notes sociologist Dana Fisher in *American Resistance*, by supporting bottom-up, geographically diffuse organizing and the formation of loosely affiliated networks that mobilize and connect people. Crowdsourcing, which uses online tools to enable any participant to submit an idea to solve a specific problem, is expanding the innovation capabilities of foundations, suggest Kiko Suarez, vice president of communications and innovation at Lumina Foundation, and

Alph Bingham, a cofounder of InnoCentive. In Germany, for instance, a digital platform, #WirVsVirus, engaged 28,000 citizens in a 48-hour hackathon to develop ideas about how to address Covid pandemic challenges.

Resistance to business as usual. A widespread distrust of top-down, centralized institutions and organizations—and awareness of their limitations and failures—inspires the exploration of alternative models for taking action. This is especially true for younger generations, as columnist David Brooks points out: "The emerging generations today . . . grew up in a world in which institutions failed, financial systems collapsed, and families were fragile. Children can now expect to have a lower quality of life than their parents, the pandemic rages, climate change looms, and social media is vicious. Their worldview is predicated on threat, not safety."

Journalist Ezra Klein points to this generational shift in US federal policy realms: "Washington is run by 20- and 30-somethings who run the numbers, draft the bills, brief the principals. And there is a marked difference between staffers and even the politicians whose formative years were defined by stagflation, the rise of Reaganism and the relief of the Clinton boom, and those who came of age during financial crises, skyrocketing personal debt, racial reckonings and the climate emergency. . . . In general, the younger generation has sharply different views on the role of government, the worth of markets and the risks worth taking seriously."

A majority of young foundation staff, according to a 2018 report, feel their institutions are not in touch with the needs of the communities they support and nearly three-quarters say the communities they serve do not have a voice in decision making.

"There is a generational shift in America toward increasing justice and collective responsibility," argues Malia Lazu, a lecturer at MIT's Sloan School of Management. Younger generations, especially Millennials, embrace a culture of collective action, which resonates with the inherent communality of networks.

Barriers to Scale

Even though social innovation networks are proliferating, it's commonly said that they rarely achieve impact at scale. "Despite scale being a large focus of conversations, blogs, articles, and conferences, the do-good industry is still failing to bring the rigor and depth needed to make the desired impacts on social issues," declares Greg Coussa, founder of Spring Impact, an organization that helps social ventures scale up. A typical observation comes from a trio of leaders of IDEO, the global design consultancy that a decade ago introduced the design-thinking approach to the social sector: "While many social-impact design efforts over the past decade have demonstrated innovation in tackling social challenges, far fewer have demonstrated change at scale." In a two-year study of how nonprofits, philanthropists, and community groups increasingly engage in cocreation—open innovation, design competitions, crowdsourcing and other approaches—scholars Joanna Levitt Cea and Jess Rimington conclude that "few of the results lead to system change or profoundly shake up what is considered possible."

Innovation networks seeking big social change face daunting obstacles to success. They must convert their audacious goals and ideas into actual innovations. They must test the innovations they've designed and then revise them according to the real-world feedback received. And, of course, they must meet the challenge of implementing innovations at scale. Along the way to success, networks will likely have to address the skepticism, indifference, and opposition of or competition from other people and organizations. They will have difficulty raising money and encounter problems making their ideas and strategies work well.

Many social innovations fall into a "'stagnation chasm,' where proven ideas get stuck before they are able to maximize their impact," observe Deiglmeier and Greco. Their research identified three barriers that block scaling up: inadequate funds for growth, even as the costs of getting to scale increase; the complexities of managing multi-sector collaborations that are often needed for social innovation scaling; and the difficulties of attracting and retaining the functional and technical expertise to broker innovation development. There's an additional barrier, identified by Heather McLeod Grant, cofounder of Open Impact and an expert in network building: local nonprofits, she observes, "often don't have enough power or resources to take on larger systemic issues by themselves. . . . working in silos [keeps] them from tackling more complex, systemic issues."

Networks that overcome these high hurdles may yet stumble when it comes to scaling up what they have created. It's more than likely they will have to persist for many years—even decades. There are few shortcuts on the road to social impact.

Knowing about and experiencing these challenges doesn't stop people from trying. Their personal passion for the change they want is too compelling to set aside. This powerful desire is the starting point of most social innovation networks: people connect and align with each other around a motivating goal for change, creating a collective pool of skills, knowledge, creativity, and other capacities. But beginning a social innovation network journey doesn't necessarily prepare you for what awaits along the rest of the way.

Filling the Know-How Gap

Knowledge about what social innovation networks do and how they do it, and especially how they reach high-scale impact, is not exactly well-developed and broadly shared. "Surprisingly little is known about social innovation compared to the vast amount of research into innovation in business and science," is how the Young Foundation put it some years ago, noting a "lack of reliable knowledge about common success factors and inhibitors." More recently, scholars Christian Seelos and Johanna Mair report little improvement in the situation: "Research on the role of social innovation or how social enterprises actually innovate has been scarce. The lack of a shared understanding prevents learning, accumulation of knowledge, and consistent decisions."

But developers of networks for social innovation do not have to work in a knowledge vacuum. With so many of us working in networked ways, a body of know-how is constantly being created and expanded, at least implicitly.

Connect > Innovate > Scale Up provides the founders, members, managers, and funders of social innovation networks with a great deal of what is known about what has worked in many contexts and how to apply it. What to know about navigating through the twists and turns that are characteristic of the social innovation journeys taken by networks. How to achieve scale.

Below is a list of the networks whose stories are included in these pages. (Full disclosure: networks marked with an * have at some time contracted with one or more of the coauthors for consulting and evaluation services; see end note for details). Although some of these networks have become formal organizations, such as nonprofit corporations, they are mostly made up of webs of people—groups of the like-minded—that expand, shrink, and morph as they connect, align, and collaborate to achieve social impact. We gradually introduce the networks throughout the book—four in chapter 1, several more in chapter 2, and so on—and then draw on all of them to illustrate framework themes and advice for practitioners.

Networked innovation involves many people, but the network stories we tell present just a few of the countless network entrepreneurs who are involved. This efficiency in story telling should not be taken to undercut the theme of collaboration; indeed, many of these innovators emphasize to us that "it's not just me, it's the network!"

- Ascend at the Aspen Institute*
- Biophilic Cities Network*
- Campaign for Free College Tuition*
- Carbon Neutral Cities Alliance* (global)
- Community Independence Initiative
- Energy Efficiency for All*
- Financial Health Network*
- Good SAM
- Health Care Without Harm* (global)
- High Line Network
- Individual Development Accounts (networks of networks)
- International Step by Step Association (Europe and Central Asia)
- Nebraska Community Foundation*
- OpenNews*

- Opportunity Finance Network
- Project ECHO (global)
- RE-AMP*
- Salmon Nation*
- Talent Innovation Network of West Michigan*
- US Green Building Council (LEED)
- US Water Alliance*

Our collaborations, reflection, and research into the insights of many others in the social innovation field deepened our understanding of how social innovation networks develop and succeed. They reinforced our recognition that these are complicated efforts that blend tight discipline, improvisation, and evolution. And they heightened our appreciation of the remarkable magic of social innovation. It harnesses the power of vision, creativity, and ideas, of alignment, collaboration, and grit. The power of standing together, of putting hope into practice.

Social innovation is demanding, uncertain, and prolonged work. Those of us who have chosen this work, or stumbled into it, can benefit from knowing the many lived experiences, practical knowledge, insights, and stories of other practitioners. The know-how feeds hope and confidence. It guides thought and action. Most important, it proclaims something we all want to hear: you are not alone and you can make a difference.

CHAPTER 1

Networks Seeking Large-Scale Impact

Entrepreneurs and inventors are no smarter, no more courageous, tenacious,
or rebellious than the rest of us—they are simply better connected.
Andrew Hargadon

People around the world are afire with an intense desire to change the way things are—the pervasive injustices and other ruinous failings of modern systems. There is so much to fix, but there's nothing simple about fixing it.

Many of the alarm bells that are ringing loudly signal "wicked problems" that defy easy, one-shot solutions. The Covid pandemic, food insecurity, climate change, homelessness, racial injustice, and the lack of economic mobility: despite the urgency for change, there may be great uncertainty about what the solutions are and how to implement them.

These types of problems are systemic. They have multiple, linked parts that depend on and affect each other. They require responses in which many people and organizations must change their minds and behaviors. They likely need more than one intervention, and it takes substantial resources to reach the desired scale of change. Innovators addressing these issues, note leaders at IDEO, must "adopt a more systemic lens and intentionally coordinate multiple interventions with multiple actors to create more enduring change."

In the face of wicked systemic problems, social innovation requires the courage to stand up to business as usual and to tolerate the uncertainties of achieving success. The change process needs resources—money, creativity, and time. It takes tenacity to stay on a course full of curves and surprises, a journey that may last for a decade or longer. It cannot be done without new ideas about how things could work much better, and without the skills and discipline to turn these ideas into tangible innovations that gain traction and scale. All of this can rarely be achieved without relying on networks of people and organizations.

Innovation loves company, but it's not just a matter of having a lot of people involved. It's a matter of orchestrating and catalyzing, of organizing many moving parts—people, ideas, resources, partners—and adjusting them as the innovation-making process unfolds. Networks provide unique organizing models for this work. They are built on connections, alignment, and collaboration among participants. They provide conditions critical for innovation: "blue sky" that offers room for research and idea formation; testing grounds for the necessary proofs-of-concept; real-world laboratories for prototyping and modifying inventions; and more. Networks can be highly flexible and adapted to the sequence of different innovation-development tasks and the discoveries that emerge during the process. They nurture innovators—supporting them, protecting them from opposition, challenging them to revise their vision and approach.

Networks offer enabling settings for system-changing social innovators and their efforts. But developing and scaling social innovations that transform systems most effectively depends on network leaders—founders, members, managers, and investors—recognizing, designing for, and dealing with crucial variables:

- Which system should they target for change? Which system-changing approaches should they pursue?

- Which types of social innovations should they develop? Which innovation-development processes should they use to create scalable innovations?

- Which scale should they seek and what scaling pathways should they follow?

- Which network models should they use? How should they sustain and evolve their networks?

- Which roles should network leaders play?

Taken together, these variables present social innovation networks with a complex landscape of choices and decisions as they take the journey of systems change driven by social innovation. We have worked with many networks that are navigating through this decision-terrain toward scale. Each takes its own journey, made distinct by context, personalities, and other factors. But useful patterns emerge when we look across the networks and their experiences.

This chapter describes the voyages taken by four networks that are achieving notable impacts and are striving for greater scale. We selected them because they are quite different in significant ways and thus present an initial, diverse portfolio of social innovation networks producing and scaling innovations.

- The US Water Alliance is driving equity and other community-centered practices into water systems in 28 cities and counties with more than 25 million residents.

- The Campaign for Free College Tuition is helping to advance public policy changes that now cover 25 states and 1 million college students, with much more impact on the horizon.

- The Talent Innovation Network of West Michigan is spreading its evidence-based innovation for hiring and promoting employees to businesses with roughly 90,000 jobs in one region of the US.

- OpenNews is engaging thousands of journalists in bringing crucial changes into the news media profession—elevating the voices of people of color and of technologists ready for the digital-media age.

These networks tackle different systems, create different types of social innovations, follow different pathways to scale, and develop different network models for collaboration. But, as we'll show after the story telling, their separate journeys reveal practical knowledge about how networks produce social innovations that transform systems.

Water Equity

Mami Hara is part of a small band of people striving to transform the US water industry. They work in a technical, engineering-driven sector that operates mostly in hard silos—separate entities for drinking water, stormwater, and wastewater—and focuses mainly on building and maintaining physical infrastructure and managing financial costs. The water innovators envision a radically different water system. It would help communities meet their environmental, economic, and social goals, not just provide the usual water services. It would ensure that everyone is able to access and afford water supply and services. It would secure

Mami Hara

the water system's long-term sustainability by using an integrated, rather than a siloed, approach to management of water.

While Hara was at Philadelphia Water, where she became chief of staff, she did the grunt work to set up the first annual summit, in 2011, of a new organization called the US Water Alliance. It had been created by a few water-industry people, mostly water utility managers, who wanted to talk, learn, and collaborate outside of the dominant engineering mindset—something they were not getting from the sector's professional associations. Not surprisingly, given the water industry's makeup, the Alliance's work at its inception was steered mostly by white, male utility leaders and water experts. They focused mainly on water-management issues, especially the development of a silo-busting "One Water" approach.

Much less attention was paid, however, to the larger vision for change: engaging the community in setting water system goals and addressing issues of water equity. When Hara—Japanese American, a landscape architect by training, and advocate for community-centered approaches—attended early Alliance summits, she says, "I felt like an outsider myself. It felt like a private club. I didn't feel like I had any intellectual or social home there."

Until 2016, that is. When the Alliance gathered in Atlanta that June for its 3-day annual summit, it was opening up to new, transformative possibilities. Nearly 500 people from 31 states attended—many of them community leaders, environmentalists, and racial- and economic-justice advocates from outside the water industry. Workshops included topics not usually offered to water system professionals, including "An Equitable Water Future," "Affordability and Water," and "Building the One Water Movement." The summit "was truly a watershed event," says Michael Mucha, chief engineer and director of the Madison Metropolitan

Sewerage District, an Alliance member. "It was unlike any conference I have ever attended. The diversity of attendees and topics contributed to very different conversations and brought a far deeper meaning and understanding to the work I do."

The shift to an open, collective approach began in late 2015 when the Alliance board hired a new CEO, Radhika Fox, who had extensive experience in policy development and community advocacy at San Francisco's water utility and PolicyLink, a premier institute for racial and economic equity. Fox championed a vision of the Alliance as an inclusive national network of water-system stakeholders—community organizations, environmental groups, agricultural interests, labor unions, researchers, artists and other culture bearers, as well as utilities and government agencies. This expansive diversity of participants would connect and collaborate to develop, spread, and institutionalize transformative changes. The Alliance website captures the vision succinctly: "We are driving a One Water movement—an approach to water stewardship that is innovative, inclusive, and integrated."

Radhika Fox

Fox brought the skill set needed to pull off this approach. "I remember when Radhika got the job," says Hara, who in 2016 became CEO of Seattle Public Utilities and in 2020 became chair of the Alliance board. "She is very persuasive and visionary. She expanded the profile of who was included in the Alliance's conversations. She has enormous credibility as someone who can connect across sectors and bring people in who'd never had a voice before." Fox hired staffers with the capacities, energy, and knowledge to design and implement inclusive collaborative processes. She worked to ensure a diverse and focused board of directors and to develop governance alignment around a new vision for the Alliance. "There are go-getters on this board," observes Oluwole (OJ) McFoy, general manager of the Buffalo Sewer Authority and the board vice president. "The rebuilding of the Alliance that was performed over the last few years was essential to gaining the trust of community organizations, utilities, and philanthropic organizations."

Under Fox the Alliance redesigned its annual summits into large-scale, diverse gatherings that inspired participants. Before the 2018 summit in Minneapolis, recalls Emily Simonson, the Alliance's director of strategic initiatives, the gatherings involved "a lot of people and organizations that we knew. For Minneapolis, we started thinking about the summit as a way to engage new people, bringing in everyone we could touch."

Fox also persuaded several national foundations to support new initiatives, adding financial resources to the roughly $1 million in membership dues collected annually. And she plunged into the mostly uncharted waters of water equity.

Not long before Fox joined the Alliance the Flint water crisis had become national news. The lead poisoning of water in the majority-Black city of nearly 100,000 people, 40 percent of them living in poverty, became a massive public health crisis and a national racial-justice scandal blamed on state officials' efforts to save money. Even as city residents complained about the water's color and smell and tests showed serious pollution problems, the state denied there was reason for concern. The national water sector's response was disjointed, and many leaders were silent or defensive. "Flint's story is not unique," Fox says, "but the tragedy and media attention there made a lot of people in the water sector realize we didn't have a good understanding for talking about what racial equity looks like in the context of water."

For more than a year, an Alliance team engaged more than 150 people—academics, environment and justice advocates, water-utility managers, philanthropists, tribal leaders, and other stakeholders—in discussions about ways to make water management processes and outcomes equitable. "It was a collaborative conversation," says Simonson, hired by Fox after working on urban water

Emily Simonson

issues at the US Environmental Protection Agency. "We wanted to connect all the different aspects of how equity shows up in the water space, showing that they are all part of the same story. We wanted to show who was doing what, what the bright spots were. That way you start to see the cracks in the system and where smaller interventions might add up."

The Alliance developed a definitive 64-page briefing paper, "An Equitable Water Future," released in 2017 and disseminated throughout the water sector. "As a nation, we face multiple water resource challenges," it declared, citing a lack of access to safe, reliable drinking water, decaying water infrastructure, and more. "Those most affected are often lower-income people, communities of color, children, and the elderly, among others. The impacts of water stress on physical and mental health, child development, and economic mobility are cumulative." The report identifies new practices, backed up with actual examples, that local water utilities can use to create social, economic, and environmental benefits for everyone.

With the equity framework in hand, learning teams in seven cities—made up of water utilities, community leaders, environmental advocates, and other stakeholders facilitated by Alliance staff—wrestled with how to apply what was being learned. They launched new efforts to make water services affordable and accessible and to create economic opportunities, while promoting new dialogue and understandings among stakeholders. "Every aspect of running a water utility is an opportunity to advance equity," notes Simonson. "The teams prioritized based on what was urgent or timely for them and moved to other topics over time."

The learning team for Buffalo, a majority-minority city of about 250,000—half the population it had in 1950—with a poverty rate of 30 percent, produced the first local roadmap for water equity, but not without difficulty. The team struggled to build trust between the utility and community group leaders at the table, recalls the sewer authority's leader OJ McFoy, an engineer born and raised

OJ McFoy

in Buffalo. "When it came to trust, we started out as a 3 out of 10 and I would say we got to maybe a 7 and then fell back to a 6. During our equity journey there were rifts and arguments. The push from community leaders was that the utility wasn't changing fast enough. We pushed back: 'What are you talking about? We are moving fast!'" But, McFoy adds, the process allowed the participants to develop their understanding of each other and to realize that neither side had all of the answers. "That's the big thing about convening and taking the time to talk and listen, to be authentic and work together to create a common solution. I love being in that space because it's when we get real and get to solve problems."

Buffalo's roadmap for water equity identifies priority actions for tackling affordability, water quality, infrastructure, workforce development, and waterfronts. "Drinking water and sewer rates are unaffordable to some segments of the population," it states, "especially those on fixed incomes. The Buffalo water system, which traditionally discounted rates for low-income customers, revised its rates to make them more equitable for residential users. During the Covid pandemic in 2020, it issued a moratorium on shutoffs for non-payment of water bills, forgave all financial penalties for non-payment, and helped arrange more affordable payment plans. It also started to look for federal government partners and funding, recognizing that federal programs support low-income household access to food and heating but not water.

Buffalo also prioritizes actions to further increase the diversity of the water sector's workforce, McFoy says, which is a way to support local economic opportunities. When he was hired into the utility in 2006, he notes, "I was the eighth person of color in the utility out of more than 200 employees. I thought, 'Come on. This is not 1956, it's 2006!'" Today, though, people of color make up 37 percent of the utility workforce, up from 4 percent in 2006, and the executive leadership team is 50 percent women and people of color. Now the utility is partnering with other local organizations to ensure that Buffalo adults have the educational credentials to qualify for jobs in water and other sectors that are and will be available.

After the Alliance issued its briefing paper and worked for more than two years with the original seven learning teams, its water-equity efforts reached for greater scale of impact. "We heard from everybody on the task force that they wanted to stay together, they liked being connected," Simonson recalls. "We decided to create a larger network that is all about making the use of an equity lens a standard practice of the water sector." In September 2020, Fox sent an e-mail blast to 14,300 recipients announcing formation of the Water Equity Network with an initial 17 cities and counties. By 2022 the number expanded to 28 cities and counties serving about 25 million residents. The Alliance provides them with information about equity-oriented practices, technical assistance, facilitation support, access to experts, and connections to other utilities.

Hara, whose Seattle utility joined the equity network, says that the Alliance's equity work "aims to become a cultural reference beyond the network's own membership, influencing the wider culture of the water sector. We can point to it and say, 'Look, it works.'"

Boosted by its signature efforts on water equity, the Alliance has evolved, expanded, diversified, and developed system-scale influence. Alliance members and participants are building a common identity, says strategic initiatives director Simonson. "No matter where they come into the Alliance, they are beginning to share a similar identity as 'One Water champions.' Whether they agree or disagree on things, they have this common element of wanting to achieve our shared grand vision. There's a feeling that being in the Alliance is part of being a leader in the water sector."

By 2022, the network's dues-paying membership has increased more than 50 percent to 131 members—70 of them utilities, plus 61 nonprofit organizations, unions, and water businesses. The utility-members touch nearly 15 percent of the US population, about 50 million people. In a 2020 survey, members said their top value proposition for being in the Alliance was "to connect to a network of changemakers at the top of their game." The Alliance's latest summit, in Austin in 2019, gathered more than 1,000 people from across the nation. Eight of the Alliance's 13 board directors are people of color and in late 2021 Mami Hara became the network's new CEO.

In early 2021 Radhika Fox accepted President Joe Biden's appointment to run the Office of Water in the U.S. Environmental Protection Agency—a crucial federal position regulating and investing in water systems nationwide. A few days later Biden signed executive orders requiring federal agencies to assess equity impacts of their policies and programs. Fox's appointment, says Hara, "is validating and affirming for the Alliance and its mission. We put into practice the significant network building and culture changing strategies she's bringing to this new job. It's a contribution the network is making to the nation."

During a virtual going-away party, nearly 100 guests celebrated Fox's accomplishments and sent her to Washington, DC, with a collective assurance. "You're not alone," said a longtime friend and colleague.

"Everybody on this call is committed to your success. We're not just on the sidelines cheering for you, we're walking with you."

Tuition-Free College

Back in 2012 two policy wonks—septuagenarians and longtime friends—decided their next policy-change effort would focus on "free college," the elimination of tuition for community colleges and public four-year colleges nationwide.

"We started with a question about what we could still do while still alive to further our lifetime cause, which is and was making American democracy work," recalls Morley Winograd. His co-conspirator, Doug Ross, proposed that in their 70's they should take up something they had never done. "We settled on the issue of economic oppor-

Morley Winograd

tunity since without it, democracies as diverse and large as ours can't maintain the support of the electorate," says Ross. "And then we decided that the key to economic opportunity in today's global economy was a college education. Then we concluded that the key to more people getting a college education was improving access, especially for children from low-income families. To do that we had to reduce the financial barriers that kept people from getting access."

Ross adds that they thought "the time was ripe for this change. We saw the growing tension between the needs of a knowledge economy and the levels of education in the country as analogous to those that generated universal primary education in the 19th century and universal high school in the first half of the 20th. We picked free college because we thought it was good policy, but also because we thought it had the advantage of strong historical and economic tailwinds. We wanted to not just fight the good fight, but to win."

Morley Winograd and Doug Ross didn't know much about the higher education system and its policies. At the time, only a few states were moving toward a tuition-free approach. It would be two years before Tennessee adopted a pioneering statewide free-tuition program for its community and technical colleges.

By 2022, though, the network that Winograd and Ross established nearly a decade earlier, the <u>Campaign for Free College Tuition</u>, could count 25 states that had established free-college programs. The Tennessee Promise had enrolled a total of 88,000 students and covered $115 million of their college costs. In Michigan, where a free-college policy breakthrough was engineered in 2020—aligning a Democratic governor, Gretchen Whitmer, and a Republican-controlled legislature— more than 150,000 residents had registered online to have their state government pay for community college classes they planned to take. Between February and May 2021 about 70,000 adults applied to "Michigan Reconnect" to have state government pay all of the tuition for their upcoming community college classes. The surge added to the 83,000 essential workers who had been accepted in the fall of 2020 into another new state program, Futures for Frontliners, which provided them with free community college.

Ross, a former state senator, state commerce director, and assistant US secretary of labor in the Clinton administration, had led the drive for Whitmer's initiative as the governor's senior advisor for Michigan prosperity. He lined up allies in the state's business community to press Republican lawmakers for adoption of the free-college legislation. It

Doug Ross

was one of the most visible actions of the small, highly decentralized network that he and Winograd, a former state Democratic Party chair and policy advisor to Vice President Al Gore, set up with their allies to influence policy making.

The network is bipartisan and lean: no full-time staff, no office, just volunteers, advisors, some contractors, and a post office box. One founder, Harris Miller, former head of the Association of Private Sector Colleges and Universities and a former congressional senior staffer, figured out how states could afford to pay for free college by using existing federal funds to supplement their funds. "The federal government actually already spends enough money in support of higher education to cover tuition for every public college student in America," explains the network's website.

Another founder, former Michigan Governor James Blanchard, was instrumental in resolving a debate in the group about how ambitious its advocacy for free college should be. "We had to decide how big to go: whether or not we should go all the way and advocate free tuition for both 2- and 4-year public colleges or do something less than that like advocating for limiting tuition prices," Winograd says. Some members of the group wanted to get control of tuition prices by linking them to the cost-of-living; others wanted free college, period. "Doug and I were in Blanchard's office. He jumped up from his desk chair, pounded on the desk, and said, 'Go big, go free, or go home! Unless you have a large-scale ambition, it's not worth doing.'" That became the network's mantra. About half of the group quit due to the decision, but those who remained were joined by other people attracted to the bold advocacy.

The network floundered at first. A loose affiliation of a few elected officials and free-college policy enthusiasts, it reached out to organizations of politically active Millennials. "Since the policy would benefit younger generations, our strategy was to make an alliance with them," recalls Winograd, coauthor of three books about the impact the Millennial generation will have on America. "We met with a half-dozen Millennial organizations and got turned down by every one of them. They said, 'We don't know who you are, and you didn't involve us in starting this.'"

But the network did discover several ways of attracting the interest of state-level elected officials and policymakers. It held well-attended workshops around the country and connected influential supporters to undecided policy decisionmakers, sometimes governor-to-governor. For instance, legislators in Connecticut told Winograd that the state's governor did not favor free-college policy and their fellow lawmakers did not want to vote for something that might be vetoed. He passed the information along to the governor of neighboring Rhode Island, Gina Raimondo, who was co-chair of the campaign's advisory council. "She said, 'I'm having lunch with him next week. I'll talk to him.' And she did. We called our friends in Connecticut and said, 'Get on the governor's calendar to talk about the legislation.' He told them he didn't support it but wouldn't veto it." That paved the way for adoption of the policy. "We used one hub in the network to get another hub to do more than they otherwise might," Winograd observes.

Another time Winograd called the president of the West Virginia Senate, a Republican, who had advocated for a free-college program that was rejected by Republican legislators due to lack of money. "I said, 'What do you need?' He said, 'I could use a lot of op-eds. I have to convince people in the state.'" So, the network wrote advocacy pieces and got them circulated in the state. Eventually, the Republican-controlled legislature passed the program, unanimously in the Senate. "Now," Winograd says, "people ask the senator, 'How did you do that? That's a policy that Bernie Sanders is for!'"

The network conducted and publicized research, including public opinion surveys that found a large majority of the public supported free-college policies. It published guidance for candidates running for state elected offices and created an extensive briefing book to help advocates design free-college policies and make the case in states. These materials provided a framework that detailed several versions of free-college policies. "We understood from our work in state politics that 'every state is unique,' at least as far as the politicians working in it are concerned," says Winograd. "Any attempt to design a model state law is doomed to failure and is a complete waste of time." The network's briefing book declares that states can follow more than one path to make their colleges tuition free.

The network allied with RISE, providing some start-up capital to the nonprofit that supports students in organizing campaigns for free college, ending student hunger and homelessness, and getting out the vote. "In California, RISE made free college policy happen," Winograd says. Then the student organization started spreading into other states. "RISE has a much bigger budget than we do," he adds. "We work in tandem. They operate independently, but cooperatively when it comes to planning."

The network also piggybacked on positive developments, including President Obama's decision to push for federal policies for free community college.

It's often difficult to determine who and what most influenced the adoption of policy changes, and the free-college network mostly stays in the background—connecting, arming, and advising advocates. But the network has obviously played a significant role in the policy changes that have occurred. "It's happened faster than we thought it might," Winograd reflects. "When we started the network in 2014 our first strategic plan said maybe by 2018 there'd be three to six states with free college."

With 25 states already on board, the network carries on. "When 50 states have this," says Winograd, "then we'll be done."

In February 2022 came another policy victory. New Mexico's governor, Michelle Lujan Grisham, co-chair of the campaign's advisory board, signed legislation that later in the year will provide free college for an estimated 34,000 students.

Talent Supply Management

One number stands out when Bill Guest describes the social innovation that TalNet is moving into the world: 10,000. It's the number of times that the employer that piloted the innovation, called evidence-based selection (EBS), used it to hire or promote employees.

Mercy Health, a nonprofit health care system with 9,000 employees in west Michigan, found its evidence-based selection results compelling. It achieved a 23 percent reduction in the first-year turnover of new hires and a 16 percent reduction in the time spent on hiring processes. And it doubled its number of non-white employees—an increase to 20 percent of its workforce, about the same portion as the population in its service area. The improvements drove cost savings and productivity gains and indicated increased employee satisfaction. By 2021, Mercy Health's parent company, Trinity Health, was expanding the use of EBS into the 22 states where it employs about 130,000 workers. The results also impressed other employers in west Michigan; 30 of them, with a total of about 90,000 employees in the region, signed up with HireReach, one of TalNet's initiatives, to use EBS.

It has taken 15 years to get to this point, from the spark of a fuzzy system-change ambition to a well-tested innovation that is scaling up deliberately and catalyzing other innovations. "We struggled against all kinds of odds," says Guest, former automotive engineer, systems thinker, data geek, and cofounder and facilitator of TalNet. "Now everywhere we turn, it's going well. It makes the work a joy."

Bill Guest

TalNet is short for the Talent Innovation Network of West Michigan, a cross-sector assemblage of employer associations, higher education institutions, K-12 education entities, workforce development government agencies, nonprofit organizations, and several philanthropic foundations. A self-described "network of talent system innovators," TalNet's 10 founding organizations are aligned around a common social cause: "to accelerate economic mobility in West Michigan by improving the quality of career decisions in education, training and job selection." The talent-management system they are tackling is enormous; the west Michigan region, 13 counties anchored by the city of Grand Rapids, contains more than 30,000 businesses, 800,000 jobs, 83,000 students in college, and 400,000 children and youth.

The network's lead innovation goes by a wonky description: "evidence-based talent supply chain management." Talent supply refers to the system that employers throughout the US use to recruit and hire tens of millions of employees and that nearly everyone uses to prepare for and find jobs. "Everybody has a stake in the talent system," says Guest. "Everyone is a student, or the parent of a student, or an employee or employer."

Talent management is actually a system of systems made up of employers' workplaces and human resource processes, labor markets for employment, K-12 and higher education, and workforce development for training and job placement. A talent system fuels the economic success of companies that need employees with particular skills and provides people seeking jobs with opportunities for economic mobility, career advancement, and well-being. It supports the economic prosperity of a region's workers, businesses, families, and communities.

But the nation's talent supply system is widely acknowledged to be broken. Its labor-market component, in which job vacancies are filled, doesn't function well to match supply and demand. Typical hiring practices don't effectively assess the competencies of job candidates or how well candidates match the skills companies need; therefore, they don't predict how well candidates will perform in the jobs. They often allow biases and stereotypes to seep, unconsciously and consciously, into hiring decisions, which penalizes people of color, women, older candidates, and anyone else who is considered "different."

Meanwhile, the system's education component—K-12 and higher education—doesn't prepare most students with the skills that employers are looking for. The massive pipeline of schools and workforce development entities that moves millions of young people from school to work doesn't effectively guide them in their education, job training, and career decisions.

Together, these talent system problems result in less-than-optimal job performance, high and costly employee turnover rates at companies, low diversity of the workforce, and low job satisfaction of employees. The system's chronic difficulties, apparent for decades, have attracted dozens of national, state, regional, and local problem-solving efforts and large amounts of government and philanthropic capital.

But TalNet brings something new to the table—evidence. "We are measuring skills that matter and we are doing it fairly and objectively," explains Guest. This sounds much simpler than it is. Most employers are not very precise about what competencies are required to do their jobs well; they are more instinctive than analytical. Most of their hiring processes rely on types of evidence, like work experience, education degrees, and references that, according to industrial psychologists, are weak predictors of a job candidate's performance. Instead, it takes a combination of structured interviews and tests that examine cognitive skills—critical thinking and problem-solving—personality traits, such as integrity and conscientiousness, and career interests to generate a reliable, objective, and valid predictor of job performance.

Part of the TalNet origin story dates back to 2010 when Thomas Karel, a top human-resources executive in the Trinity Health system, told Guest that his organization wanted to dramatically improve its talent system to ensure it hires only the best employees to serve patients. "Tom said, 'I want an evidence-based selection process that we use every time, and we don't override.'" Guest recalls. "Afterward, I got in my car and thought, 'Oh, man, I've been working on this sort of problem for years, but I don't know if we can do it or not.'"

They did do it, starting with the Mercy Health pilot and its 10,000 EBS transactions. TalNet's innovative evidence-based selection solution provides employers with methods and tools that change their hiring models. Employers meticulously identify the knowledge, skills, training requirements, education level, compensation, and other features of the jobs they have. Typically, an employer's many jobs will boil down to a small set of "job families," jobs with similar characteristics that can be assessed in similar ways. Then employers determine which assessment tools and methods to use to examine job candidates, focusing on tests and structured interviews. They standardize the use of assessments by their human resources staff and hiring managers so that hiring processes are fair, objective, and valid. They adopt TalNet's "compensatory rating system" that bundles a candidate's various assessments into a single "whole person" rating (1 to 5 stars) that takes into account cognitive skills, personality traits, career interests, online reference checks, and historical behaviors evaluated by interviews.

Guest uses a sports-film analogy to explain the essence of the EBS solution. "Have you seen Brad Pitt in *Moneyball*?" he asks, explaining that it's about the way baseball teams select their players, their talent system. Pitt plays Billy Beane, the baseball executive who abandoned the traditional model of player selection that was based on hunches and biases and favored powerful homerun hitters. Instead, Guest notes, "Beane paid attention to data analysis of games that showed that players who got on base frequently were more important for winning. And they were cheaper to hire than the home-run hitters that everyone was pursuing. The analysis provided Beane with a version of evidence-based assessment. When he hired players with a documented ability to get on base, his team set a record for winning games and did better than teams with more expensive payrolls."

The EBS process fundamentally changed Mercy Health's understanding of how to hire employees. "Before the pilot," Guest says, "they had a sense of what made a good performer and they hired based on that. But when we did the job analysis and also the analysis of employee performance, what we found was that there are additional specific competencies that make the difference. So, they started testing and hiring for those too."

TalNet is the latest configuration of social innovation collaborations that started 15 years earlier in west Michigan. "Hundreds of people have contributed to improving the talent system," Guest says. For nearly two decades, business leaders and educators in the region organized studies and initiatives. In 2005, they obtained a $15 million grant from the US Department of Labor to develop national-scale innovations in workforce development—an effort that supported Guest's early engagement in changing the talent system.

TalNet was designed to usher the EBS solution and other talent-system innovations to a new level, starting by building a critical mass of employers using the solution so that evidence-based selection becomes a regional standard. In 2019 two TalNet partners launched an initiative called HireReach, with financial support from the W.K. Kellogg Foundation, to expand use of the EBS solution in the region. They recruited 30 employers in the region, including prominent employers such as Steelcase—a global furniture manufacturer—the YMCA of Grand Rapids, Mercantile Bank, and the City of Grand Rapids.

The idea of establishing a network to reach regional impact came from Luis Lugo, director of community initiatives for the Doug and Maria DeVos Foundation in Grand Rapids. A self-described "recovering academic," Lugo has led the foundation's investment in the network, $3 million by 2022. He says he was impressed by Guest's

Luis Lugo

approach and the ripeness of the talent-supply effort. "I've always been inclined to systems thinking. Bill thinks systems, so we were really simpatico. He has a track record of on-the-ground experience and working well with a variety of partners."

To Lugo, using a network structure was a way to build on readiness in the region for significant investment in changing the talent-supply system. "There were already organizations on the ground"—education, workforce development, and employer entities—"with track records of working on the systems," he explains. "We were not starting from scratch. So why form yet another organization? Instead, we could help to link the organizations, because the real payoff is in aligning them. Bank on their good work, don't displace them or take the focus off of them. Help them to realign their resources through collaborative efforts."

The EBS solution is an essential starting point for larger scale system change because it changes employers' practices, Lugo says. If employers won't change their hiring practices, he continues, little else in the talent management system can change. When a critical mass of employers changes hiring practices and precisely defines the skills needed for job success, those skills can then be communicated to other players in the talent supply chain: workforce organizations, higher education and K-12 schools. Today the network uses its evidence-based approach to support aligned change in the region's education and workforce development systems. A CareerPoint team is developing a career pathways project to establish a seven-step process that helps students and adults match their interests and abilities with training, support, and career opportunities. A SkillSense team is creating common definitions and tools that people can use to develop and document their soft skills, such as communication and teamwork abilities. A JobSync team is defining career qualifications by distilling massive amounts of occupational data to provide practical information to individuals, educators, trainers, and employers. And IncludeAll is working to advance leadership practices of diversity and inclusion, ensuring that each TalNet innovation has a strategy and metrics for advancing these goals in the talent system.

Each of these innovation-development efforts, along with evidence-based selection that is already spreading among employers, is part of a larger approach to developing a radically changed regional talent-management system that better serves children and adults.

"No other region in the country has attempted this scale of transformation," says Guest. "West Michigan can set an example for the country."

Newsroom Communities

Three years before the *Los Angeles Times* hired Sandhya Kambhampati as a data journalist—an investigative reporter who mines databases for stories— she was tapped unexpectedly to join a small network of journalists specializing in using digital technology. She had applied for the position with OpenNews, which was introducing data miners and software

Sandhya Kambhampati

coders into newsrooms, but she figured she was too young and inexperienced to be accepted. "When I got the call that said I was a finalist, I said, 'Are you sure? Why me?'" The network told her that a small nonprofit news outlet in Germany wanted her to work there. "We did a Skype interview and the next thing I know, I was getting a visa and moving to Germany. It happened so quickly." For 10 months she worked there as a network fellow, investigating the poor quality of care in nursing homes and other stories. "I worked with newspapers across Germany doing data analysis."

Now Kambhampati is an active leader in the growing OpenNews network, mentoring other journalists, creating tools for news managers to use, blogging, attending annual conferences. In early 2021 she helped with the network's new effort to increase the racial diversity of newsrooms, supporting the creation of an online "safe space" for people of color and women in journalism to meet and talk with each other.

OpenNews began life about a decade ago as an experimental fellowship program, created by the Knight Foundation and the Mozilla Foundation, which supported development of open-source software. The goal was to embed dozens of technologists in news organizations. It was a way to strengthen the technology-journalist talent pipeline while shifting the culture of newsrooms to embrace the new digital world and accelerate much-needed digital innovation in the media.

Ben Welsh

Back then, only a few hundred employees in US journalism could be described as technologists. But the news business was on its way to being "fully transformed by the Internet," says Ben Welsh, editor of the data and graphics department at the *Los Angeles Times* and a participant in the OpenNews community. Today, news about current affairs is distributed online globally 24 hours a day to computers and mobile devices, often for free, and with audio, video, graphic, hyperlinks, and interactive enhancements. This provides fierce competition with what traditional newspaper, television, and radio outlets typically provide. In 2008, more Americans reported getting their national and international news from the Internet than from newspapers. By 2021, *The Washington Post*, a leader in the digital shift, had about 3 million digital subscribers and more than 100 million monthly unique visitors to its website. In contrast, circulation of its daily printed edition maxed out at a little more than 300,000, half the number in 2013.

For Welsh, trained as a reporter, the shift to a digital news model was career changing. "I was one of the last cohorts to be inducted into the journalism field with the older generation approach. But I was seeing what the next era would be like and realized I needed to evolve." He learned how to write software code and joined networks of web developers. In the mid-2000's, Welsh explains, "the transformation was just gathering steam, moving beyond boutique experimentation. In major newsrooms small digital teams were starting to make things happen on the web." Several major newspapers—*The New York Times* and *The Washington Post*, in particular—began making the transition on their own. But many smaller news entities haven't had the awareness or resources to advance, and their economic survival is at stake.

Over the years, OpenNews expanded its network-oriented activities to engage a growing community of technology-journalists, not just a small set of fellows. It developed a website for information and communication, a repository of digital tools, low-cost hack-a-thons, other sponsored events and convenings, and an annual conference, SRCCON. By 2016, more than 1,100 journalism technologists—including software engineers, data scientists, and visualization/infographic designers—had participated in network activities and were creating freely available software and other tools used by an array of newsrooms worldwide. Meanwhile, journalism schools at universities started to reshape their courses to train a new generation of digital technology journalists.

Participation in OpenNews continued to increase. In 2021, the News-Nerdery collaboration space in Slack, which OpenNews staff help administer and moderate, had 4,600 participants. By then, the network's main focus on bringing technologists into the media had evolved. The network's 2020 report, "Vision25: Building Racial Equity in Newsrooms," positioned OpenNews and two partner organizations as "a catalyst in a social change movement that seeks to build journalistic institutions where newsrooms are actively anti-racist and collaborative, and journalists of color feel like they truly belong." Just a few months later, *The New York Times* released a report on diversity and inclusion that acknowledged its newsroom culture and systems "are not enabling our work force to thrive and do its best work. . . It is particularly true for people of color, many of whom described unsettling and sometimes painful day-to-day workplace experiences."

"My peers and I could see the momentum that OpenNews' organizing had among the younger generation," Welsh says. "The emphasis on software has diminished. OpenNews is becoming a safe space for underrepresented voices to organize and make change. The support gives people a way to talk about and negotiate their struggles."

More than 100 journalists, including Kambhampati, are involved in developing the network's
racial-equity initiative, says Sisi Wei, OpenNews'
co-executive director, who is orchestrating the
effort. Wei, like Kambhampati, feels passionate
about making sure journalists of color and software coders are treated equitably and valued in the

Sisi Wei

journalism profession. After working almost 10 years as a technology-journalist who coded, reported, and managed data-visualization projects in prominent newsrooms, she started to work at OpenNews in 2020.
Two weeks into the job transition, she blogged that the change "feels like
moving from working for one, amazing newspaper, to being able to work
for all of journalism."

Wei, Kambhampati, and Welsh are part of a growing community and
are committed to helping others in the community. For them, Open-
News—an open, sprawling network with no membership eligibility
requirements or obligations—makes possible crucial new developments
in the news business like open-source digital technology and racial diversity and inclusion. The network is scaling up within the professional field
of journalism. In such a network, creating a sense of belonging is critical,
says Wei. "A main goal of OpenNews is to identify and remove the sense
of loneliness, while bringing new skills into the industry."

In OpenNews, what the community says it values drives the use of
network resources. "When we survey people about what they care about,
diversity is incredibly important to our community," says Wei. It's up to
network staff like Wei to enable participants in OpenNews, but not dictate
to them. "I'm not telling them what do to," Wei says of the racial-equity
initiative. The network uses a "light structure to create impact," she contin
ues. "My role is to create a framework with them and bring them together.
I will help document it and turn the things they are doing into things for
other people to use. We want those who care about this to own it."

Sandhya Kambhampati certainly cares. "I engage a lot with Open-
News. It's a good support system; like-minded people who will help you
out," she says. "Any time OpenNews asks me, I will help, because they
helped me so much. I care deeply about OpenNews." The sense of isolation that once prevailed for her as a technology-journalist of color

has changed. "I feel like everywhere I look, the OpenNews community is there."

A Maze of Choices

We've told the stories of these four social innovation networks to set up the frameworks in the chapters that follow.

In some ways the networks are quite different. They were initiated and are led by different people with different life experiences. They have tackled different systems, created different social innovations, sought different scales, and developed different capabilities. They have faced different barriers and navigated through different turning points. They have had different impacts.

But the networks also share similarities: passion, collaboration, and time—characteristics you're likely familiar with in your own work. The wonderful people involved have an enduring passion for taking on seemingly impossible missions. They build powerful collaborations with many others to make change happen. Their efforts persist for many years to approach success.

The networks have something else in common. They display the main features of the complex landscape through which social innovation networks pass on their way to large-scale impact. It's a setting that presents innovators with predictable choices with a range of options. These choices force decisions that fundamentally affect the network's performance. Understanding this landscape of choices and options can help social innovation networks anticipate and make decisions that enable their efforts to build enduring collaborations with transformative strength.

The choices are about five elements of large-scale transformation: systems, social innovations, pathways to scale, network models, and leadership roles.

Systems

Social innovation networks have to get clear about which systems they target and which system-changing levers and approaches to use.

The networks we described have targeted huge systems for change: water management, higher education finance, talent supply, and journalism. The systems are quite different from each other, and this has implications for how change-agents proceed. A talent-management system, as we've seen, is a mashup of labor markets, workforce development entities, K-12 school systems, higher education institutions, and numerous employers' human resource units. The professional field of journalism is spread across numerous news enterprises, a few of them large and well-resourced businesses, most of them struggling to cope with dramatic changes in the business brought on by digital technologies. The water management system is highly fragmented into thousands of local water utilities, some very large, many quite small. Its knowledge and learning processes are dominated by large trade associations for water professionals. The higher education financial system is a hodgepodge of state and federal government and higher-ed institutional policies and funding sources.

These systems include a private market (employers and job seekers), a professional field of practice (journalism), and public institutions (water utilities, public colleges, and K-12 education). The differences between these types of systems inevitably affect the types of innovations worth creating.

Social Innovations

Whatever system they target, networks have to determine which type of social innovation to develop and how to produce them.

The US Water Alliance, for example, creates experience-tested knowledge about what changes water utilities and their stakeholders should make and how to make them. It demonstrates this know-how at real-world sites and then shares it with the water sector using information products and sometimes assisting those who want to make changes.

OpenNews targets the personnel/culture parts of journalism field/newsrooms system, and the innovations it is developing are practices. It brings together and into the news media field a critical mass of people who have been kept at its margins: people of color and digital technologists.

In contrast, the Campaign for Free College Tuition pursues public policy changes by state and federal governments, while TalNet produces tools and practices—solutions—which employers embed into their own processes to change the performance of their hiring systems. Solutions are not information and advice about what to do; they are products, including software apps, or services, such as financing and data tracking and analysis, or business models—all of which actually make change happen.

Creation of these different types of innovations requires networks to employ different innovation-development processes and build different capabilities. Sooner or later along the way, they will encounter the challenges of scaling up.

Pathways to Scale

Networks have to identify the pathways to scale they will take with their social innovations. This starts with clarifying what type of scale they pursue. Is it a market, a field, or a government? The Campaign for Free College Tuition targets governments, which formulate policies for financing public colleges. The US Water Alliance targets the field of water management—especially, professional water utilities, while OpenNews engages the journalism field of practice. TalNet is scaling its evidence-based selection solution in the labor market. Often, though, system changers wrestle with more than one scale.

For each of these scales there is a unique pathway. Networks take new products and services into markets. They grow new practices within fields and persuade governments to adopt policies. Each pathway has distinct factors for success.

As innovation networks move from developing and testing innovations to scaling them, the fundamental nature of the network changes.

Network Models

System changers have to figure out which model of network to develop and evolve. There are many options, but systems-changing innovation networks tend to need a design that can continuously develop innovations and then shift to moving innovations to scale. They also need to be able to mount additional activities, such as leadership development, consulting, and movement building, using additional networks.

As their tasks become much more complex, networks may change their underlying design to be able to coordinate the growing number of participants conducting multiple functions. They may become "networks of networks" and "strategic hubs," which allow them to manage complexity while maintaining the flexibility and other desirable characteristics of a network.

Leadership Roles

Finally, leading social innovation networks involves several key and somewhat unique roles. Leaders have to enable social innovation development processes and a supportive and creative network culture. Sometimes they get deep into the weeds of developing a particular innovation.

They have to help innovators build the strong relationships within the network that enable innovation development, and they have to build connections with outside partner organizations needed for taking innovations on pathways to scale.

They have to lead strategically—drawing on insights from outside and inside of the network.

And they have to tell the most compelling story of the network—to members, partners, and investors.

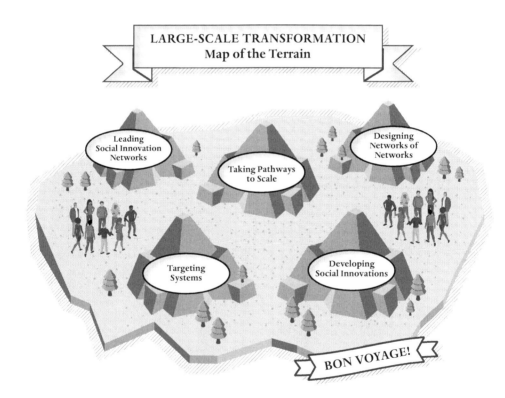

Networks & Seeking Scale

The frameworks described above may seem like a strictly linear progression—from systems to innovations to scaling and models—but the action rarely unfolds in a straight line. Social innovation efforts to change systems are characterized by ongoing, recurring, and shifting challenges, a dynamism that intensifies the challenges of navigating through the maze of choices we've sketched.

The drive for systems change may not start with a system analysis. Social innovation networks arise in different ways. Many, as we explained in *Connecting to Change the World*, emerge from a mash-up of like-minded people and organizations that share a problem. They get together to see what they might do and invent a common path forward. Their understanding of the system is probably more from experience and intuition than analysis and assessment. These and other networks may have an instinct about a social innovation to create, but not because they have a deep understanding of the system. Other networks start less impulsively; they are engineered into existence, the result of analysis, planning, and negotiation, processes often required and funded by philanthropic investors. But the system analysis that they develop may need to be enhanced and revised.

The system itself can be a moving target. As the US Water Alliance pursues best practices for One Water approaches, new technological products and government regulations are being introduced into the water system. For the Campaign for Free College Tuition, the 2020 election of a new US president changed who the policy decision-makers were in the higher education finance system and introduced new policy preferences and priorities. A "policy window" opened at the federal government level, but within a few months it closed when the Democratic majority in the US Congress could not agree on adopting free-college policy.

The scale of a change effort may shift. Bill Guest and colleagues spent years working to develop a "national laboratory" for workforce development in west Michigan but shifted their sights to the regional scale in west Michigan after the DeVos Foundation, located in the region, expressed interest in investing in work at that scale. The 2020 presidential election affected the Free College network's strategy for scaling. "We're busy changing focus from state governments to the Congress," Morley Winograd reports. "It's quite a reach for us; a federal focus requires new tactics, new partners. But when circumstances change enough, the thing to do is to do your plan over."

Many system-changing initiatives may need to produce more than a single social innovation in order to achieve transformation. The social innovation network may serve as a catalyst of multiple interventions in a system. This is the case, for instance, with the US Water Alliance; water equity is just one of a half-dozen major efforts. In 2021, the network also had initiatives to respond to water-sector stresses caused by the Covid-19 pandemic, advance a blueprint for federal policies, support change-management leadership, consolidate small utilities, build climate resilience, promote collaborations between artists and water utilities, and operate a national campaign championing public investment in water infrastructure.

Or a system intervention may be one of a number of efforts developed by multiple networks and organizations with similar aims. TalNet, for example, is one effort among several to shift the west Michigan's talent-supply system. "I think about it as a community," says Guest. "We don't think we're the center of the world. And we don't want to step on other people's innovations."

Finally, networks that undertake system-changing social innovation may need to evolve and even change dramatically. OpenNews morphed from a network concentrating on technology-journalism to a network also focusing on racial inclusion in the news media. The US Water Alliance shifted from a small, exclusive network of water-management professionals into a large, inclusive network of water-sector change agents. These sorts of shifts may affect a network's purpose, strategies, innovations, and model.

Different kinds of systems and scales, social innovations, pathways to scale, and network models: these are main features of the complex, shifting landscape through which social innovation networks must navigate on their way to large-scale impact. That's exactly what the four networks we've described are doing: steering toward systems change. So are other networks that we'll introduce.

Whatever these networks' origins, maturity, and capabilities, at some point they had to develop an understanding of the system they have targeted. They had to identify levers they could move to change the system. And commit to a general approach for engaging the system over the long run.

Targeting the system: that's the next stop in our exploration of this stirring and daunting space.

CHAPTER 2

Targeting Systems for Change

We live in a moment of profound possibility and disruption. A moment that is marked by the dying of an old mindset and logic of organizing. . . . What is being born is less clear.

C. Otto Scharmer

In the 1980s Gary Cohen had a college degree in philosophy and was making a living by writing guidebooks. "I could tell you where to get the best cannoli in New York's Little Italy, find an undiscovered bistro on the Left Bank, or sign up for the coolest walking tour of Amsterdam," he recalls. Then a friend asked him to write a guidebook about something deadly serious: toxic chemicals and communities impacted by chemical contamination.

"As I began traveling around America," Cohen says, "I met people sitting around kitchen tables, moms and dads, who were asking, 'Why does my son wake up coughing? Why does the water taste so bad? Why does my daughter have a rare form of cancer?'" These people "had no money, no technical expertise and little political power, but they

Gary Cohen

were brave and tenacious because they were fighting to protect their family's health."

When a pesticide factory in Bhopal, India blew up in December 1984, killing thousands of people and unleashing decades of trauma, Cohen immersed himself in the environmental health and justice movement. "While the Bhopal disaster was called an 'accident,' there's nothing accidental about the system that created it," he notes. "It begins by externalizing the harm to this community and internalizing the profit. And it makes people expendable." Just a few years later the first alarms sounded about how burning fossil fuels was warming the planet, changing the climate, and threatening people's health. These impacts hit Cohen profoundly: "As a Jew growing up in the post Holocaust generation, learning what can happen when people are made expendable by either governments or corporations operating outside of any moral parameters deeply impacted me."

What could be done to change the situation? "I asked myself: what institution in society is powerful enough to bring a more evolved ethic into this collective trauma? Over time, I realized the answer: the healthcare industry. It is the one sector of our society that has a healing mission." But, Cohen understood, the healthcare sector itself was implicated in the problem. "It's a major chemical polluter, poisoning the environment and communities and contributing to the very diseases that its facilities are set up to treat."

It's also an enormous system—by 2022, a $3.8 trillion industry in the US alone, the nation's largest employer, with nearly 800,000 companies and more than 6,000 hospitals that handle 36 million patients annually. How could the performance of such a sprawling, complex, and essential system be impacted? Where would you even start?

Leveraging Systems

The great but elusive prize for those seeking to change a system is this: finding leverage—the small shifts that produce big changes in the system. It's young David using a slingshot and stone to fell the giant Goliath. A smaller, weaker underdog defeating a bigger, stronger adversary. Or, on point, a network of people with miniscule resources and power taking actions that transform an established system with far more resources and power.

"This idea is not unique to systems analysis—it's embedded in legend," explains Donnella Meadows, an environmental scientist known for seminal contributions to the discipline of systems thinking. Meadows, in her posthumous book, *Thinking in Systems*, calls this idea a *leverage point*: "The silver bullet, the trimtab, the miracle cure, the secret passage, the magic password, the single hero who turns the tide of history. . . . We not only want to believe that there are leverage points, we want to know where they are and how to get our hands on them. Leverage points are points of power."

A system is a set of things that work together to create behaviors and results that the individual parts cannot produce by themselves. A system may contain sub-systems, interacting parts that themselves are systems, and may be described as a "system of systems." Humans have been perceiving, thinking about, analyzing, and creating systems for millennia: astronomic, biological, mechanical, ecological, technological, economic, and other types of systems. But our book's focus on systems change is *social systems*, those created by human beings to arrange how people live and work together. Each of the networks we've described so far is working on a different social system: water supply, higher education, employment, and news media. The undesirable outcomes produced by these, and other, modern social systems have become serious, large-scale obstacles to human well-being.

Social systems are complex and have a life of their own. As Meadows puts it: "Social systems are the external manifestations of cultural thinking patterns and of profound human needs, emotions, strengths and weaknesses. Changing them is not as simple as saying 'now all change,' or of trusting that he who knows the good shall do the good."

Bill Guest was an engineer developing industrial-process systems before he cofounded TalNet to deal with talent supply, a social system. He worked on the first emissions control systems for automobiles, part of a team that put a computer on an engine for the first time in the world. "It's commonplace now," he reflects, "but back then inventing this was like putting a man on the moon." Guest was general manager of a corporation that invented the forward-looking sensor for cars. "We had more sensors on more cars than anyone in the world. We were driving around Europe in self-driving cars before Google existed." He also developed the system for a robot assembly line. Creating technological systems like these, Guest acknowledges, isn't as difficult as reshaping social systems: "Building robots was a lot easier than fixing the talent system."

When it comes to changing social systems there have been two schools of thought. The reductionist approach divides a system into its components and assumes that the whole system can be changed by focusing on and optimizing the parts. But social systems involve highly complex interrelationships between individuals, groups, and organizations and may defy reductionist thinking. People use their rational abilities, Meadows explains, "to trace direct paths from cause to effect, to look at things in small and understandable pieces, to solve problems by acting on or controlling the world around us." But complex systems problems—the undesirable behaviors of systems—don't always yield to a rational, reductionist approach.

Systems thinking, an alternative to reductionism, seeks to understand and improve the dynamic interconnections among the parts and looks for a small set of ways to leverage them.

In the 1960s Meadows joined a team at the Massachusetts Institute of Technology that was developing solutions to global problems by applying new computer-based tools for modeling the often non-linear, changing relationships between the parts of a social system and how they affect the system's behavior. But she says, she and other practitioners made a "terrible mistake." The tools of systems thinking were "born out of engineering and mathematics, implemented in computers, drawn from a mechanistic mind-set and a quest for prediction and control." Complex social systems turn out to be "inherently unpredictable. They are not controllable. The goal of foreseeing the future exactly and preparing for it perfectly is unrealizable. The idea of making a complex system do just what you want it to do can be achieved only temporarily, at best."

Instead, Meadows says, "We can't control systems or figure them out. But we can dance with them!" A system's future can be "envisioned and brought lovingly into being. Systems can't be controlled, but they can be designed and redesigned. . . We can listen to what a system tells us and discover how its properties and our values can work together to bring forth something much better." To help others dance with systems Meadows identified a dozen generic leverage points, places to intervene in a system. (See Appendix A for full list.) The most powerful lever is the mindset or paradigm out of which the system arises. A society's paradigms, Meadows explains, are the shared ideas in the minds of society, assumptions and beliefs, about how the world works. From them, the system's goals, power structure, rules, and culture develop.

The Power of Mindset Change

Mental models are the "bedrock upon which a system is built," explains Motaz Attalla, a former program officer at the Garfield Foundation, who worked with grantees and partners to support system-change efforts. "We often hear people talk about changing the criminal justice system, the health care system, the education system, the foster care system," he says. "When people name those systems, they're generally referring to the current institutions and regulations that form the structural layer of a sector (or system). The focus is on how it operates to deliver a service or function and, naturally, impact a lot of people's lives. But these institutions and regulations aren't the system in its totality."

Other systems changers have reached similar conclusions. Mental models are "foundational drivers of activity in any system," say John Kania, Mark Kramer, and Peter Senge in "The Water of Systems Change." Underlying a social system's reality is a set of ways of thinking, beliefs, ambitions, perceptions, relationships, skills, norms, and rules—what Christian Seelos, director of the Global Innovation for Impact Lab at Stanford University, calls the system's "behavioral architecture."

Mindsets have another, less noted, power when it comes to systems change. They are the seedbed from which system changers grow the innovations they will use to change the system. Innovations carry new mindsets into systems. This is a critical process for successful large-scale system change: develop new mindsets, use them to produce innovations, then use innovations to take the mindset into the system in ways that solve problems, which leads systems players to change their mindsets and seek additional innovations.

The networks we've presented all pursue mindset change to change systems. The US Water Alliance, for example, promotes a broad "One Water" mindset shift for the national water sector, with an emphasis on community engagement and water equity, rather than just technical and financial management of water systems. "Water agencies are being redefined and reimagined as anchor institutions as utility leaders expand the scope of their mission," rather than just providing a commodity service and minimizing engagement with the communities they serve, a 2021 Alliance report observes. TalNet works with multiple, interdependent

systems, starting with the transformation of employer hiring processes—a mindset shift that emphasizes relevant, demonstrable, and objective capacities of job seekers—and seeks to align the K-12 education,
workforce development, and higher education systems around an
evidence-based model.

These are just a few of the numerous mindset or paradigm changes
that system changers around the world have initiated. Some are very
broadly applicable, while others are narrower in scope. A 2020 report by
the FrameWorks Institute, "Mindset Shifts: What Are They? Why Do
They Matter? How Do They Happen?" sketches some of the different
types of mindsets: "There are foundational mindsets like individualism,
which shapes thinking across social issues. There are mindsets that apply
to specific social issues, like economic naturalism, which holds that the
market is driven by natural forces that are outside of intentional control.
There are definitional mindsets, like competing models of marriage as
being about commitment versus exchange. Some mindsets provide
models of how the natural world works, like the idea that nature stands
in delicate balance that, if disrupted, can lead to irreparable harm, or the
competing model of nature as self-repairing and durably resilient." Identifying a desired mindset shift is just a first step toward transformational
change. Whatever type of mindset shift the agents of system change are
trying to push into a system, sooner or later they are bound to encounter
a truth that Meadows acknowledges: "It's one thing to understand how
to fix a system and quite another to wade in and fix it."

Wading Into a System

Gary Cohen didn't know how to dance with the health care system. "I
knew nothing about the sector." But he and the band of friends and
colleagues attracted to the cause did know this: physicians pledge to
uphold professional ethics, first framed as the Hippocratic Oath more
than 2,000 years ago, in which they commit to do no harm. "It seemed
important to focus on that," Cohen says. "What does the oath mean in a
world where kids are being born with toxic chemicals in their bodies,
where food systems are spreading disease? The US Environmental Protection Agency was saying the health sector was the largest source of toxic
dioxin emissions—from medical waste incineration—and a big source of

toxic mercury emissions. The sector's own facilities and supply chains were unwitting accomplices in damaging the environment and people's health."

The sector's ethic was a paradigm-mindset lever, and focusing on that lever led Cohen and allies to a system-change approach. They assumed that people in the health care sector did not understand the harm they were causing—and would change their minds and behaviors when informed that their practices conflicted with their espoused ethics. They chose to push on that lever in a particular way. "We could have taken the typical NGO advocacy approach: expose them, blame them, shame them, make them change,'" Cohen recalls. "But we said no to that, that's not the play here. The thing to do is to partner with this sector. Bring the latest environmental health science to their door. Get them to understand environmental health and justice. Help them on a long journey toward a sustainable, toxic-free, low-carbon future."

Instead of assaulting the system, they would dance with it. "We were very conscious about highlighting and documenting the problem and its impacts, with strong science, and showing them the alternatives. The whole chemical framework of the health care sector was wrong, and we were going to blow it up."

In 1996 the group formed a nonprofit, Health Care Without Harm— putting right into its name the mindset shift it wanted to see—and began to engage major health care organizations. "There was denial from the American Hospital Association," Cohen recalls. "They said, 'We have experts, we have this covered.' We said, 'Who are they?' It turned out to be two guys who sold waste incinerators to hospitals. We said, 'Maybe you need a second opinion.'" At the same time, Cohen continues, "There was enormous pushback from the chemical industry. They infiltrated our conference, they partnered with medical manufacturers to undermine us. They called us Health Care Without Shame."

The network started by building the healthcare sector's awareness of the damage it was causing. It organized a Mercury Awareness Day and a thermometer swap with a hospital in Boston, substituting more than 1,000 mercury thermometers with digital alternatives, an effort that gradually spread to 5,000 US hospitals.

Early on, Health Care Without Harm forged partnerships with Catholic Health Care West and Kaiser Permanente, the nation's largest integrated health care system. "We had God and size on our side within the first year," Cohen notes. Initial probes based on the leverage point of scientifically informed ethical behavior had led to aligned relationships with leading players in the system. "You couldn't ask for better partners," Cohen says. "When the chemical industry said we were Greenpeace in sheep's clothing, we said, 'Come and talk to the nuns about that.' These partners provided the initial anchors within the system. We weren't just outsiders anymore."

Health Care Without Harm partnered with the Environmental Protection Agency to gain the cooperation of the American Hospital Association and the American Nurses Association in reducing medical waste incineration. The federal agency didn't have regulatory authority to force hospitals to change behavior, and the association wanted to avoid new regulations. The four entities launched a voluntary effort, Hospitals for a Healthy Environment, to educate all hospitals and then pharmacies about the problem and to seek voluntary changes. "We had enormous scale from the get-go," Cohen recalls. "Within a decade and with almost no regulation we had closed 4,000 medical waste incinerators and eliminated the market for mercury-based measurement."

As the network expanded and took on additional challenges—the food system and climate change, for instance—other health care organizations started to engage with it. "As we grew, we got more and more validators," Cohen notes. "It went from organizations that were mission-aligned with us, like Kaiser Permanente, to those who wanted to follow the mission-aligned leaders: big nonprofit hospitals, then the for-profits, then the US Veterans Administration came in."

With sectoral relationships expanding, the network had a critical structural decision to make. "If you want to do systems change," Cohen explains, "You don't want a big building called Health Care Without Harm. You want the work to be done *by the people inside the system.* We decided from the get-go we were not going to be a big organization. We were going to build an ecosystem."

The distributed structure enabled Health Care Without Harm to scale up globally. "These toxic chemicals are global pollutants," says Cohen. "If we shut every US incinerator and they build 1,000 incinerators in India, there's no net gain." In Europe, the network engaged with Green Parties in parliamentary systems to enact pollution-eliminating policies. Elsewhere in the world—Buenos Aires and Manila, for instance—it partnered with local hospitals to eliminate use of mercury. These initial relationships catalyzed other partnerships, just as they had in the US.

By its 25th anniversary, the system-changing network was operating in more than 70 nations. A legally binding global treaty has been adopted to phase out mercury thermometers and blood-pressure devices. More than 22,000 health care institutions in 34 countries are committed to reducing their greenhouse gas emissions; 80 percent of network members' facilities are purchasing certified green chemicals; and more than 90 manufacturers are eliminating toxic chemicals from the furniture they make for hospitals. The World Bank is working with Health Care Without Harm to figure out how its lending programs can support climate resilient health systems in low- and middle-income countries. And in early 2021, the network released a global roadmap for decarbonizing the healthcare sector.

"We no longer need to convince people of the value of our work," Cohen notes. "People are coming to us, and we are struggling with managing all the opportunities presenting themselves to us."

Health Care Without Harm has danced with the system for more than two decades—identifying system leverage points, implementing partnership strategies for making scalable changes, and adopting a highly distributed, global structure. The network's role with the system has evolved. "The thing we're able to do is say to the system, 'Here's the next thing to work on, and the next thing,'" Cohen says. "Mercury, climate change, food systems. We've created a whole sustainability platform for any health care system. Here are 10 doors you can enter, which do you want to focus on? Anyone working on sustainable health care anywhere in the world—they're in our network or just one step away. We've become system orchestrators."

Approaches to System Change

Partnering to change a system—associating with it—as Health Care Without Harm does, is one of four system-changing approaches that innovation networks use.

Approaches for Changing a System	
Associate	Engage with the system to inform, promote, and support change.
Adversary	Seek to change the system against its will. Often occurs when system changing is done through public policy shifts.
Alternative	Create a new system designed to solve the problem and/or to lure the existing system into changing itself to address the problem.
Authority	Change a system's performance by aligning and coordinating the efforts of leaders with power over various parts of the system.

Acting as an *associate* encourages the system to change itself. In California, for instance, a network of 13 philanthropic funders pooled $9.2 million and teamed up with other stakeholders to partner with the community college system. They wanted it to provide educational opportunities to the state's numerous incarcerated and formerly incarcerated students. They served as "a trusted advisor, present to lend expertise, put in the necessary time, and ensure that the work was done," according to Rebecca Silbert and Debbie Mukamal, co-directors of the effort. "The team was available to accomplish what the public stakeholders lacked the capacity to do, whether that was drafting a new policy, identifying a shared hurdle and presenting the solution to the decision maker who could make the necessary change, or following up on promises made." Between 2014 and 2019, the state's community college system went from no face-to-face teaching in state prisons to holding in-person classes for 6,000 students in 34 of the state's 35 prisons. "It resulted from deliberate actions and policy changes made by a group of stakeholders working in partnerships with each other," the co-directors report.

Acting as an *adversary*, the second approach, tries to force the system to change. Change agents act as "warriors," says Steve Waddell, lead staff at SDG Transformations Forum and a frequent writer about large-scale systems change. They push "for widespread change, trying to influence others through their pressure and advocacy. . . . They focus on gathering strength through followers and supporters."

A third approach, acting as an *alternative*, involves bypassing the system to establish another choice. Change agents, explains Waddell, "are not fixated on destroying the old. . . . Their energy is devoted toward creating the new." A prominent example of this approach is the worldwide development of alternative financial institutions—microlenders, community development banks, loan funds, and credit unions dedicated to financing that helps low-income, low-wealth, and other disadvantaged people and communities join the economic mainstream. "Our field started as a small grassroots movement to counter discrimination in banking and investing," says Lisa Mensah, president and CEO of the Opportunity Finance Network, a nationwide web of community development financial institutions (CDFIs) that invest in people and communities left behind by the mainstream financial system. "The earliest CDFIs were created to provide financial services and support to people that banks wouldn't or couldn't serve," Mensah continues. "We've grown into a $222 billion industry that works to address longstanding disinvestment, the racial wealth gap, and persistent poverty."

A fourth approach, using *authority*, is tried by people who have direct power over a system—leaders, owners, champions, stakeholders. They align, redesign, and coordinate with each other to change the system's performance. The "collective impact" practice developed and promoted by FSG, the global social-impact consulting firm, is an example of align-to-change efforts by system insiders, often at the local level of a system. Waddell calls this "the popular but complicated strategy of 'Let's get all the stakeholders in the same room and figure out how we'll work together for change.' It depends on the willingness of everyone to change [because] we all hold values, beliefs, and ways of understanding that have to change."

These four approaches are not permanent states or mutually exclusive. As Waddell notes, "As a transformation progresses, the comparative importance of each" changes in response to "the particular circumstances and environment that transformation confronts."

The Adversarial Approach

The Campaign for Free College Tuition has followed an adversarial approach—seeking to force the system to change. From its beginning, the Campaign's advocacy for government policies that eliminate public college tuition payments ran into opposition from the higher education system. College presidents "hate the idea of free college tuition," says Morley Winograd. "The higher ed financial aid folks also hate us, not only because we will put them out of a job, but because our argument that the best way to get everyone enrolled in college is to make it free runs counter to their business model. Their business model says to make college relatively free to poor folks by providing manipulated scholarships and using a lot of hocus pocus to cover up the fact that the only way the middle class can pay for college is to go into debt."

At the same time, Winograd notes, the free-college network has important allies in the higher education system: "In many states community college presidents have led the charge for free college tuition because they can use the legislative process to get funding they might not otherwise get." And many of the nonprofit organizations trying to increase college enrollment and completion remain mostly neutral about the Campaign's effort. "They have other more specific agendas, but don't see us a threat—we're more like someone whose cause would send them more students to work with."

Overall, Winograd concludes, "It's a mixed bag, but the bottom line is that most of the higher education system can't handle our constant criticism of the status quo."

This sort of conflict is par for the course when social entrepreneurs use policy innovations to drive system change. The "owners" of the system resist the changes or seek to weaken their impact, rallying their allies and using their established relationships with elected officials to press for the status quo. "One way to deal with policy resistance is to try to overpower it," says Meadows. "If you can wield enough power and can keep wielding it, the power approach can work, at the cost of monumental resentment and the possibility of explosive consequences if the power is ever let up."

The Alternative Approach

Another time-honored approach to systems change is to create an alternative system, like the field of community development financial institutions described earlier. This is called "changing a system by building a system" by Seelos and Johanna Mair at the Global Innovation for Impact Lab. Below we take a brief look at two distinct system-creation efforts, one emerging in a vast bioregion, the other initiated in New Mexico and now operating at global scale.

Spencer Beebe

The instinct to invent something new runs deep in Spencer Beebe, a serial social innovator. "I'm a contrarian," Beebe declares. "If existing stuff is so great, why are things falling apart?" Animated as a young man by a desire to protect and restore the natural environment, Beebe worked in The Nature Conservancy (TNC) to assemble and fund major land preservation projects in the Pacific Northwest and Latin America. He left TNC and became president of Conservation International, which pioneered the first debt-for-nature swap that resulted in the 336,000-acre Beni River Biosphere Reserve in Bolivia. Then he created Ecotrust, dedicated to helping local communities build capacity to meet their economic and social needs while replenishing the natural resources on which they depend. Prosperity based on natural-world processes became Beebe's pursuit. He worked closely with elders of Haisla First Nation to build a coalition of ex-loggers, environmentalists, regional scientists, and elected officials that convinced a timber company to renounce logging rights to the largest intact coastal watershed in North America, the 800,000-acre Kitlope River Valley. He created the world's first environmental bank, ShoreBank Pacific, to make loans to small- and medium-sized businesses in the Pacific Northwest.

Then came Salmon Nation. "We took two words that sound crazy when you put them together and literally reimagined human enterprise in relationship to the life-support systems in a particular area," Beebe says. The geography of Salmon Nation stretches along the Pacific Ocean and across local watersheds from the Sacramento River in California to the Yukon River in Alaska. It is a vast bioregion defined by natural boundaries and dynamics and diverse human cultures comprising 30 million people. The presence of the Pacific salmon provides the best biological indicator of natural, social, and financial health. The bioregion's "estuaries, its coastal plains, rugged mountains, forests, farmlands, and grasslands are home to vibrant cities . . . busy rural towns, public and tribal lands; and host a hotbed of creativity and enterprise that adds up to a $1.5+ trillion bioregional economy," explains a 2019 essay Beebe coauthored with Christopher Brookfield and Ian Gill. "It is a nature state, as distinct from a nation state."

Salmon Nation, Beebe says, "is a mental framework that says—whoa, we have to start rebuilding the whole economy from the bottom up in a way that restores and maintains soil, climate, social equity. Right now, we are destroying the very life-support systems of which we are a part. Salmon Nation is a mental reframing of people and place and the economy of that place by organizing around natural systems, not political lines and colonialism." Existing systems in the bioregion do not serve local people well. "Our focus is on rural, Indigenous and urban 'edge' communities; on lesser-served places and markets; on remarkable people doing remarkable work," the Salmon Nation essay explains. "We believe these places and people—near enough to resource centers, yet far enough away to preserve alternative viewpoints—are well positioned for development and demonstration of new approaches to living that make more regenerative use of natural, social and financial capital."

The edges, Beebe expands, "are places where people are feeling more independent, self-sufficient, more contrarian, more able to free themselves from traditional expectations. They are an enormous source of creativity." People at the edges, he continues, "express a fractal of deep systems change." A fractal is a pattern—human creativity and resilience, in Salmon Nation's case—that can repeat itself at larger (and smaller) scales.

The "human-powered natural system" that Salmon Nation's founders envision "aims to shift mindsets in our bioregion, helping people move from individual preoccupations that feel besieged and lacking in control to being part of a regenerative fabric of active, creative and more locally and regionally engaged people." The Salmon Nation alternative will be "a more appropriate superstructure for bioregional nation building," Beebe adds. "We're trying to prove out the idea now."

Salmon Nation is still in infancy. But Project ECHO, a new system developed by a physician in New Mexico, has spread across the world.

ECHO's founder, Sanjeev Arora, a liver specialist, was deeply frustrated by his inability to treat all the patients who needed his care, especially people living in poverty and in remote rural areas. The waiting list to access his university clinic was 8-months long and many patients' conditions worsened during the delay; some died. Fewer than 5 percent of the more than 35,000 people in the state infected with the hepatitis C virus were being treated. Arora wanted to solve the problem, but the existing healthcare system offered few solutions.

"The traditional medical model," explain Tamara Kay and Jason Spicer in a 2021 article about Project ECHO, moves "rural patients to urban and university medical centers." It maintains strict controls over training of medical specialists, preventing clinicians—doctors who have direct contact with patients—who are not trained as liver specialists from accessing that knowledge and helping to treat patients. "The approaches of emerging telemedicine and for-profit medical education companies had not solved the access problem," they report. In addition, the typical telemedicine model in which one doctor advises another about a particular patient is difficult to scale up widely.

Arora says he started thinking "How do I really take my talent, treating patients, and help a massive number of them?" The answer he developed was to create a "telementoring" system—a new way to virtually train clinicians in remote areas to treat and manage complex health conditions. Project ECHO "turned the medical model on its head," say Kay and Spicer, "It moved medical knowledge to patients in rural and remote areas." Arora traveled across New Mexico to find primary-care clinicians interested in participating in weekly telementoring sessions to learn how to treat patients with hepatitis C. The sessions used case-based learning as the practical training model and promoted best practices backed by evidence. ECHO also monitored outcomes by collecting data and evaluating activities. "Together, these features foster a community of practice in which everyone teaches and learns improved methods," Kay and Spicer observe.

Within a year of starting the project, Arora's patient waiting list was down to just two weeks long. A 2011 study found clinicians trained by

ECHO had the same cure rates as doctors based at the University of New Mexico hospital. The model increased the access of underserved patients to medical services they needed, often through local clinicians they trusted. "They get better care and there is better adherence to the treatment," says Arora.

That was just the beginning in Project ECHO's development as an alternative system. By 2020, it had a global network of more than 800 clinics and programs worldwide and had trained 96,000 practitioners. Its training had expanded beyond liver treatment to address diabetes, chronic pain, opioid-use treatment, and scores of other health issues. And ECHO adopted the goal of reaching 1 billion lives by 2025.

The key to the new system's remarkable growth was the innovative design of ECHO's organizational model. ECHO "is highly decentralized and organized as a network of partners around the world, who have minimal legal and governance ties to one another and no financial ties to the headquarters," Kay and Spicer report. "The hundreds of local partners—ECHO clinics, which emerge through local actors, not replication efforts by ECHO—agree to abide by ECHO's standards and to fund and cover their own costs. ECHO, meanwhile, freely gives its partners its training materials and other intellectual property, access to teleconferencing and research, and opportunities to engage with other partners. Partners may modify the ECHO content to meet their local needs." In other words, ECHO is a "diffuse collective of autonomous clinics joined by a mission to disperse best health practices."

The Authority Approach

Using the associate, adversary, or alternative approaches, the networks we've described seek to change a system from the outside-in. Sometimes, though, the drive for change comes from within the system, from people running or investing in the system. "Those who are in positions of power and authority and are committed to change" can direct the changes they want, observes Waddell. "But that often requires fundamental disruption in the structures that give them power and authority in the first place. They typically have a missionary's zeal . . . since such work involves overcoming immense inertia to break up and reinvent organizations and structures to become something very different."

In 2006, a cross-section of regional Cincinnati's leaders in the education, business, government, nonprofit, and philanthropic sectors committed to pursue a common, long-term agenda to provide high-quality education to every child in urban neighborhoods. Strive, as the initiative was called then, was "an unprecedented partnership among institutional leaders," recalls Jennifer Blatz, president and CEO of StriveTogether. The arrangement became known as "collective impact," heralded by John Kania and Mark Kramer in a seminal 2011 article in *Stanford Social Innovation Review*, the most popular article in *SSIR*'s history. "Unlike most collaborations," they wrote, "collective impact initiatives involve a centralized infrastructure, a dedicated staff, and a structured process that leads to a common agenda, shared measurement, continuous communication, and mutually reinforcing activities among all participants."

TalNet looks something like this—an effort to align the power of leaders in education, workforce development, and employment systems around a shared (and disruptive) vision and change effort in the west Michigan region. The network is made up of people in leadership positions of key organizations in the systems: business associations, 2- and 4-year colleges, government workforce entities, and intermediate school districts serving local K-12 schools. These system insiders spent years building relationships and examining the performance of their systems, committing to a new mental model and goals, and initiating systems-change processes, starting with evidence-based selection for employee hiring and promotions. "The leaders work for different organizations, but we have a common commitment, and we listen to each other," says Bill Guest. "Each is innovating their part of the system, but they are curious about the others, and they dialogue with each other so they can make connections between the parts."

More recently at Strive, leaders have shifted from a nearly exclusive focus on institutional leaders to also include community voice, authority, and ingenuity in the collective. "Institutional leaders must empower residents and grassroots leaders as peers with shared authority, shared responsibility, and shared accountability," explain Blatz, Byron White, executive director of StrivePartnership, and Mark Joseph, an associate professor of community development.

Understanding Systems

In the process of engaging a system, you want to build your understanding of how the system works. You have to define the boundaries of the system and the drivers of system behaviors. You have to uncover the various perspectives people hold about the system, what the system's power centers are, and what the leverage points for change may be. This is true whatever type of social system you're dealing with, such as a market like health care, a professional field like journalism, or a community-based system like K-12 education.

"Enacting system change requires observation, careful probing, and reflection," say Seelos and Mair. Building trust and rapport with the leaders and stakeholders of a system can lead them to share with you the system's "secrets," aspects of situations and problems that are not readily visible. Other ways for networks to come to understand a system and find its leverage points use analysis and lived experience, as well as strong intuition, to develop insights. Combining these methods can deepen understanding and also provide a check on information they reveal. For example, the lived experience of people who live in poverty can serve as a check on the formal analysis of poverty data that misses nuances in how multiple factors on the ground prevent economic mobility.

Ways to Understand a System	
Intuition	Change agents have an instinctive feeling, rather than rational analysis, about how the system works and its leverage points.
Analysis	Change agents gather data and expertise, using various tools, such as system map-ping, feedback loops, and recognition of typical leverage points, to understand how the system works and where its leverage points may be.
Lived Experience	Change agents tap into the experiences and voices of people within or affected by the system, which provides unique information about the system.

Jennie Curtis wanted a system analysis. After a few years as executive director of the Garfield Foundation, she was unsatisfied with the funder's grantmaking. "I had the feeling that something just wasn't right with what we were doing," recalls Curtis, an experienced manager of international humanitarian programs and former Peace Corps

Jennie Curtis

volunteer in Thailand. Garfield was distributing about $3 million a year, making grants to nonprofit organizations to advance a new idea, sustainable consumption. "These were really good opportunistic grants, but our grantees were not talking to each other even though they were doing complementary work. And there was very little discussion among funders about aligning and collaborating their work in this area. That was frustrating!"

Curtis's conversations with others led her to try a new approach: systems thinking. "We wanted to understand the system we were trying to change in a way that would help us to understand how our grants could make a collective impact."

Creating "systemic awareness," explain David Sawyer and David Ehrlichman at Converge, which supports social-impact networks, "helps to shift attention away from organizational silos and toward the ways that people and organizations interconnect."

Seeing the system forces that are at play, explain Kania, Kramer, and Senge, "requires that changemakers look beyond any single organization to understand the system by identifying all of the actors that touch the issue they seek to address. One must then go further to explore the relationships among these actors, the distribution of power, the institutional norms and constraints within which they operate, and the attitudes and assumptions that influence decisions. These are the conditions that significantly impede or enable social change."

Curtis brought together 20 leaders from foundations and environmental advocacy organizations to map the electricity sector in the Midwest and understand what was holding back the growth of renewable energy in the region. "The systems mapping process unfolded over the course of a year, and, frankly, it was a difficult journey," she recalls. The project, named the Renewable Energy Alignment Mapping Project or

RE-AMP, "was hard work, time-consuming and required faith that the process would yield a useful outcome. Even so, each step of the process uncovered some intriguing insight that kept the participants curious and engaged."

The systems map produced by the group, with support of consultants, was based on more than 35 interviews and data analysis, focusing on systems and sectors that produced, transported, marketed, consumed, and regulated energy in the region. One realization from the analysis was that recent progress on energy efficiency and renewable energy had been negated by the new construction of just one coal-burning plant.

During the process the group shifted its focus from boosting renewable electricity production to reducing carbon emissions of the region's entire energy system in response to climate change. It identified four key levers that could change the system: retiring the existing 70 coal plants in the region; stopping proposals for 25 new coal plants; greatly increasing demand and availability of renewable energy; and steadily reducing electricity consumption through efficiency measures. Then the group designed working groups and action plans with specific targeted goals for each leverage point.

By the end of the systems-mapping year, says Curtis, "the group had co-created a complex systems map, collectively identified a set of interventions informed by the map, solidified relationships, and decided unanimously to work together to deploy collaborative strategies that would advance renewable energy *and* stop the advancement of climate change." The group decided in 2005 to organize as a network with decentralized structures, shared leadership, and multiple ways to connect and communicate. Its motto: "Think Systemically and Act Collaboratively." Funders that had been involved in the process committed more than $2 million to start the work, on top of the $500,000 a year for five years that Garfield committed for RE-AMP. In the wake of the collaborative process for systems analysis, Curtis says, "the RE-AMP network was born."

By 2022, RE-AMP contained more than 130 nonprofit and funder organizations in nine states; had regranted $25 million in support of climate action in the region; and could claim numerous state policy victories and coal-plant closures. And the network continues to refine its system map; now called the "Equitable Deep Decarbonization Framework," it covers additional systems such as transportation, food, and local decision-making power over energy.

Like RE-AMP, each of the networks portrayed in chapter 1 undertook a type of system analysis, often focused on particular aspects of the system's performance. Bill Guest and others in western Michigan spent years studying the talent supply system, which is a complex mashup of education, employer, and workforce systems. They concluded that employer hiring practices were the critical leverage point to change. Radhika Fox's team at the US Water Alliance assembled a detailed understanding of inequities in water systems, tapping expertise around the country. Morley Winograd and the Campaign for College Free Tuition supported essential analyses of the cost of making college free in each state, and they armed candidates for state office with policy advice. And OpenNews initiated research that identified a "social tipping point" for the journalism industry: if 25 percent of the 88,000 newsroom employees and newsrooms in the US stood up for racial equity in journalism, then social change would happen. The network explained that "instead of aiming at a threshold of representation within newsroom staff—plenty of organizations are already working toward that worthy goal—our goal is to create an industry threshold that leads to lasting systemic change."

In each case, increasing the network's understanding of the system revealed leverage points that became the focus of the network's strategy for system change.

Lived Experience

Systems-change analyses are not just based on data and expert information. One's understanding of a system can also be based on a different kind of evidence: the lived experiences of those within or impacted by a system.

At OpenNews, for instance, Sandhya Kambhampati and Sisi Wei weren't just reading studies about racial inequities in US newsrooms, they had both experienced the culture of journalism as women of color. Kambhampati, born in New Jersey to immigrant professionals, remembers the first journalism conference she attended: "Nobody looked like me at this conference. I was one of very few Indian people there." Now she works through the network to spark conversations about race in newsrooms.

Doug Ross, cofounder of the Campaign for Tuition Free College, had established a charter school district in Detroit, filled with thousands of African-American students, most of them from families living in poverty. He had wrestled for years with the challenges of inspiring students who assumed they could not afford to go to college—and with scrounging up scholarship money to pay a small fraction of the families' post-secondary education costs. Now he works to change the financial system that keeps qualified students out of college or loads heavy financial burdens onto them.

Significant experiences can come from any aspect of one's life. Dana Bourland, senior vice president for environmental program at the JPB Foundation, opens her 2021 book, *Gray to Green Communities*, with a personal revelation: "By the time I was 17, I had moved 11 times." Why was this important to share? "My experience living in different homes and different communities and working in different environments have all been inputs into how I view the world and how I understand how systems work," she explains. The experiences were just Bourland's first exposures to the housing system. She also volunteered with Habitat for Humanity, worked to track racist housing policies that destabilized neighborhoods, witnessed the unhealthy impacts of inadequate housing while in the Peace Corps in Belize, engaged with communities to write housing action plans, and helped develop the nation's first green-building standard for affordable housing.

When Bourland lived in a green-certified building in New York City she wore a bracelet designed to detect hidden chemical exposures in the living environment. "Much to my horror my wristband detected 11 chemicals, including persistent, bioaccumulative, and toxic ones. They sound as scary as they are." Bourland looked for the system that

Dana Bourland

allowed this to happen: "Those life-threatening toxic chemicals . . . are ingredients chosen to be in those products by manufacturers. But manufacturers of building products and materials do not have to disclose those ingredients to the consumer." Only 300 of the 80,000 chemicals in products have been tested and only nine of them have been banned, she reports. "This is not because only nine are harmful but because the testing process is so ineffective."

Bourland doesn't just rely on the understanding gained from her own lived experiences. "Talking to practitioners to understand their experiences also shapes my understanding of the system," she says. "I feel like I'm always truth testing my assumptions about the systems to see what I'm missing." For example, she spent time in Albuquerque, New Mexico, at the Sawmill Community Land Trust, a 27-acre industrial pollution site converted by community activists into green development with 93 affordable ownership homes and three affordable apartment complexes set within a neighborhood with community gardens, playgrounds and a plaza. Learning about the locals' experiences helped Bourland understand that it wasn't enough to create green housing; green development had to consider a community's entire set of activities. This included where the materials for housing come from and what they contain, which allows them to be considered "green." Prior to the site's redevelopment a functioning sawmill on site had used formaldehyde to create particle board, which was then transported to developments. This is what led to the contamination and prompted the community to gain ownership to clean up the site.

Due to her experiences with the housing system, when national environmental organizations were seeking funding for federal policy work, Bourland suggested instead that they demonstrate to utility companies that affordable housing could be a part of the solution for reducing carbon emissions. Otherwise, it was clear to her that housing would be left out of a federal agenda. To reach scale, she knew it would be necessary to connect organizations' efforts. The organizations then created a national network—Energy Efficiency for All (EEFA)—that would increase people's access to affordable and healthy multi-family homes by assembling leading environmental nonprofits and state coalitions of housing, health, energy efficiency, environmental, and community advocates that have not typically worked together. By 2021, EEFA partners' activities had resulted in more than $454 million in new funding, mostly from utilities, for energy-efficiency upgrades of apartments.

Lessons from lived experience can be combined with data-and-expert analysis to reveal a system's leverage points. However, achieving a blend may require networks to address the tendency of analytic, scientific, and professional frameworks to discount and ignore the value of lived experiences of people impacted by a system. This often occurs when people of color, Indigenous people, and people with low incomes are a part of the system in question.

"When we enter an institution or a sector, there usually isn't a space for understanding our lived experience," explains Olivia Roanhorse, COO of Roanhorse Consulting, an Indigenous women-led think tank. "We come with our own knowledge and perspectives, but it is ignored." Instead, says Roanhorse, a citizen of the Navajo Nation and

Olivia Roanhorse

former vice president of programs for the Notah Begay III Foundation, "we go into western institutions and have to shift *our* frameworks and worldviews to understand what the institution values. It's hard to show up as your authentic self when you were purposely not allowed to be a part of the creation of the system and it continues to devalue your perspectives."

Opening up to the lived experience of people for whom a system was not designed brings new insights about a system. But this requires ways of engaging that are not often used. Roanhorse provides an example from her work as an evaluation researcher for an innovative partnership between a financial institution and community organizations that provides capital to people of color—individuals, businesses, and communities—that have been historically excluded from financial services. "In all our research we always ask questions that center those most impacted and allow them to talk about who they are, their lived experiences, and what's important to them. In our evaluation of the project, one of the questions we asked the Native borrowers was, 'Did you feel cared for in accessing and using the loan?' For typical financial institutions this question might be seen as a general satisfaction query, but for this project it was clear that it had deeper meaning and reflection on what a financial system could and should be for excluded borrowers. The overwhelming response from borrowers was, 'Absolutely, I felt seen, not just by my community, but by the financial institution—for the first time.'

"This is important because, in 2021, the Federal Deposit Insurance Company reported that one in six Native American and Native Alaskan households were unbanked; they were unable to be served by a bank or similar financial institution," Roanhorse says. "This left them to turn to predatory lenders who take advantage of these community members, charging interest rates as high as 250 percent in some states. Which ensures a harmful and generational cycle of debt and extraction. The innovative partnership's effort gave them an opportunity to see that these financial institutions could be used for good and *did* value who they are. It wasn't transactional; there was an actual person in the institution who cared about them, who wanted them to succeed. This is how to start to build trust in a thoughtful and respectful way."

Melissa Herman, a Dënësųłinë journalist in Edmonton, Canada, who focuses on local stories of Indigenous innovation, notes that much Indigenous culture passes traditional knowledge orally. "A common concern is that, when recorded, documented, and shared with exclusivity, traditional knowledge loses authenticity." In addition, language barriers may interfere with tapping into Indigenous experiences. For instance, Herman says, the term "industry" in the Dënësųłinë language denotes destruction, loss, and extermination—a meaning that creates tensions when industry representatives try to consult and work with the Indigenous communities. Despite the difficulties, she adds, it's critical to develop ways in which "the voice of Indigenous people is amplified and respected; where we control our own narrative."

A striking example of including lived experience in systems-change work is seen in the efforts of Ascend at the Aspen Institute, a national network of nearly 460 organizations seeking to end the cycle of intergenerational poverty. Ascend consistently brings the voices of parents with low incomes into decision-making about policies and

Marjorie Sims

practices for the human services system in which they participate. "We engage parents as experts—they know better than anyone how and why family supportive programs fall short," explains Marjorie Sims, Ascend's managing director and a national leader in expanding gender-equity policies and women's philanthropy. "As one parent said, 'Who better to identify the cracks in the systems than the ones who have fallen through them?'"

Since 2011 Ascend has invested in conducting focus groups with diverse sets of parents from across the nation, and it pays parents who serve as advisors in its multiyear initiatives. "We build partnerships with parents," says Sims. "Their experiences and recommendations are strategic guidance for our work. To do this, we honor, respect, and hear parents, and ask them to share their recommendations. And we compensate parents for their time and expertise with stipends—for taking time off from work to be our thought partners, out-of-pocket costs, and their time spent providing the expertise from lived experience."

Networks & Systems Change

Networks are well suited—even essential—for system-change work. They can provide the multiple perspectives, data, and lived experiences that are needed to come to understand how a complex system works and can be leveraged to change.

"Systems change isn't something that one or two organizations can do on their own," says Jennifer Berman, former partnerships and training officer at the Garfield Foundation. "The practice requires multiple organizations with different perspectives to come together to create a shared understanding of the current reality (at a deeper level), agree on where they collectively want to go, and where and how to intervene to change the underlying dynamics." Garfield's work to establish RE-AMP, says David Sibbet, who facilitated development of the network's first action plan, "was an unprecedented kind of collaboration between NGOs and foundations in the environmental funding world. We had changing members, limited funding, rapidly evolving politics, emergent strategies, and no offices."

You also need a network to change a system, not just to understand it. "Because of the complexity of system architectures, many change proposals rely on collaborative initiatives," observe Seelos and Mair. "But collaboration introduces additional complexity and requires aligning resources, competencies, strategic priorities, and ideologies about effective and legitimate means and ends across partners from different sectors."

From our work with social innovation networks we offer advice concerning systems change.

Advice for System-Changing Networks

- Embrace the complexity of social systems.

- Patience is a necessity.

- Be the systems change you want to cause.

- Practice continuous learning about the system.

Embrace the complexity of social systems. "There are no cheap tickets to mastery," cautions Donella Meadows. "You have to work hard at it, whether that means rigorously analyzing a system or rigorously casting off your own paradigms and throwing yourself into the humility of Not Knowing." This is great advice! Recognize the difficulties and tackle them humbly. Be aware, warns Christian Seelos, of the tendency to overestimate "our ability to intervene in and change situations for the better."

And don't leap to conclusions. Systems changers must avoid the "tendency to prematurely specify and enact solutions that are not effective or likely make situations worse," Seelos urges. They have to be "more humble and willing to explore and learn, rather than to base decisions on the assumed superiority of our existing knowledge, technologies, and strategies." He and Mair cite studies of professionals trying to change complex systems and warn that "experienced professionals with high ambitions tend to quickly decide on system interventions but spent little time trying to understand system dynamics and characteristics."

Funders, these concerns are for you, too. Seelos notes several system-changing "pathologies" of the philanthropic sector: "an obsession with technical solutions, a sense of urgency to demonstrate large-scale impact, and the formulation of strategies with prespecified objectives designed by people who are not part of the target system."

Eleni Sotos, former senior program officer at Garfield, points out other ways that philanthropies' behaviors can be antithetical to system changing: "Funders commonly maintain a laser focus on specific projects that aim to yield measurable outcomes within a short period of time. This practice prioritizes reporting predetermined outcomes to foundation boards to assure them that their investments are producing immediate results. This approach is problematic when addressing complex problems because foundations typically propose their own theory of change and rarely analyze or align their strategies with other foundations working on the same issues. Going deep to analyze, understand, and address troubled systems can't happen within the confines of a one-year grant cycle, one organization, or one strategy."

Patience is a necessity. Systems change is a long game. You may have noticed that most of the networks we've described so far have been at it for one or two decades, and even more. "To act systemically is to commit to surviving the short-term expression of a problem, agree on a short-term fix, and then engage with the longer-term game," says Motaz Attalla. "Recognize that the time horizon for change might be two generations!"

Be the system change that you want to cause. "Any organization's ability to create change externally is constrained by its own internal policies, practices, and resources, its relationships and power imbalances, and the tacit assumptions of its board and staff," argue Kania, Kramer, and Senge. "Funders also often embody traditional power dynamics based on wealth, race, gender, and status, which can limit their ability to support deep inquiry into such conditions externally."

Otto Scharmer, in his *The Essentials of Theory U*, quotes Bill O'Brien, late CEO of Hanover Insurance, on the same theme: "The success of an intervention depends on the interior condition of the intervener." Interior conditions—"the sources from which we operate both individually and collectively"—are a blind spot in current approaches to leadership, Scharmer continues. "The essence of leadership," he explains, "is to become aware of our blind spot . . . and then shift the inner place from which we operate as required by the situations we face."

Practice continuous learning about the system. Systems can be moving targets; they change. As the US Water Alliance pursues best practices for One Water approaches, new technological products and government regulations are being introduced into the water system. For the Campaign for Free College Tuition, the election of a new US president changed who key policy decision-makers were in the higher education finance system and introduced new policy preferences and priorities.

At the same time, one's understanding of a system may evolve. Eric Stowe, CEO of Splash, a nonprofit focused on safe water for families worldwide, recounts a potentially disastrous revelation about a system in China. Splash had worked closely with Chinese government officials for five years to provide safe water to every orphanage in the nation, 700 of them in all. By 2012, Splash was close to finishing the project, with only 20 orphanages to go. "Imagine my unfiltered shock when the government informed us that there were actually more than 500 orphanages still left on the national roster," Stowe recounts. The "new" orphanages were the most sensitive and remote ones in China, he says, and Chinese officials had been unwilling to share their existence with Splash until they were comfortable the situation wouldn't be politicized or proselytized. Splash faced an immense funding gap and questions from its staff, board, and donors about its apparently weak planning for system change. Splash managed to redesign some of its funding and reassign staff to engage with the expanded system, but Stowe reflects, "it took at least three years to relearn our rhythm and regain our pace in China."

One's understanding of a system may also change due to the lived experience of innovators who are engaging the system. As RE-AMP has progressed, for example, network members have used their experiences in seeking to change the Midwest's carbon-producing systems to expand their analytic understanding of the system. RE-AMP calls this a "living system analysis"—a framework that "informs and is informed by action. Members act strategically on the strongest aspects of our analysis, while also working to increase our knowledge. This improved knowledge spurs more action, in a virtuous circle of analysis and action."

―――――――――――

As you develop a deeper understanding of what makes a targeted system tick and adopt an approach for using levers to change the system over the long term, you will have to figure out how to turn these insights into actions that gain traction. This means converting the mindset you want to spread in the world into social innovations—policies, practices, tools, models, and the like—that will instigate change in the system you've targeted.

A social innovation is like a Trojan Horse. It is designed and built to breach the walls of the system, carrying and releasing an unseen force, mindset shift, to achieve transformative change. Social innovations that produce the desired results are the most effective agents of mindset change. But they must be developed and deployed in ways that overcome the uncertainties of the innovation process.

CHAPTER 3

Developing Social Innovations

Innovation done right is more than a good idea or a "eureka!" moment—
it's a patient process of iteration, learning, evaluation, implementation,
and, importantly, scaling up what works.
Muhammad Musa & Judith Rodin

I t was life changing for me," says Bob Friedman. A colleague had introduced him to a professor of social work, Michael Sherraden, who had given him three chapters of his draft manuscript to read. "Michael's whole framework made sense of things; it was profound. I had a mental epiphany. In his proposed Individual Development Account, I saw the simple, central, building block of a truly inclusive and progressive investment system."

Bob Friedman

Sherraden's book, published in 1991 as *Assets and the Poor: A New American Welfare Policy*, revealed to Friedman and many others a fundamentally different way of thinking about how to reduce poverty. "Instead of focusing welfare policy on income and consumption, as we have done in the past," Sherraden wrote, "we should focus more on savings, investment, and asset accumulation." He defined assets as "the stock of wealth in a household," in contrast to income which is "the flow of resources in a household" and is associated with consumption and a standard of living. "Assets are the key to economic development. Individual and family development is not built on receiving and spending a certain amount of monthly income. Rather, development is built on planning for the future, accumulating savings, investing, using financial assets to support life goals, and passing along assets to offspring."

Assets, Sherraden argued, "have a variety of important social, psychological, and economic effects. Simply put, people think and behave differently when they are accumulating assets, and the world responds to them differently at the same time." Accumulating assets creates an orientation to the future, increases personal efficacy and social influence, provides a foundation for risk-taking, and has other positive effects.

Sherraden noted that "the nonpoor benefit from elaborate systems of asset accumulation"—including massive federal subsidies and policies—while the poor, especially people of color, "typically receive very few assets from any source and accumulate few assets over the long term." The GI Bill, for example, offered college tuition, home loans, and unemployment benefits to veterans, but administrators excluded Black veterans. Federal public housing programs instituted racially segregated housing. The Social Security Act initially excluded agricultural and domestic workers, who were disproportionately Black.

Sherraden proposed to introduce "institutionalized asset accumulation processes into the welfare model," noting this would require a new structure for the poor to use. The mechanism he suggested was called the Individual Development Account or IDA. Most simply, IDAs would be financial accounts for each individual into which deposits would be made—from an individual's earnings, government matches and subsidies, and other sources. Revenue could be withdrawn by the individual for designated purposes such as paying for post-secondary education or job training, starting a business, purchasing a house, and other asset-building activities. "IDA accounts would introduce real assets into the lives of many poor people who would otherwise be without them," Sherraden argued. "IDAs would enable the poor to bring their own cards to the table and make their own deal."

Sherraden's comprehensive analysis of failed welfare policies and his call for IDAs expanded the track that Friedman had been pursuing. "I had been working for 10 years to build in the US the microenterprise field with its asset-building tenets—that people, including poor and Black people and women and immigrants, are assets in and of themselves. They are entrepreneurs, investors, and creators of wealth who deserve and would do good things if invested in. But they confront barriers and penalties for asset acquisition. Michael's asset framing offered a way to build assets through home ownership, education, saving, and investment as well as through entrepreneurship."

Born into a wealthy family in San Francisco, Friedman describes himself in his 2018 book, *A Few Thousand Dollars: Sparking Prosperity for Everyone*, as "an accidental inheritor of privilege. White privilege. Male privilege. Wealth privilege. Family privilege. I was born into a rare extended family, who afforded me every opportunity to develop whatever skills and pursue whatever interests I desired." He went to Harvard and then Yale, where he prepared to be a lawyer, graduating debt free. But he found a different life-passion. "I was a non-practicing lawyer. I love justice, not the law," Friedman explains. He established a nonprofit organization, the Corporation for Enterprise Development (CFED, renamed Prosperity Now). His family's assets, he acknowledges, meant he could "afford to found a nonprofit, even when I knew little about what building a nonprofit required. It meant I could devote my life to creating for others some measure of the opportunities I was given."

Sherraden's ideas started to get attention. Friedman's colleague, Janet Topolsky, edited portions of the book into a CFED publication that fed a national audience of social policy innovators. The Washington Post's William Raspberry championed the assets-building idea in his columns. "Pretty soon," Friedman remembers, "Jack Kemp [then-director of the US Department of Housing and Urban Development for President George H. Bush] was waving the book around." The first national conference on IDAs in Chicago, organized by Friedman and Sherraden, was sponsored by a score of national nonprofits and foundations. Another groundbreaking tome, *Black Wealth/White Wealth*, by sociologists Melvin Oliver and Thomas Shapiro, detailed the staggering disparities in private wealth due to race.

But exactly what should Individual Development Accounts look like? How would they function? Would they work to help people get out of poverty? Asset building might be a system-changing leverage point—but it would have to become more than a compelling concept.

Types of Social Innovations

IDAs involve two types of innovations: one, a new practice, which incentivizes and organizes financial savings by families that have low incomes;

the other, new public policies to support the spread and use of IDAs.

First came the practice, as numerous nonprofit organizations and philanthropies undertook the development and use of IDAs. Friedman, Sherraden, and colleagues spread the IDA concept and information about how to design and deploy IDAs. Many change agents do this: disseminate practical knowledge about innovative practices—what to do and how to do it—using reports, webinars, conferences, and other methods. The US Water Alliance, for instance, developed a framework for the many practices that utilities can use to improve water equity and it pioneered methods for utilities and their stakeholders to co-develop local roadmaps for achieving greater water equity. The Carbon Neutral Cities Alliance, a global network of 22 cities, produced a "game changers" report on seven leading carbon-reducing practices that other communities could use. In mid-2021 Health Care Without Harm released a "Climate Impact Checkup" tool that, it says "any health care facility in the world" can use to determine its operations' carbon footprint, pinpoint targets for reductions, develop plans, and measure the impact of their actions.

This know-how is often spread through a "community of practice," a peer-learning cohort that convenes for participants to learn together how to use the knowledge and customize it to their own situations. The Alliance uses its Water Equity Network of 28 cities to implement practice knowledge and demonstrate to the rest of the water sector the practices' feasibility and impacts. The Biophilic Cities Network—Arlington (Virginia), Austin, Milwaukee, Norfolk, Pittsburgh, Richmond, Phoenix, Portland (Oregon), Reston, San Francisco, St. Louis, and Washington, DC, plus 12 international cities—has been promoting innovations in city planning and design to produce more vibrant nature-filled cities. It has been supported by philanthropic grants and the in-kind contributions of advocates. In 2021 the network offered a four-week course, taught by experts, for people interested in learning how to implement biophilic concepts—for a fee of $615.

The second type of IDA innovation is public policies that provide funding for IDAs, a key goal of advocates. It's a crucial way to put the far greater financial resources of governments into IDA development and use. Many system changers develop policy initiatives that they seek to have adopted by elected officials. The Campaign for Free College Tuition

introduced public policy innovations, aimed primarily at state governments. RE-AMP, Ascend, and Energy Efficiency for All—networks
mentioned in chapter 2—all pursue policy changes as a way to radically
alter a targeted system's performance.

Although most policy innovations focus on a specific policy realm,
such as energy or human services, some innovations target the public
governance system itself in attempts to change political power. They may
focus on changes in representation and voice in government decision-making processes. For example, in 2015 Seattle voters approved the
creation of "democracy vouchers," the nation's first city-based public
financing for elections. The program allows Seattle residents to donate
their voucher's money from an earmarked property tax to support participating candidates running for mayor, city council, or city attorney—a
way to counter the influence of large donors.

Practice know-how and public policies are just two types of social
innovations. Another is goods and services—solutions, not just information, that users can put to use. "The product or service itself creates a
social benefit," explain the authors of "The Many Roads to Revenue
Generation," based on a decade of research on how social innovators
generate revenue. The product approach, they add, "is becoming increasingly popular among nonprofits" precisely because it can generate
income.

TalNet provides employers in west Michigan
with a solution—tools and processes, not just
advice—that they can use to implement evidence-
based selection of employees. The many charter
schools established in the US by Doug Ross and
others are another example of a solution: actual
schools that enroll students, not just practice
knowledge that existing schools may adopt. In 2021, reports Erika Owens,

Erika Owens

co-executive director of OpenNews, some news organizations that were
impressed by the way OpenNews operates—its inclusive values and peer-
to-peer learning and decision-making processes, for example—asked the
network to provide a new service: coaching for their executives. "They
say, 'You work in a way that we can't work. Coach me in this way.'"

(There's a fourth type of social innovation, promotions that use educational and communications processes to influence the personal behaviors of large numbers of people. But we are not familiar with networks that have used this and it does not seem to have strong system-changing impacts. See Appendix B for a description of promotion innovations and their scaling pathway.)

These types of social innovation—practices, policies, products—are the main outputs of social innovation networks. Producing each of them poses different challenges for networks.

Types of Social Innovations	
Practices	Knowledge about promising or proven new practices and tools and how to apply them.
Policies	New or revised public policies (laws, regulations, investments, programs, services, administrative rules) and government power relationships.
Products	New goods or services or business models—solutions—which users can obtain and use.

Key Features of Systems-Changing Innovations

A 2019 analysis of "big bets" on social change made by philanthropies uncovered a key factor that prevents nonprofits from obtaining sizeable investments: "lack of clarity on what enduring results a big bet could credibly achieve, often undermine[s] donors' willingness to take the plunge." Having a relationship with donors—"getting lunch with the right billionaire"—matters, note the report authors, a trio from the Bridgespan Group. But big-bet philanthropists "want to create change that solves or significantly ameliorates a problem," they continue, and "social change leaders, in pursuing exceptionally large gifts, tend to place the heaviest emphasis on the enormity of the problem and on the moral imperative to tackle it rather than on the specific results their efforts could achieve and the specific and logical path to accomplish their goal."

It is critical to be clear about the potential and enduring outcomes and credible pathways to scale of social innovations. Not just for fundraising, but also for the innovation-development process for designing and testing innovations. "A credible pathway . . . contains a few elements," observe the Bridgespan leaders: "A simple logic of the pathway that does not involve a major leap of faith; milestones and processes needed to reach the arrival point; evidence that suggests it will work, based on what's been learned from the pilots, prior work, external research, or the examples of others."

Social innovations that networks produce are most likely to have a credible path to substantial impact if they meet three criteria:

They have systems changing leverage. The innovation must carry a clear, different mindset that is disruptive to business-as-usual in the targeted system. "Big social challenges require system transformation," notes Zia Khan, the Rockefeller Foundation's senior vice president for innovation. "This requires a paradigm shift in how people think about solving a problem and their role in driving a solution.

The innovation must be able to achieve large, measurable improvements of the system's performance. A small improvement, say 5 to 10 percent, may be desirable but it is not likely to transform a system. TalNet's performance data with Mercy Health—a 23 percent reduction in the first-year turnover of new hires and a 20 percent increase in the diversity of its workforce—helped persuade other employers to sign up for its HireReach solution. An innovation's superior performance also includes improved cost effectiveness in producing the results.

They are financially sustainable. The innovation must have a business/economic model that is sustainable, meaning that it is based on reasonably predictable revenues and generates enough income to allow ongoing investment in scaling the innovation. It may start with philanthropic funding, but eventually must find customers or government agencies willing to pay for it. A scalable solution, says Kevin Starr, who directs the Mulago Foundation, must have a strategy "that identifies who is going to replicate the model at really big scale and who is going to pay for all that replication."

They are scalable. The innovation must not be highly dependent on contextual factors that may not exist elsewhere. Instead, it can be applied in many other settings. "Design explicitly for scale," urge Rahul Nayar, Asif Saleh, and Anna Minj, in an article about how social innovations can leverage government resources. "When the potential for widespread impact is considered from the initial conception, it can drive important decisions about inputs, activities, human resources, costs, and complexity."

(For questions to ask about whether potential innovations meet these basic criteria, see Appendix C, Assessing the Potential of Social Innovations Under Development.)

Stages of Innovation Development

No social innovation is born fully ready to have large-scale impact.

The ongoing development of IDAs from a concept in a book to widespread practices and public policies follows a typical—and messy—process for the development of a system-changing social innovation. It starts with a powerful mindset change and the idea for a particular innovation. But, as Bob Friedman says about the IDA concept that Sherraden sketched, "At some point we had to move beyond concepts."

The innovation-development process is often described as a funnel: wide at the opening, narrowing along the way, and extremely narrow at the end. Many ideas are seeded at the outset, but after they are tested against innovation criteria and weeded out, few remain to grow to scale. A striking example of the funnel process at work occurred with the digital platform, #WirVsVirus, initiated in 2020 in Germany to identify ideas for responding to the Covid pandemic. As Johanna Mair and Thomas Gegenhuber report, the open-innovation hackathon attracted 28,000 participants. That was the wide end of the funnel gathering ideas. During a 48-hour period, participants generated 1,500 ideas. A week after the hackathon, roughly 600 experts evaluated the ideas and then assembled a jury of 48 experts from government, business, media, academia, and the civil sector that selected the 20 best solutions. The hackathon organizers also backed additional ideas, providing 130 innovator teams with opportunities to network with experts, exchange knowledge, and request resources from supporting companies. Wrapping up the process, they held a public event that showcased 66 solutions the teams developed. The funnel had narrowed considerably the original pool of ideas.

Social innovation, like business innovation, its commercial counterpart, is a developmental process with an underlying logic. It follows a set of distinct stages: (1) concept development, (2) design and prototyping,

(3) operations, and (4) scaling. In the business sector, this step-by-step process is known as "stage gates"—at each stage, the innovation must meet certain criteria before proceeding to the next stage.

Here's the stage-gate process for social innovations in a nutshell:

- **Concept Development.** Disciplined social innovation networks combine insights and research to form the core concept around which they design an innovation.

- **Design and Prototype.** Innovation networks design and test—prototype—the innovation's feasibility and impact, with feedback usually resulting in the need to redesign and retest, maybe several times.

- **Operations.** Innovation networks design and launch a full-scale operational model from the tested prototype, with a revenue strategy and plan for long-term sustainability.

- **Scaling.** Innovation networks spread the innovation—practice knowledge, policies, or products—into the world through applicable pathways.

This may seem simple, but it isn't. All too often, social innovators and their investors don't have the discipline to follow the process. They may be satisfied with fuzzy ideas that it turns out can't be converted into operational models. They may leap from a concept to a scaling model without testing it thoroughly. If they do prototype the concept, they may not test it carefully enough to learn where it goes wrong or needs improvement. They may fall in love with their innovation and ignore the negative feedback they get during prototyping. Or they may try to operationalize or disseminate an innovation without having thought through how it might be sustained economically over the long run. When Kriss Deiglmeier and Amanda Greco studied 10 major social innovations, they found that barriers to scaling up were "most troublesome between the piloting phase and the scaling phase," creating "a 'stagnation chasm,' where proven ideas get stuck before they are able to maximize their impact."

The innovation process may look linear, step-by-step, but it usually isn't, especially in the design/prototyping stage. As soon as an innovator "goes into the field" and starts testing a design, new information shows up that can rapidly change the original innovation conception. As IDEO leaders explain, the innovation-development process involves "multiple cycles of exploration, prototyping, refinement, measurement, and optimization . . . to ensure that our solution not only succeeded in the pilot phase but also had a clear pathway to scale."

An implication of the stage-gate process is that innovation networks must develop a level of comfort with the idea of "failing early and failing often." Most early-stage innovations do not make it to the operational and scaling stages. "During most parts of an innovation process," note Christian Seelos and Johanna Mair, "it's not clear whether and when an innovation will succeed. . . . Working through the process is like riding a rollercoaster; it's full of ups and downs and sudden swerves in one direction or another." Failure is an important part of the innovation process and can provide valuable information for future innovation development. "Innovation is essentially a matter of learning," Seelos and Mair advise. "Innovators who expect success from innovation efforts will inevitably encounter disappointment, and the experience of failure will generate a blame culture."

Deliverables from Each Stage of Innovation Development

Concept Development	A defined innovation hypothesis and concept, with an analysis of why the opportunity for innovation exists; a written description of the innovation, including its primary features and benefits; and a broad understanding of the resources required to make it a testable reality.
Design & Prototype	A refined design for the innovation, including strategic, user, market, technical, and financial analyses, and working prototypes of the innovation, with performance characteristics verified by users. (This stage often involves several iterations of design-prototype-design-prototype cycles.)
Operations	All of the operating capacities needed to implement the innovation are established, including production processes, talent, business models, capital, and positioning. These may differ depending on the type of innovation.

Scaling	Plans and implementation of efforts to spread/grow the innovation, customized to the type of innovation being scaled and the type of system that has been targeted. There are several distinct pathways to scale.

Concept Stage: Making an Innovation Hypothesis

The networked innovation-development process begins with the formation of concepts and ideas, aka ideation. Sherraden kicked this off for IDAs, much as Radhika Fox did for water equity at the US Water Alliance, and Gary Cohen did in the years when Health Care Without Harm was being born.

An innovation concept is not just a statement of need or a description of a problem or opportunity, which is where many social innovators begin. It's an idea about how to meet a need, solve a problem, or seize an opportunity, based on intuition, analysis, and/or lived experience, that provides the starting point for developing an innovation. For systemic impact, it articulates a mindset shift and offers an innovation hypothesis, a proposed starting point for further investigation about which particular innovation might create the desired impact.

An innovation hypothesis is a version of what could be created and why it will change things. It offers insight into why the targeted system is operating the way it does and how the dynamics of the system can be leveraged in a fundamentally new way. It needs to be specific and actionable, and describe metrics to show whether it's working. It's essential to develop a clear *innovation hypothesis*; when you encounter new information, for instance in the prototyping stage, having a well-defined hypothesis allows you to determine whether the new information puts into question the hypotheses or just calls for an adjustment in how you test the hypothesis.

An innovation hypothesis describes:

• The system that innovators seek to affect.

• What is known about the leverage points in the system— elements of the system where a relatively small input can have a large impact.

- How the hypothesis would move a leverage point.

- What knowledge and other sources inform the hypothesis.

- What it will take to test the hypothesis.

- What kind of evidence will be used to conclude whether or not the hypothesis is valid.

- If the hypothesis proves correct, what getting to scale would look like, and what it would take to achieve it.

  (For more questions to ask see Appendix D, Assessing an Innovation Hypothesis.)

Innovation hypotheses can come from just about anywhere. Mauricio Lim Miller, founder of the Community Independence Initiative, got his radical idea for changing the welfare system by thinking about the way his mother had raised him (see sidebar: Momma Told Me). Fox and the staff at the US Water Alliance engaged in discussions with 150 people in the water sector to develop a framework for water equity. Doug Ross developed the design for a new charter school in Detroit by visiting schools around the US that were successfully educating his target enrollment, African-American students from urban families with low incomes.

Scott Bernstein, founder of the Center for Neighborhood Technology, current president of the American Council for an Energy-Efficient Economy, and a serial social innovator for four decades, describes his approach to developing innovative ideas: "I would look for things that already operated at scale—a high volume of trans-

Scott Bernstein

actions—and examine the regulatory and other requirements they couldn't ignore." What if those drivers could be changed—retrofitted—in ways that produced stronger social benefits? "Or I'd look for organizational forms that were working at small scale and people trusted, and ask, 'Why aren't there more of those?'" What if the models could be replicated? "Or I'd look for the need to invent a service—like energy audits for buildings—that was not being provided, but for which there would be demand." What if something new could be developed and supplied?

Momma Told Me

An unexpected question from a stranger left Mauricio Lim Miller wondering what he really knew from the nearly 20 years he'd spent working to reduce poverty in San Francisco and Oakland. Miller was the executive director of Asian Neighborhood Design, a community organization that worked to improve employment opportunities in poor neighborhoods, and

Mauricio Lim Miller

was praised in President Clinton's 1999 State of the Union message.

The inquiry came from the mayor of Oakland, the famously free-thinking Jerry Brown, the state's former governor. Brown telephoned Miller out of the blue to complain that professional welfare bureaucrats and service providers—social workers, administrators, and other workers—would get most of the money in a $10.2 million proposal to help some of the community's toughest kids. "Poverty pimping," Brown called it. Miller served on the board of the public entity that had drafted the plan.

After Miller agreed with Brown that the professionals were the only people guaranteed to benefit from the proposal, the mayor popped the question that propelled Miller on an innovation path that has run for two decades. "He said, 'If there were no bureaucratic rules and regulations, and you had all the money to use, what would you do to get families permanently out of poverty? Come tell me what you'd do.' He gave me a month."

Right away Miller realized he didn't have an answer to Brown's question. "I'd been working with poverty for 20 years, but always inside the box. You just kept pushing in the box." Most anti-poverty programs, Miller says, including those he ran, don't help poor families permanently. "If anything, they only make the conditions of poverty more acceptable." But Miller thought he knew someone who could help. A month later he met with Brown.

"He turned to me and with no greeting he asked, 'So, what would you do?'" Miller responded: "I don't know what I would do. But my mother figured out what to do to get me out of poverty, and I think every mother, father, or guardian will know the best way to get their own families' lives together." Miller had turned to his mother, Berta, a Mexican immigrant with a third-grade education and two divorces. "She knew what she had done to get me out of poverty." After Miller's sister had a baby at age 17 and left school, Miller's mother decided he would go to college and get the family out of poverty. "She told me I had a choice: doctor or engineer. We weren't sure what engineers did, but we knew they made money." After a brief stint as an engineer and a military tour of duty in Vietnam, Miller began working as a community activist focusing on gang kids.

Thinking of his mother's approach to his upbringing sparked Miller's insight: "Every poor family I knew, knew what they would do to get out of poverty."

Miller told Brown his radical innovation hypothesis centered on the power of networks and people leading their own change: "I have been studying our history, how Harlem and the Chinatowns were built, and how the Irish and others came to dominate certain occupations. It took friends coming together and helping one another, referring one another into jobs. Instead of employing social workers as helpers, I will enroll groups of families who are friends so they can help each other. I think it takes a group to get out of poverty, not a program. . . . From the funds we save by not hiring social workers, we will provide resources directly to families based on what they do for themselves and others."

To develop this concept, Miller created the Family Independence Initiative in 2001, now named the Community Independence Initiative, to demonstrate that just giving people a social worker or a bit of money, like a dollar to the homeless, will not bring about fundamental change. He insisted that governments and nonprofits have to stop playing the leading role and, instead, just backstop the efforts that the people themselves were taking, every day and everywhere. Rather than making handouts, the power of people to help each other, peer-driven change, would unleash more effective and sustainable solutions. "Even though I had been running social welfare programs in Oakland and San Francisco for 20 years, now I was proposing no program, just empowerment of group efforts."

In 2022, Mauricio Miller's expanding efforts are in 10 different countries, activating thousands of local residents to help each other bring about the change that *they* want.

Michael Sherraden's deep analysis of the human services system took many years of systematic social-science research. But his powerful and contrarian insight about the power of asset building for reducing poverty also came from personal experience. Sherraden had never had much savings until he became an assistant professor at Washington University and began to receive quarterly statements for the retirement account that came with his job. He went to a meeting to learn more about the accounts, not expecting there would be many other people there. But, as Bob Friedman reports in *A Few Thousand Dollars*, the room was packed with faculty. "Asset-holding," Sherraden reflected, "has a way of grabbing people's attention. They, like he, had been given an asset of growing value. . . . It did not escape Michael's attention that these accounts, although called 'private,' were in fact created by public policy, with substantial public subsidies through tax benefits." At the same time, Sherraden's research involved interviews with welfare recipients who noted that they were not given any assistance in saving for the future and if they did save even $1,000, they could lose their welfare benefits. "Michael reflected on the duality of these policies—some people were encouraged and subsidized in building assets, while others were discouraged and penalized. . . . And then he designed and tested potential solutions."

Sherraden was hardly alone in developing these ideas. In *Assets and the Poor*, he acknowledges the contributions of more than 70 people—his *network* of academic colleagues, policymakers, welfare recipients, friends, and family members who provided suggestions, encouragement, discussions, ideas, and questions in the development of the IDA concept.

A number of factors for success in the conceptualization stage have emerged in the work of social innovation networks, including:

Practice co-creation. Collaboration with stakeholders, users, and customers can greatly enhance the innovation-development process, starting with conceptualization. Networks can be ideal settings for bringing together the right mix of collaborators and creating the conditions for productive, inclusive collaboration. As leaders at IDEO note: innovators "must shift from mere consultation to co-creation, in which those who will ultimately benefit from and/or deliver a solution can shape the outcome at each stage of the design process. . . . We must build a space that enables those with lived experience of the issue at hand to participate fully."

Joanna Levin Cea and Jess Remington in "Creating Breakout Innovation" caution that effective cocreation requires power sharing: "While many crowdsourcing, open innovation, and consultation processes ask stakeholders to provide input, relatively few share power. Sharing power means distributing the functions of decision making, creation, implementation, and evaluation among the process participants, and dissolving once rigid divides between designer and consumer, expert and beneficiary."

Apply ideas from other fields and other unexpected places. Look to other fields to find ideas that may have innovative applications in your field. For instance, Erika Owens at OpenNews is thinking about her earlier experiences in community organizing in Philadelphia to imagine potential new services that the network might develop. Mauricio Miller's idea for radically reinventing human services came from his mother's experiences as a parent (see sidebar, Momma Told Me). Cross-fertilization provides food for the associational thinking that the authors of *The Innovator's DNA* say is a key skill for developing innovative ideas (see sidebar, Five Skills for Developing Innovative Concepts).

Start with the end in mind. Address getting to scale early in the innovation-development process. While the problem of scaling doesn't need to be tackled until the innovation has demonstrated that it can work, the requirements for scaling need to be considered as early as possible in the innovation development process, preferably starting at the concept-development stage. Many innovations achieve their performance outcomes based on conditions that cannot be replicated at scale—such as excessive financial subsidies, unique local circumstances or relationships, one-time policy opportunities, or unique talents or personalities—without any consideration of how these contextual limits will be overcome in the scaling process.

Frame the concept for success. How the concept is framed can matter when it comes to attracting the interest and resources of other parties. We noted in chapter 2 that a network of philanthropies helped the California community college system provide educational opportunities to the state's numerous incarcerated and formerly incarcerated students. The changes were not framed as a criminal justice strategy. Instead, they were presented as a higher education initiative because, as Rebecca Silbert and Debbie Mukamal report, "the goal was to change the public

Five Skills for Developing Innovative Concepts

Concepts for system-changing innovations arise from human creativity. It's common to believe that creativity is a genetic endowment that someone does or doesn't have, or that it's a mental process, a way of thinking, which can be learned. But the authors of *The Innovator's DNA*—Jeff Dyer, Hal Gregersen, and Clayton M. Christensen—offer a quite different explanation. Their research with hundreds of business innovators found that creative ideas spring from five "discovery skills" that are the basis for developing innovative concepts:

Associational thinking. This is a cognitive skill: making connections across seemingly unrelated questions, problems, or ideas. "Innovative breakthroughs often happen at the intersection of diverse disciplines and fields." Associational thinking is sparked by the four other skills, which are behavioral.

Questioning. Innovators' "questions frequently challenge the status quo . . . They love to ask, 'If we tried this, what would happen?'" They ask questions "to understand how things really are today, why they are that way, and how they might be changed or disrupted. Their questions outnumber answers and are valued as highly as answers."

Observing. Innovators "carefully watch the world around them—including customers, products, services, technologies, and companies—and the observations help them gain insights into and ideas for new ways of doing things."

Networking. Innovators "spend a lot of time and energy finding and testing ideas through a diverse network of individuals who vary wildly in their backgrounds and perspectives. . . They actively search for new ideas by talking to people who may offer a radically different view of things."

Experimenting. Innovators "explore the world intellectually and experientially, holding convictions at bay and testing hypotheses along the way. They visit new places, try new things, seek new information, and experiment to learn new things."

higher education system and to incorporate these new students into the existing higher education structure, rather than to create a new criminal justice project. Beneficiaries were students who happened to have criminal records, rather than 'offenders' in a new recidivism program."

Prototyping Stage: Designing and Testing

Sooner or later concepts for innovation, however they have been developed, need to be proven to work. This is usually done by designing the idea into a prototype and testing it. "At some point," recalls Bob Friedman, "I decided that ideas are one thing, but we needed to see something in practice. A real IDA. We needed a systematic, rigorous demonstration so we could produce evidence."

For IDAs the main test was the American Dream Demonstration or ADD. The demonstration started in 1997; $14 million in total grants from a dozen national foundations enabled experiments at 14 sites with community-based organizations as partners. Their IDA programs provided each of 2,378 account holders—most of them women of color living in poverty—with up to $2,000 in matching funds for savings they deposited, and also gave them financial education. The project lasted five years and was subject to rigorous evaluation that, Friedman says, "proved that the poor can save a few hundred dollars a year—rates that, proportionately speaking, exceed those of higher-income families—if that saving is structured and made easy and rewarded." Half of the participants saved money in their accounts, accumulating more than $1.12 million in savings. Within two years of starting their IDAs, a third of the participants had used savings to obtain assets—paying for education, purchasing or repairing a home, starting a small business, or saving for retirement. Large majorities of account holders said that because of their IDAs they felt more economically secure and more confident about the future.

"We proved that there is a savings capacity among the poor," recalls Lisa Mensah, who at the time was a program officer at the Ford Foundation, which put substantial funding into the demonstration. "I got to put real zeroes behind the dollars," she says, with the support of Melvin Oliver who in 1996 became a vice president at the

Lisa Mensah

foundation and pushed the assets-building approach for poverty reduction. Mensah, who grew up as one of the only African-American girls in a small Oregon city, had a professional background in banking and has focused her career—split between Ford and the Aspen Institute and now as CEO of the <u>Opportunity Finance Network</u>—on closing the racial wealth gap in the US. "I was a momma of the movement for 25 years."

The prototyping stage is often the most chaotic and unpredictable time for an innovation. It requires that innovators combine rapid adaptation, gut instinct, ruthless rigor and openness to surprise. Some innovation designers adopt a "rapid prototyping" approach in which they conduct short-term, low-cost trials with frequent design changes. Sometimes prototyping results will push an innovation back into the concept stage, forcing the innovator to rethink the premises upon which the innovation is based. It almost always results in the need to revise the innovation that's being tested because feedback loops reveal the strengths and weaknesses of the innovation design.

The testing of the GoodSAM app in the United Kingdom followed a pattern of successive revisions. GoodSAM alerts off-duty doctors, nurses, paramedics, and qualified first aiders when someone near them has a life-threatening medical crisis. Conceptualized in 2018 by a neurosurgeon, Mark Wilson, the app had a volunteer community of 25,000 responders, whose actions helped to reduce the response time when emergency services were needed to provide basic life support. But before the app scaled up, it had to be redesigned several times, as Alicia Clegg explains in "Smartphone Samaritans."

In its first iteration, members of the public could use the app to issue an alert. But this required people to have downloaded the app onto their phones, which limited the number of patients that could be helped. The second version integrated the app into the typical process that regional ambulance services used for responding to cardiac arrests. But its usefulness had to be demonstrated. "When the ambulance services saw how good the functionality was and that there was a pool of people ready to volunteer, it became much easier to get them around the table," recalls Ali Ghorbangholi, who developed the app. With the integrated approach, it became necessary to ensure that volunteers were vetted for competence, so they had to be trained and assessed to perform CPR. Local ambulance services, not GoodSAM, may choose to limit the volunteer community to their own staff or specific partner organizations such as fire and law enforcement agencies. On the technology side, the app at first could not bypass the silent mode on phones. Developers worked with Apple and Google and made GoodSAM the world's first app to give users the option of overriding silent mode.

TalNet also made significant adjustments as it tested its evidence-based selection solution. Its redesign reduced by more than 50 percent the amount of time it took for users to implement the solution, taking it down to 5 months. The network also managed to cut the cost of analyzing each employer's job requirements, once in the thousands of dollars, to almost zero.

The US Water Alliance made a different kind of adjustment when it prototyped a process for initiating water equity practices. Working with water utilities and community organizations in a seven-city piloting taskforce, it realized that forging successful local collaborations—critical for water equity—depended on addressing the power imbalance between community members and the large water institutions. "Not only do community groups tend to be significantly under-resourced, leading to gaps in funding, staffing and capacity to take on extra work, the experiences and wisdom they gather from the front lines are often valued less than government bodies or institutions," states an after-action report, "Water Equity Taskforce: Insights for the Water Sector." The Alliance offered stipends to community leaders as compensation for their time and also paid for their travel and lodging for in-person learning exchanges. But that wasn't enough to level the power differential. "After the first learning exchange among cities, the Alliance received feedback that teams were not hearing from community groups as much as they would like. It was clear that despite the intentionality in the Taskforce design, it still needed explicit structures to elevate the voices of community members." So, the Alliance redesigned sessions to provide dedicated time for community groups to share their views. The second learning exchange included a panel of community leaders discussing their experiences in policy and program development.

Prototypes are probes that help you more deeply understand the system you are seeking to change. If you are working with a highly complex system, it is often impossible to know everything you need to know to gain leverage. Prototypes allow you to get intimate knowledge of how the system works by interacting with it on an operating basis. A system may change its behavior in unpredictable ways in response to your innovation, and you can't know what these ways will be until you get out there and test what you've designed.

Factors for a network's success in the prototyping stage include:

Design for user interaction. Here's how designing things typically occurs, says Piyush Tantia, chief innovation officer at Ideas42, a social enterprise that uses insights from behavioral science to design solutions: "We use our creativity to brainstorm a few big ideas, experts decide which one they like, and then investors bet on the winner." What this leaves out, he continues, is "insights into how people interact with their environment and each other under different conditions." This is crucial for designing social innovations because they typically depend more on human interactions than on the physical product or service. Vaccines, for instance, are technological products. But whether, how, and when people get vaccinated—social issues—is a key part of whether a vaccine will be successful. Turning to behavioral science can provide valuable insights into how people react to specific elements of their context, Tantia says. "We can use behavioral science to anticipate which solutions are likely to suffer from behavioral problems such as low adoption by participants or misperception of choices."

A related lesson comes from practitioners of human-centered design. IDEO leaders were piloting sites for DIVA Centres in Zambia, places where teenage girls could hang out with their friends, with a nurse present to answer questions, especially about sex and contraception. It was an effort to expand young women's access to reproductive-health care. But the centers' initial design was critically flawed. It focused too narrowly on just reproductive health. "While the social sector is frequently divided into actors that address these issues individually, girls themselves experience them holistically," report Jocelyn Wyatt, Tim Brown and Shauna Carey. "For a teenage girl access to contraception and choices about sex and relationships are intrinsically linked to the other areas of her life. Creating systemic change in the opportunities young women have to shape their lives will require coordinated efforts within and beyond access to reproductive-health care." Since 2014 the redesigned centers have served more than 400,000 young women, who adopted contraceptive methods of their choice.

Build relationships. Prototyping is a great way to build supportive networks and partnerships, and should be structured to "harvest" these relationships in productive ways. In many cases, key players will listen politely to your ideas and even give you useful input, but they won't engage with you until you are doing something that connects concretely to their professional work. As these new partners connect with you, their views will often also drive additional changes in your innovation design.

Beware of premature exposure. One of the difficulties of the social sector is that it often ends up conducting its design/prototyping process in a "fishbowl" with too many unrealistic expectations. There can be a need to show results much too early, and too many people end up weighing in on the design too early in the process. This can cause more confusion than clarity. Social innovations are often publicly "launched" at the prototype stage in a way that puts them under a level of public scrutiny that actually constrains innovative thinking and responsiveness to feedback. Changes in direction and design are perceived as "failures" or "mistakes" instead of being seen as a natural part of the process.

You need to protect innovators at this stage, keeping them as much "under the radar" as possible and allowing them to "fail early and fail often" in a way that maximizes learning and improves innovations. Expectations for results and outcomes should be kept modest, and stakeholders should be reminded that the innovation is still a hypothesis that has not yet demonstrated "proof of concept."

Manage funders' expectations. Innovations often go through four or five generations of design in the design/prototyping phase, a timeline and process that can be difficult for many philanthropic investors. They may expect predictable results and that the innovation's development will proceed smoothly from design to launch. The key here is to get investors to focus on the potential *outcomes* instead of the innovation design, and not to worry if the innovation design changes rapidly.

(See Appendix E, Prototyping Questions to Wrestle With)

Operations Stage: Managing and Implementing

In late 2021 TalNet was putting the finishing touches on operationalizing its first innovation, an evidence-based selection (EBS) solution that employers could use to implement a fair, objective, data-driven system for making better hiring and promotion decisions. It had successfully prototyped EBS with one large employer, which over the years applied the solution to 10,000 hiring and promotion transactions.

Through the HireReach initiative, it was taking the EBS approach into dozens of enterprises in west Michigan and needed to establish a complete operational capacity. Delivering the innovation to a growing number of employers required 12 distinct, interlocked components. The HireReach Academy would be a five-month learning-and-doing session for participating employers to develop and launch their customized EBS process. But to pull off the academy, HireReach needed to have a recruitment system to attract employers; an application form for employers wanting to participate; a baseline assessment of each employer's talent selection practices; a design for the academy; and much more. It needed ongoing management and staffing capacity, which would be provided out of a new nonprofit organization called Strategic Workforce Solutions. It also hired a software engineer who had worked with employee assessments to turn its instructional material into an online platform with automated test taking and scoring, creating a learning management system for customers to use.

At the operational stage, innovations like EBS for talent are made ready for "prime time." All of the core operating capacities needed to implement the innovation are established. At this stage, the challenges of innovation development transition from invention to execution, no matter what type of innovation is being developed.

- Public policies are formally adopted by a governing entity and, if necessary, government budgets are appropriated and staffing is put in place to implement the policies. In Michigan, for instance, state government created a website through which people could apply for free community college—and tens of thousands did. The state legislature appropriated funds to cover the cost of eliminating tuition.

- Solutions—products and services—are put into final production, with processes, budgets, and staffing. Quite often, a new enterprise is created to enact the operations, as in the case of the nonprofit that will carry the HireReach solution into the talent-selection market.

- Practice know-how is packaged into attractive information products—guidebooks, curricula, frameworks, tools, lessons learned, and the like. Instructional models such as webinars and workshops are designed to support users in applying the knowledge. Communities of practice—groups of individuals or organizations focused on using the innovation—are often assembled so practitioners can learn with and from each other about using the know-how. The US Water Alliance's Water Equity Network of 28 cities does exactly that. The know-how that has been developed by earlier prototyping cities requires utilities and community groups to "build meaningful, trusting relationships and adopt new ways of thinking and working," as the Alliance reports. Operationally, this means building new capacities for long-term collaboration and systems change within the participating organizations. Doing this usually entails profound changes in the organizations' cultures. Alliance teams had to listen to each other, build trust and mutual understanding. Their leaders had "to come to the table without pride or ego and with humility and vulnerability," the Alliance says. In the network, city teams learned how to "embrace participatory interactions where utilities and community groups have an equal stake in setting priorities and making decisions together."

Depending on the type of social innovation that's been developed, a network may decide to launch operations itself, or establish an enterprise that will do the operations, or partner with other entities that operate the innovation. Products and services are often produced and delivered through an organization model, usually a social enterprise. Public policies operate through government entities, although these may contract out or partner for some of the work. Practice know-how typically informs operations of ongoing networks and organizations.

The factors for success in the operations stage boil down to four building blocks that innovation networks must develop: strategic purpose, processes, talent, and capital.

Ensure that the innovation's strategic purpose is clear. Strategic purpose provides clear direction on key questions such as: What is the innovation trying to do and which users and allies does it need to engage?

Under what conditions can it succeed? What risks must be managed? Backers of IDAs found themselves in a tangle of strategic purposes that ranged from supporting nonprofit community-based providers, or engaging private financial institutions, or seeking government policies that incentivized savings. And pushing for policy support generated opposition from advocates for poverty reduction who were concerned that asset building would supplant already insufficient welfare support. "We were vilified," recalls Mensah. "At the time," she says, "the Bush administration was trying to go private with Social Security. The worry was that nice Black women like me would lend progressive credibility to efforts to end Social Security, replace it with all these little savings accounts, and we'd have no social insurance for the poor."

Detail the processes that will produce the innovation for use. The network must be clear about precisely how the innovation is to be produced and delivered, as we saw TalNet addressing. The federal government lacked this knowledge when the Clinton administration and Congress adopted an initial IDA initiative, Friedman points out. The accounts were time limited and, he says, "controlled by restrictions included in legislation developed before there was any operating IDA program." It was built on "the delivery capacity of nonprofit organizations and community largesse." And its goal of 10,000 IDA accounts was "simply inadequate in a country where 200 million people or more lack an economic place to stand." According to Mensah, "Using community organizations was never the plan for scale. How are all these millions of people and their kids going to buy houses and other assets on the backs of nonprofits? It's a great infrastructure for demonstration, but the wrong structure for scaling."

Staff the processes with the necessary talents—and build collective culture. Detail what skills and expertise are needed to implement the innovation and put qualified people in place. This building block includes the collective culture of individuals involved in the processes—the shared values and mindsets, trusted leadership, and reward systems that further enable production.

Ensure there's enough capital to launch operations—and know where future money will come from. "Social innovators face a convoluted and often elusive path to mobilize the resources needed to amplify the impact of their work," note Deiglmeier and Greco. Nonetheless, innovation networks must secure enough money to put into place the operational building blocks and the working capital needed to commence operations. And they must determine their longer-term economic model for generating revenue to cover costs.

Re-Designing Innovation Operations

Nearly three decades ago a network of foresters, environmentalists, community leaders, and some forestry businesses pioneered a certification process to ensure that wood products come from sustainably managed forests. It was a social innovation product designed to enter and impact global forestry markets. The network formed the Forest Stewardship Council (FSC), which by 2022 had certified 565 million acres of forestland worldwide, equivalent to 30 percent of all the land in the US.

But back in 2001 the fledgling nonprofit and its innovation were in trouble because of the design of its operations. As the Ford Foundation, a major donor to the FSC, reported at the time, the nonprofit membership organization had hundreds of members, had established the integrity of its certification process, and had been endorsed by environmental groups worldwide. Thousands of wood and wood-containing products bore the Council's trademark logo. But there were major operational problems. Because its world headquarters was in Oaxaca, Mexico, FSC leaders had trouble raising the Council's visibility and maintaining communications with players in the forest industry. "Organized as a classic NGO, it could not function at the speed of business," Ford summarized. The FSC was having difficulty building demand for certification in the Congo Basin, Southeast Asia, China, and other critical places in the forest world. Even though it was providing discernible commercial value to the forest products industry, it was not financially self-sufficient and had to find grants to keep running.

A strategic planning process laid out these challenges and resulted in a Council commitment to revamp operationally. It moved its headquarters to Bonn, Germany, and raised enough additional one-time philanthropic funding to expand its efforts and support a transition to a sound financial basis.

Scaling Stage: Pathways to Scale

Nearly 30 years after Sherraden's manuscript first turned his mind, Bob Friedman can see IDAs dispersing across America and scaling up. Today, he says, the IDA field, contains "tens of thousands of organizations and individuals all across the nation, devoted to financial capability, inclusion, and asset-building—and is growing on all sides."

It's been an incremental progression. By 2001, some 400 community IDA programs had 10,000 account holders, and 31 states and the District of Columbia had passed IDA-related legislation. A nine-year federal program funded an IDA program in which 21,512 refugees saved more than $30 million and leveraged loans—which enabled them to purchase vehicles, homes, education, and more. The US Department of Housing and Urban Development opened and partially funded more than 75,000 IDA accounts. By 2006 about 600 programs in all 50 states delivered IDAs.

Policies supporting asset building by individuals, Oliver and Shapiro note, "moved from something nobody heard of or knew anything about in 1995, to being a main player and topic of conversation at the policy table"—and they were being institutionalized, so progress didn't depend on just a few social entrepreneurs. All told, notes Friedman, "hundreds of thousands of Americans have used IDAs," with more than half of them using their savings to purchase homes, start businesses, or go to college or job training.

Meanwhile, IDA account holders have expanded the use of assets to provide themselves with emergency savings cushions, retirement savings, preparation for citizenship, and other uses. New applications of the IDA concept include "baby bonds," accounts for newborns into which governments place seed grants—larger ones for poorer families—that grow through investment and are available for use when the babies reach adulthood. "At the root of the racial wealth gap, and wealth inequality in general, is capital itself," says economist Darrick Hamilton, founding director of the Institute for the Study of Race, Stratification and Political Economy at The New School. "Baby bonds are specifically aimed at giving people that seed capital, that asset that passively appreciates over their lifetime."

In Maine, since 2009, 116,000 children have been awarded a total of

$58 million for accounts. In 2018 Pennsylvania became the first state to adopt legislation to create accounts for all children—about 140,000 annually—with $100 seed deposits. Oklahoma opened college savings accounts with grants of $1,000 each for more than 1,300 children, chosen at random, between 2007 and 2019.

But these developments have not realized the ultimate scale that Friedman and other advocates wanted: universal IDAs, a savings account for every American. At least not yet.

Scaling up IDAs always depended on securing an enormous amount of government funding. "The greatest barrier to universal IDAs is funding," Friedman acknowledges. "A few thousand dollars for a million Americans is billions. A few thousand dollars for hundreds of millions of Americans is hundreds of billions."

But even as IDA scaling seems to have plateaued, the system-changing mental model shift toward asset building that is embedded in IDAs has gained momentum. "No longer is the field of asset development focused on one product, the Individual Development Account," Friedman explains. "Now it encompasses a range of products and services, from credit-building savings groups to financial coaching. Nor is the field based on freestanding, privately supported nonprofits. Financial inclusion practices and policies are being integrated into education, social service agencies, housing services, and even the tax system."

In late 2021, for example, New York City opened college savings accounts for about 70,000 public school kindergarteners, with a $100 deposit for each and financial incentives to induce parents to add to the savings. The city committed $15 million to the initiative through 2025, matched by $15 million from the Gray Foundation. This added to the nearly 1 million children's savings accounts already established in 36 states.

The elements of a wealth-creating system for the poor are evident. "It is time," Friedman says, "to take the proven principles, lessons, and results of matched savings, IDAs, and other wealth-building tools to scale." He has hope because "the times have changed. People are talking about wealth and the racial divide in ways that are fundamentally different from 30 years ago."

It's not unusual for system-changing networks to work on multiple types of scale. The scaling of IDAs has taken several distinct paths. Nonprofit organizations developed their own IDAs based on the practice knowledge that Sherraden, Friedman, and others developed. Eventually they formed communities of practitioners that share information, experiences, and advice. IDAs were also promoted by public policies of state and federal governments, which offered incentives and other support. And players in financial markets—banks, community development financial institutions—began to offer IDAs as products for customers.

These three types of innovations—practices, policies, and products—are main elements in our overarching framework for getting to system-changing scale. Because there's much more to say about the multiple pathways that such innovations take to scale, we devote the next chapter to this topic.

Networks & Social Innovation Development

The 30-year arc of the IDA social innovation involves a rolling cast of many people and organizations in different and evolving configurations. "The whole growth of the IDA/asset-building field is the story of networks," Friedman observes. "My whole strategy—intentional and unintentional—was to reach out and bring people together who were attracted to the concept. There was the annual IDA Learning Conference, which morphed from 150 people at the first one to more than a thousand at the later conferences, all increasingly diverse in race, gender, role, and sector. The American Dream Demonstration, and community-based practices, public policies, and private markets for IDAs—there was never any top-down command-and-control. And the participants wouldn't take orders even if there had been. There are federal, state, regional, and local clusters of players that are working together and feedback loops and different funding sources—all learning and growing together, all working on different aspects of IDAs, but with multiple and strong research, policy, funding, and practice efforts. The whole nature of the 'field' was and is a network."

For networks moving social innovations through stage gates, in addition to the requirements at each stage, there are several lessons learned about navigating the overall and often turbulent process of innovation development.

Advice for Networks Developing Social Innovations

- Build an ongoing innovation-management system, not just a one-time effort.

- Be willing to rigorously interrogate your own ideas.

- Follow the money.

- Prepare for the long run.

- Recognize that failure = learning.

Build an ongoing innovation-management system, not just a one-time effort. System-changing efforts usually need to produce more than a single social innovation to achieve transformation. Therefore, social innovation networks may need to serve as the developers of multiple, linked interventions in systems. They are actually in the innovation management business. Even if they start up to produce a single innovation, they find they have to do much more innovating over long periods of time to impact the system they've targeted. They have to build a sustained capacity for innovation.

This is the case with the US Water Alliance; water equity is just one of a half-dozen major efforts it pursues for systemic change in the water sector. In 2022, the network also has initiatives that respond to water-sector stresses caused by the Covid-19 pandemic. It is advancing a blueprint for federal policies and supporting change-management of utilities' leadership. It advises on consolidation of small utilities and helps utilities to build climate resilience. It promotes collaborations between artists and water utilities and runs a national campaign championing public investment in water infrastructure.

Be willing to rigorously interrogate your own ideas. Social entrepreneurs are often action oriented and impatient. But a balance needs to be struck between "shooting from the hip" (rushing into the field before you have clearly articulated or researched your innovation hypothesis) and "analysis paralysis" (thinking forever and never doing anything). The concept stage, for example, requires a certain level of patience and discipline in continuing to ask hard questions about your hypothesis, rather than jumping to the design of the innovation. Many would-be social innovators start by working from an innovation hypothesis that is far too vague and abstract. They may not acknowledge the uncertainties they face in the innovation-development process, or have not developed sufficient knowledge of the system they target, or have no real hypothesis about scaling. These are all potentially fatal flaws.

Follow the money. You have to know how much innovations will cost to implement. Scalable and financially sustainable social innovations cannot be developed without detailed knowledge of costs. Many social entrepreneurs lack the financial management skills, systems, and discipline to develop innovations that can eventually support themselves financially. Knowing what the "unit of production" is, exactly how much it costs, what that cost consists of, and what the key cost drivers are: this information is critical for the innovation development process.

Prepare for the long run. Most entrepreneurs and investors seriously underestimate the time and cost of developing and launching social innovations that have the potential to transform the performance of systems. Serious innovations that end up getting to some scale may take one or more decades of experimentation, refinement, and support to achieve success.

Recognize that failure = learning. Innovators get attached to their ideas and it can be difficult for them to let go, even if an idea fails to measure up to its potential. Pulling the plug is typically perceived by others as a "failure" rather than as a smart and disciplined move to conserve scarce innovation capital and talent. It is important to build a culture within the social innovation network of rapidly learning from failure and rewarding those who make the hard decision to stop investing in a failing idea and move on to the next opportunity. Don't let wishful thinking override feedback.

For system-changing networks, the first three stages of innovation development—conceptualizing, prototyping, operationalizing—are more than hurdles that must be cleared. They are ways to evolve and strengthen the innovation under development for the ultimate stage of scaling.

We've used the word scale dozens of times in the previous pages—always as an aspiration that a social innovation network holds. Learning more about how to scale up innovations—what the pathways are and how to follow them—starts with answering this question: what exactly is scale?

CHAPTER 4

Taking Pathways to Scale

*We can't chart precise directions for each and every scaling journey.
As we travel, conditions change, and so too should our route,
our speed, our means of transport, and even our destination.*

John Gargani and Robert McLean

Scaling up is like climbing a mountain. You need to know which pathway to take to the summit and you must have the right capability for coping with the changing conditions as you ascend.

For social innovation networks seeking system impacts, the summit is whatever scale you hope to achieve. There are three main types of scales: markets, fields, or governments. The pathway you follow depends on which scale you've chosen and the type of innovation you've developed. Each scale has a distinct pathway. Some innovations, however, need to be advanced along more than one pathway.

The network capability needed for the climb is different from what got you to the base of the mountain. Innovation networks that have been conceptualizing and testing innovations are not designed to take scaling pathways. Turning an idea into an innovation is not the same as applying the tested and completed innovation in numerous settings, getting other people and organizations to accept and use the innovation. Scaling requires different skills and functions. It's the difference between developing the concept for Individual Development Accounts and establishing and operating IDAs for millions of users nationwide. Or developing an evidence-based selection model for employers and persuading and supporting hundreds of employers in a region to replace their hiring processes with EBS. Or developing a comprehensive framework for water equity and helping thousands of water utilities, community groups, and equity and environmental advocates to agree on and implement actions together.

In the beginning stages of innovation development—conceptualizing and prototyping—the network usually is a small, tightly connected group of people, what professor of innovation and entrepreneurship Andrew Hargadon, in *How Breakthroughs Happen*, calls a "collective." Further along in the development progression—operations and scaling—the network typically grows to involve many more people and organizations, what Hargadon labels a "community."

These communities undertake the main tasks of scaling up in a market, field, or government, which are fundamentally relational. "Innovators must develop relationships with those affected by the innovation and those that make scale possible," note evaluators John Gargani and Robert McLean. "The practical challenge that innovators face is how to coordinate the actions of diverse actors with multiple agendas and perspectives in a way that advances the public good." Aligning diverse actors at scale can be extremely difficult. They will have different attitudes toward an innovation, which affects the speed and ease of its progress toward scale. Some will readily embrace the change; others will not be interested at all or may oppose it.

The framework of scaling pathways that we present in this chapter is entwined with the significant adaptations that innovation networks undergo as they take on the unique challenges of scaling.

Green Buildings

Karen Weigert didn't invent the LEED rating system for green buildings. She didn't even know much about it when, in 2011, Chicago's mayor appointed her to be the city's first chief sustainability officer. "None of my work experience had gotten me into the day-to-day of LEED," recalls Weigert, who'd been a senior vice president at a

Karen Weigert

community development bank, the producer and writer of a film, *Carbon Nation*, about solutions to climate change, and a consultant with McKinsey & Company.

In 2022, though, Weigert is helping to guide LEED through its next decades of existence. In 2019 she joined the board of the US Green Building Council (USGBC), which did invent LEED. "I said yes because I was interested in meaningful change at scale, and LEED is as close as you'll find to that for buildings." She and other USGBC leaders have taken up the cause that motivated the generation that founded USGBC and designed LEED nearly three decades ago.

In 1993, as concern about global warming was heating up, there were few, if any, green buildings in all the world. Some buildings had green features—designed, constructed, and operated to reduce energy or water consumption, solar panels installed to provide clean energy, and other fixes. But buildings had not been developed to be as environmentally and socially responsible as possible. And the building sector had no standards in place to determine how sustainable a building was. That year a small group of environmentalists, real-estate developers, architects, lawyers, and business leaders met and created the US Green Building Council (USGBC) to develop a green-building rating system, which became known as LEED, short for Leadership in Energy and Environmental Design.

As a social innovation, LEED falls into the product and service category. It is essentially a standard, a set of measures of building quality, that can be evaluated and formally certified by an independent third party, the USGBC. LEED assesses the design, construction, and operations of buildings, and scores them for numerous categories including energy efficiency, water savings, waste reduction, indoor environmental quality, and materials selection. It awards certificates for varying levels of quality: from a low of certified, then up the ladder to silver and gold, and to the maximum level, platinum. After the assessment, a customized LEED plaque can be installed in the building to showcase the achievement. "It's a system that gives you concrete ways to make your building better, and any building can be better," Weigert notes.

LEED's development comes as the world moves into an enormous boom in global building stock to accommodate population and economic growth. "The largest wave of urban growth in human history," predicts Architecture 2030, forecasting the addition of 2.4 trillion square feet in new floor area—"the equivalent of adding an entire New York City to the world, every month, for 40 years."

Use of LEED spread slowly at first. It took five years for the newly formed USGBC to develop LEED 1.0 and begin to test it on 19 projects.

The public launch of the first LEED certification for new construction came in 2000. In 2003 a comprehensive set of LEED standards covering all aspects of building development and construction was launched and by 2004 there were 1,200 LEED certified projects. The next year the USGBC held its first green building conference and 4,000 people attended.

When Weigert started working in Chicago's city hall, she quickly realized that a number of architects in the city were designing new buildings using LEED and that city policies "embraced LEED as a tool for sustainability." She could see the power of the innovation: "It took something squishy—green buildings—and made it concrete. It laid out the things you did to get a label. It offered different tiers of certificates so you could keep improving." Looking around the US she saw many other players advancing LEED years after its birth. "There were chapters all over the place. The thousands of people who were participating in creating the green building sector—they'd caught lightning in a bottle."

By 2022, the USGBC says, LEED has become the most widely used building-rating system in the world, applicable to all building types and all building phases. More than 69,000 buildings in the US are LEED-certified, the most of any nation. Texas has the most LEED-certified residential projects of any state, 6,945 of them, nearly half in the Dallas-Fort Worth-Arlington region. As LEED spreads internationally, Canada and China are early adopters with more than 4,700 projects between them.

From 2015 and 2018, according to the USGBC, certified buildings worldwide saved more than $2.1 billion in costs for energy, water, waste, and maintenance. Certified projects were estimated to have required more than $100 billion in green materials. LEED now certifies communities as LEED-users, with more than 120 US cities and counties having achieve that designation. Washington, DC became the first LEED-certified city in 2017; two years later it certified the first LEED business improvement district in the world. Today the city contains more than 1,100 LEED-certified buildings.

The evolution of LEED displays the shift from a tight collective to a broad community that Hargadon identified for innovation networks. It was created and has been sustained through nearly three decades by a morphing network of participants. The innovation collective started fairly small; about 60 people attended the first meeting and a subset of them worked on designing LEED. Many other people participated in critiquing and testing the first LEED models. As LEED was operationalized, the number of people and organizations involved increased and a loose and growing community took shape. Over the years, founders departed and new players like Karen Weigert took on leadership roles.

Today the US Green Building Council's scaling community contains more than 6,000 dues-paying member organizations, more than 300 staff, 130,000 volunteers, and more than 220,000 LEED-trained and -accredited professionals. The USGBC has partner organizations such as the Center for Green Schools and Greenbuild, which hosts the world's largest annual event for green building professionals. In addition, the World Green Building Council has member councils in more than 70 countries worldwide, with a total of 49,000 members.

How does the enormous expansion in the use of LEED and other social innovations happen? What pathways to scale are used?

Scales and Levels

When we say "scale" what do we mean? And what exactly is the scale of a system?

"There isn't a universal definition of scale," report Kriss Deiglmeier and Amanda Greco in "Why Proven Solutions Struggle to Scale Up." "Scaling impact can look different for different innovations." They note definitions that cast scale as achieving impact that matches the level of need or having an impact that is far greater than the resources used. Along these lines, Christian Seelos and Johanna Mair describe scaling as "delivering effective products and services to more people and doing it more reliably, more efficiently, and with a steady improvement in quality."

Most understanding about scaling comes from the expansion of 19th century industries, the regulation of pharmaceuticals, and 21st century technology startups, observe Gargani and McLean in "Scaling Science." Drug companies obtain sole rights to an innovation and scaling it, they explain. Tech companies use lean development processes in which they "build a minimum viable product, bring it to market, learn rapidly from customer behavior, modify the product, or pivot, and repeat." But, they continue, these models "are insufficient for contemporary social innovation. They reflect an old mind-set in which organizations rather than impacts are scaled up, scaling is an imperative, bigger is better, and the purpose of scaling is commercial success."

Along with these general explanations of scale we can identify several prevalent scales that social innovators target for change: markets, fields, and governments.

Markets. One system scale is markets: sellers offering goods and services to buyers in exchange for money. A market is a composition of systems, institutions, procedures, networks, infrastructures, and government regulations that enable the exchange. Markets may be distinct from each other, with sectors and segments depending on which product or service or type of customer is involved.

Many social innovation networks take on systems that are markets. When LEED designation of buildings became desirable in the eyes of potential renters of commercial space, a market dynamic arose for green buildings. Demand and supply increased, with many customers willing to pay a premium to get access to green office space. The local water systems that the US Water Alliance engages are markets: customers pay for water services. Higher education is a market: students pay tuition for access to courses. The hiring system that TalNet works on is a market in which potential employees compete for jobs and employers compete for workers. Hospitals targeted by Health Care Without Harm also function in markets, exchanging health care services for payments by patients, insurers, or governments.

Fields. Professional fields—architects, doctors, journalists, water utility managers, human-service providers, bankers, and teachers, for example—span the globe, containing tens of thousands of people working in a variety of ways on common problems. Like markets, fields have complex enabling structures: professional associations, university departments and centers, formal networks, and more that embrace diverse perspectives, reflect multiple methods for addressing practical problems, and engage many voices and leaders. Participants in these entities usually share values, vocabulary, information, literature, and tools. They develop knowledge, individual and organizational capacities, and systems for professional development, standards, best practices, and public-policy advocacy.

Many fields have sub-fields. The field of private finance, notes a 2021 report by the Criterion Institute, "Disrupting Fields," has seen the emergence of community investing, faith-based investing, impact investing, socially responsible investing, and climate finance. Some fields are blends of other fields. For instance, the community development finance institutions in the Opportunity Finance Network apply both banking and community development know-how.

The founders of the US Green Building Council came from several professional fields and, by developing the LEED standard, hoped to introduce a system-changing innovation into their fields. Green building professionals can become LEED accredited; by passing exams they qualify to rate buildings. "People have tied their careers to LEED," Weigert notes. "LEED has grown and evolved because you had all these people working to make it relevant and update it."

The OpenNews network engages the journalism field. The US Water Alliance involves utility professionals in the water-management field. Health Care Without Harm partners with numerous professionals in the healthcare field. All of these networks are trying to change something fundamental about how their fields think and operate.

Governments. Governments are yet another distinct system scale. They have policymaking authority, processes, and resources, and make decisions that allocate public and private benefits and obligations. They have power structures that include or exclude various groups and interests. Like markets and fields, they have complex, even byzantine, structures: departments and agencies of government; legislative, executive, and judicial branches; policies, programs, regulations, investments, incentives, data gathering, and other public functions.

The USGBC reports that "more and more state and local governments are also incorporating green building into their practices and policies. Green buildings save tax dollars on utility bills and support local economic development. As more state and local governments seek to increase resilience, mitigate climate risks and reduce emissions, improving the performance of their buildings is a critical and effective strategy." New Mexico, for instance, requires new public buildings over 15,000-square feet to become LEED Silver.

Quite a few social innovations aim for government-scale adoption.

The Campaign for Free College Tuition targeted state governments for new higher education financial policies. Health Care Without Harm helped to bring about a global treaty, signed by more than 140 national governments, to phase out mercury-based medical devices.

Scales of Systems	
Markets	Sellers offering goods and services to buyers in exchange for money.
Fields	Professionals—doctors, journalists, water utility executives, human-service providers, bankers, community developers, and teachers, for example—working on problems they have in common.
Governments	Entities with public policymaking authority, processes, and resources that make decisions that allocate benefits and obligations.

These scales—markets, fields, and governments—have levels. Generally, this means local, regional, national, and international levels. Government jurisdictions in the US are divided into multiple, overlapping levels: communities (municipalities, villages, and townships), counties, sub-state regions, states, multi-state regions, and federal/national. Markets and fields can be organized at local, regional, national, and global levels.

Many social innovation networks start by targeting the local level—individual communities, large and small—within the scale they are pursuing; then they move "up" to another level. The US Water Alliance's water equity efforts engages with players in 28 cities. LEED started with individual building sites, which are a subset of the local level. Focusing on the local level makes sense for several reasons. The main scales are present and interact at the local level. So, it's possible to develop and test innovations in places and also to engage multiple scales in just one place. The local level can also be easier to work with—it's more compact, within a clear boundary, than other levels, and making change there doesn't always involve coping with the overwhelming complexities of other levels.

SCALES AND LEVELS

Levels	Markets		Fields		Governments	
Global						
National						
Regional						
Local						

The many market innovations to reduce greenhouse gas emissions that city-members of the global Carbon Neutral Cities Alliance are developing—such as building out electric-vehicle charging infrastructure, involve governments, markets, and professional fields—are being implemented at the local level, over which city governments have some control. In TalNet's case, scaling up the EBS solution is occurring at the west Michigan regional level. Scaling EBS depends on engaging employers, many of whom have employees throughout the region, so scaling in just one community would not be optimal.

Going Global: A Challenging Level for Networks

They came from around the world to a dome alongside Copenhagen's waterfront—a temporary demonstration site for sustainable housing. From as far away as Brazil, Japan, and Australia, representatives of 17 cities convened to launch a new global network, the Carbon Neutral Cities Alliance. Johanna Partin became the Alliance's first executive director in 2015—and

Johanna Partin

started to wrestle with the many challenges faced by anyone managing a network spread across the planet.

Differences in time zones—Australia and Japan, for instance, are usually 10-12 hours "ahead" of the US—makes it very difficult to find times for virtual meetings or conference calls that everyone can attend conveniently, instead of very early or very late in their day. "This was the biggest communications problem," says Partin—even more challenging than managing different languages. The network conducted business in English and, at in-person convenings, provided interpreters for members not fluent in English.

The very different governmental and political contexts of cities around the world—regulatory regimes and national strategies for energy supply, for example—is also a challenge. "Even within regions, countries are very different," says Partin. But, she adds, these differences also make connecting internationally more interesting. "People are fascinated to hear about what works in other countries. That's where the innovation comes in. Someone says, 'That might work for me.' I don't see this as a barrier; it's an opportunity." But the discussions have to be carefully selected, Partin insists. "It doesn't make sense to have cities in different countries talking about the informal waste collection sector when some of them don't have this sector. You have to curate issues and discussions thoughtfully, looking for where there's something in common."

The Covid pandemic severely limited in-person gatherings, especially when national borders shut down to prevent spread of the virus. ""People constantly say the biggest value they feel is being connected to their peers," Partin notes. "For CNCA, which is so heavily focused around the members and making them feel supported and connected to each other, you don't have enough of that when you can't meet in person."

Jumping Scales

Whatever the intended scale of a system-changing effort, it may eventually change.

A shift occurs when social innovators find they need to impact one or more additional scales. The LEED innovation started in pursuit of field scale—influencing the thinking and behavior of professions critical to the design and construction of buildings. It also pushed into market scale as demand for greener residential and commercial space increased and sparked a growth in supply that needed to be certified by someone. And it sought government scale, with public entities, such as New Mexico and Washington, DC, adopting versions of LEED, as well as other green-building standards, as part of their regulatory requirements for new buildings.

We saw this multi-scale pattern in efforts behind IDAs—which built a field of community-development practitioners in places, sought supportive state and federal government policies, and engaged the financial institutions market.

The global spread of microfinance also jumped scales. First, nonprofits like Grameen Bank, a community development bank in Bangladesh, demonstrated success in providing financial services to formerly unbanked people, and a small field of microfinance entrepreneurs arose. Governments and businesses paid attention to these developments. "Following the pioneering role of nonprofits to establish proof of concept, commercial banks entered the market, with mixed social outcomes, given the pressure they faced for profitability," observe Deiglmeier and Greco. "As the microfinance industry matured, governments created a legal and regulatory environment that encouraged transparency, market entry, and competition. The cumulative efforts and engagement across the nonprofit, private, and public sectors were critical to scaling microfinance as we know it today."

Migration into other scales is not unusual for social innovations, because many of the systems targeted for change are formed from a combination of markets, fields, and governments.

A network may also shift the level it is targeting. Bill Guest and TalNet colleagues spent years working to develop a "national laboratory" for workforce development in west Michigan. But they shifted their sights to the regional scale in west Michigan after the Doug and Maria DeVos Foundation, located in the region, expressed interest in investing in work at that level. The 2020 US election affected the level for change that the Free College network targets. "In early 2021 we changed focus from state governments to the Congress," Morley Winograd reports. "It was quite a reach for us; a federal focus requires new tactics, new partners. But when circumstances change enough, the thing to do is to do your plan over."

Pathways to Scale

Remember the main types of social innovations we described in the last chapter: products/services (or solutions), practices, and policies? Each type has a scale that it is most suited to: products for markets, practices for fields, and policies for government. And there is a particular pathway to each scale.

Social innovation networks move their innovations, and their embedded mental models, along one or more of the following pathways:

- They take new products and services to markets—supplying solutions to paying customers.

- They grow new practices in fields—spreading usable knowledge among people and organizations working on common problems.

- They influence government policies—persuading public policymakers to adopt new approaches.

Whichever path social innovators use, they must address basic questions that include:

What is the unit of scaling? The "unit" that is being taken to scale could be a practice, a product, a policy, a social enterprise, or an entire new system. Innovators must define exactly what this unit is; what the core operating systems are that support it; how much it costs; and what capacities and competencies are required to implement it effectively.

How will success be measured? Social innovators don't measure success by focusing on profits. But they have to be clear about what system-changing outcomes they will measure. "Focus on system indicators," urge Jennifer Blatz and Geoffrey Canada in "The Importance of

Place." Outcomes for individuals, instead of systems, "don't always get the full picture. We don't see the norms, policies, and practices embedded within systems. . . . We miss the role that complex systems play in creating racialized disparities in education, health, wealth and social mobility."

Gargani and McLean caution that conjuring a specific scale to please funders—like declaring 1 million lives will be saved—"can instigate unhelpful designs" in innovations. "As scale increases it may also change the mechanisms that produce impact."

Impact assessments of innovations should not ignore the complexities of working on systems change, notes a 2020 report from Rockefeller Philanthropy Advisors: "Systems change generally demands a different approach to evaluation. While popular notions of social impact evaluation tend to assume discrete projects and relatively straightforward theories of change, systems change assessment requires a more holistic view of how different types of programs complement each other, and a more adaptive understanding of program implementation."

What is the scaling business model and its economics? It costs money to scale up an innovation, usually more than it costs to develop the innovation. Social innovators must think through their business model and work up a financial strategy before they take on scaling tasks. Unfortunately, many social innovators are underinformed about how much it will cost to get their innovation to scale.

Pathways to System Scale	
Taking New Products and Services to Markets	Production and distribution of product and service innovations that are sold to customers—individuals, businesses, or other organizations--in market segments
Growing New Practices in Fields	Dissemination of tested know-how about practice innovations to individuals and institutions in professional fields that apply them
Influencing Government Policies	Advocacy for adoption and implementation of public policy innovations—laws, regulations, programs, investments--by government bodies

Taking New Products and Services to Markets

The scaling power of markets—systems for the sale and purchase of goods and services—attracts many social innovators. A market can have astonishing global reach; think of iPhones, with 2 billion sold and an estimated 1 billion active users. "I always think of innovations in terms of how much change can be met through a market-oriented logic," observes Scott Bernstein, founder of the Center for Neighborhood Technology. "You just can't build enough government services and one-off nonprofits."

When networks take innovations to market, like USGBC's LEED product, they are seeking tremendous impact but they usually encounter the many difficulties of launching and growing a new business.

In 2021 the nonprofit Financial Health Network started a new business called Attune. The network's mission is to improve the financial health of people, communities, and businesses, especially those that have been historically marginalized. It does this mainly by seeking changes in the way financial services markets perform. "Our goal is market change.," explains Jennifer Tescher, the network's founder and CEO. "If the only thing we accomplish is 200 companies join as members and are part of a community of practice, but we don't see market change—that wouldn't be success for us."

The Attune startup came with all the attendant hopes of a new product—and a significant financial cost. "Attune is a data-and-insights digital platform that enables companies and organizations to measure and benchmark the financial health of their stakeholders, customers, employees, and clients," explains Tescher. "We bootstrapped this, with probably $1 million of our own capital."

Attune emerged from the roughly eight years the network spent developing ways to measure financial health. First the network produced a toolkit for scoring financial health and put it on a website where it could be downloaded for free. Then it created a community of practice for early adopters. "Over time people got into it and wanted a technology platform that would make it seamless and easy to use," Tescher says. To help develop the platform, the network created an advisory group of six stakeholder organizations. "Every week or two we'd bring them what we'd built so far and they'd give us feedback."

In Attune's first year, Tescher says, there have been about 20 customers, purchasing two-year licenses to use the product. Some of the customers come from outside of the network's membership. Tescher expects Attune's second year to come close to financial breakeven—with revenue nearly covering expenses. But ahead lies the challenge of substantially scaling up the product in the market. "We will need more capital. But this raises business questions: Should we spin out the product? Should we raise equity capital? How much controlling interest should the network retain? How integrated should Attune be with the rest of what the network is doing?"

Attune, Tescher continues, "also raises existential questions for the network: what do we want to be? Does the network want to continue to dedicate staffing to operating the digital platform? If Attune becomes a separate entity, can the network still take advantage of the opportunities that the product might generate for influencing the market? What should the network do when competitors to Attune emerge? Is that good, a signal that the market is taking on this approach?"

Scaling through markets usually requires a business-enterprise approach that quite often means an innovation network will create an enterprise to produce and sell the solution that's been developed. An alternative to growing an enterprise is to initiate a commercial franchise model—a way to increase impact without having to increase an enterprise's size. "Social sector franchising is emerging as a promising approach," declare a trio of researchers and consultants in a 2021 article in *Stanford Social Innovation Review*. Franchising, they say, "provides a proven operating model with defined systems and processes, delivering a standardized product and/or service; it offers a common brand with trademark(s), owned by the franchisor and licensed to the franchisees, along with the operating system." The model generates fees for the franchisor for use of the brand and system and for support services such as marketing. Other scaling alternatives include licensing of products, mergers and acquisitions, and joint ventures.

Pursuing a social-business model raises questions that most for-profit businesses would have to answer: how to produce the goods, what price to put on them, how to reach customers and deliver the product, how to raise more investment capital for expansion, and more. But a system-changing network that's behind a product may not have the expertise, capacity, or capital to navigate the product into the market.

For instance, Health Care Without Harm launched an innovative business enterprise, the Greenhealth Exchange, to provide sustainable products to healthcare systems. The goal was to accelerate the sector's procurement of certified sustainable medical and other products—to make green purchasing easy. "We understood early on that leveraging the purchasing power that health care has in the society was going to be a key strategy," notes the network's founder, Gary Cohen.

But the Exchange collided with a number of market realities. Existing group purchasing organizations (GPOs), which many hospitals and other healthcare providers use, countered with their own pricing and product offerings. Many healthcare purchasing contracts bundle together a range of products, only some of them sustainable, which makes it hard for healthcare providers to buy green products on their own. Although product sustainability matters to healthcare buyers, so do price and other criteria.

These problems led Health Care Without Harm to look for a different way to expand green purchasing. It created Greenhealth Approved as an alternative, a way to certify—but not sell—products that meet certain sustainability criteria. The innovation relies, like LEED, on voluntary standards to reshape market behaviors. Health Care Without Harm helped to develop the criteria. "We can't compete with the GPOs, so instead we'll be the standard setters," Cohen explains. This, it is hoped, will influence buyers to demand that their GPOs make the green products available to them in purchasing contracts.

The standard-setting approach benefits product suppliers by allowing them to signal to purchasers that the sustainability features of their products have been vetted by a third party. This enhances their sales pitch and reduces the need for purchasers to do their own research about the products' features. To date, Greenhealth Approved has certified products in medical products, carpets, and flooring. It charges suppliers a nominal fee to cover the cost of assessing their products; if the product meets the criteria, an annual licensing fee, based on product sales, is charged for use of the Greenhealth Approved seal.

Several lessons emerge from market experiences of these and other innovation networks:

Look for low-risk, low-cost economic models to carry social innovations into markets. Entering and scaling in competitive private markets — hospital supplies, green buildings, and financial services, for example— requires more than a solution and a strategy. It takes business savvy and money, resources that may be in low supply for scaling. Especially capital. Scaling up a solution usually comes with increased costs, Deiglmeier and Greco note: "Investments are needed to upgrade technology, hire senior-level talent, and improve infrastructure." But, they continue, social innovation funders don't find these activities very appealing because "they rarely produce immediate results." They gravitate toward investing in the earlier stages of innovation development, idea generation and prototyping. Compounding the problem, most funders won't make the long-term funding commitments that scaling up usually requires.

Undercapitalized market-scaling efforts, usually in the form of a social enterprise, just don't have the financial resources to take losses as they build the capacities to produce and distribute their solutions. This leaves them scrambling for hard-to-find capital even as they try to scale up.

Health Care Without Harm is pursuing a standard-setting model for influencing markets—Greenhealth Approval—rather than the social enterprise business model it initially followed, and this tends to be a less costly and less risky path to follow.

Partnering to scale up in markets can be tricky. An attraction of partnering is to gain access the partner's existing distribution channels—networks of relationships for distributing and selling products—instead of having to create new ones, which can be expensive and time consuming. The Individual Development Account innovation would probably have scaled up more rapidly, says Lisa Mensah, CEO of the Opportunity Finance Network, if it had been aligned with private companies that financed home mortgages, college, or other "accelerators for wealth building." But, she continues, "the group behind IDAs never saw itself comfortably partnering with commercial financial interests and was wary that these companies could be focused on their own financial returns rather than on protecting the wealth-building needs of low-income Americans."

When an innovation network and its partner(s) have the necessary complementary capacities to produce and distribute an innovation, the arrangement can generate impact and revenue for the network with relatively little risk. For instance, the Financial Health Network has developed a partnership with JD Power, a 52-year-old global data analytics and consumer intelligence company. JD Power runs awards programs for industries in which it assesses and rates the performance of products and practices. It asked the network to create a methodology to analyze and score the financial health of the leading banks in the US. "They use our framework for financial health and collect the data from the banks," reports Tescher. "They put out the information product." This provides the network with a significant opportunity to project its methodology and brand into the financial services market—"JD Power connects with different people in banks than those we talk to," Tescher notes—and to make money in the process.

But partnering can also result in frustration and little more. Scott Bernstein worked for years to introduce the Location Efficient Mortgage (LEM) into the mortgage industry. "It was a captivating idea, but it never got to scale," he observes. The LEM allowed lenders to take into account a borrower's transportation costs when qualifying financially for a mortgage. This allows potential borrowers who use mass transit instead of owning a car to show they have lower monthly costs against their income, which enables more people with lower incomes to qualify for mortgages. But the pathway into the mortgage market was filled with obstacles. Bernstein's organization, the Center for Neighborhood Technology, wasn't a lender or a mortgage broker so it couldn't take LEMs directly into the market. But the mortgage industry and its government regulators weren't much help. "Mortgages are commodities that are bought and sold. The mortgage system can't tolerate much variation," Bernstein observes. A pilot program was launched with a handful of banks, but some of the lenders didn't follow through and only about 2,000 LEMs were issued to first-time homebuyers during two years. "These loans performed very well," Bernstein says. But the industry didn't pick up on the tested new product. A major lender insisted that the LEM was too hard to use. "We never found a partner to carry this into the market," Bernstein concludes.

Some partnerships give innovations instant credibility as well as reach to potential users. TalNet, for example, is developing a partnership with nonprofit Goodwill Industries to use its evidence-based talent selection innovation. Goodwill provides job training, employment placement services, and other community-based programs for people who have barriers to their employment. In 2020 alone Goodwill placed more than 126,000 people into jobs through local Goodwill offices.

Continuously improve product/service offerings. Scaling does not end with introducing the social innovation into the market. It often requires more work on the solution. "Scale and volume are crucial to making many goods and services affordable and accessible to masses of people with little purchasing power," note the authors of "The Promise of Social Sector Franchising." "Such ambition typically requires major adaptations to the original model to meet customer needs in diverse environments, to shift with evolving conditions."

Since LEED was first developed in the 1990s it has been redesigned several times and variations of the standards now form a family of products for different market segments. There's "A LEED for every project," proclaims the product website—"for all building types and all building phases including new construction, interior fit outs, operations and maintenance and core and shell." In addition to LEED for commercial facilities, schools, data centers, and other facilities, there's LEED for homes, neighborhoods, cities and communities.

HireReach, a spinout from TalNet, has improved its initial evidence-based selection (EBS) innovation by transitioning training content into a self-managed learning process, cutting in half the time that organizations need to spend learning about and implementing the network's solution. Through HireReach, cohorts of employers learn and begin to implement EBS practices. The original program occurred over 12 months and required 12 in-person, half-day cohort training sessions, as well as multiple, smaller group working sessions. The improved model cuts the time commitment to 5 months, with group meetings reduced from half days to virtual two-hour sessions. All learning materials have been organized into a learning process that allows participating teams to do much of their learning and implementation work remotely, on a schedule that works for the team.

Growing New Practices in Fields

Some social innovators focus on introducing innovations into long established fields. USGBC initiated LEED, carrying a green building standard-setting solution into the architecture, real estate development, and
construction fields. The US Water Alliance pushes a framework for water
equity into the water management professional field. OpenNews presses
the journalism field and its newsrooms to embrace digital technology
and racial diversity in personnel.

When Anne Mosle founded Ascend at the
Aspen Institute in 2011, her vision was to catalyze a
fresh conversation about breaking the cycle of
poverty that was based in lived experiences of
parents and caregivers, racial and gender equity,
and also built on what works at the state and local
levels. She had developed a big idea, a radical shift

Anne Mosle

in the mental model of the human services field. She had assembled the
support of a community of diverse philanthropists, with $10 million in
initial catalytic funding. And she had landed on a methodology for advancing change: bringing together innovative players from diverse parts of the
field to (1) exchange and explore ideas, (2) build relationships and trust, (3)
align to develop innovations in practices and policies, and (4) spread them
into government, nonprofit, and academic entities in the vast field.

These assets were the culmination of the years that Mosle spent as a
prominent leader in practice, policy, and philanthropy centering racial
and gender equity in fostering economic security and financial independence for families with low incomes. Under her leadership the Washington Area Women's Foundation in Washington, D.C., became one of the
fastest growing women's foundations in the nation. As a vice president of
the W.K. Kellogg Foundation she guided $140 million a year in invest-
ments in family economic security, impact investing, and eradicating
intergenerational poverty. In these and other roles, she'd worked on the
ground with numerous local and national organizations and Tribal
nations pursuing self-determination, inclusion, and economic opportunity. "A lot of wisdom was shared with me," she says. "I know what it's
like to be up and to be down. And on the inside and outside."

Mosle gained a perspective about the untapped potential of the human services field. "It's siloed and fragmented instead of holistic and human centered. It's situational instead of generational. And it has historically been structured to enable continuing injustice." Inspired by human services leaders at the state level, she nurtured an idea for what the field could become—by embracing an ambitious mindset of abundance. "What's most important is that the field should be centered on human potential, a two-generational approach, and equity. And it should have a mindset that models itself after the experiences of our families—so childcare, food assistance, housing, and other supports can come together to provide what families need." Mosle and colleagues packaged this idea as a "two generation" or "2Gen" approach—a mental model shift that aims to help end the cycle of intergenerational poverty by ensuring whole-family services for children and the adults in their lives, together. 2Gen is a far-reaching departure from the way human-services systems usually serve children and adults—separately, rather than as a family. "We knew that breakthroughs were needed," says Mosle, "because no matter how much we tinkered with the same old, separate service-delivery vehicles, they couldn't possibly get us to the destination we sought."

The big idea and Mosle's track record attracted substantial philanthropic support and a strong team that has persisted in the years since the startup. "They wanted to be a part of something larger that worked," recalls Mosle, who became Ascend's executive director and an Aspen Institute vice president. "They wanted to know what it would mean to go big."

Ascend developed a network structure to harness collective effort and enable participants to "spark and spread 2Gen breakthroughs," says Mosle. "We started with a fundamental question: what is the potential and power of the 2Gen approach for the field? Having impact for families and in the field was our focus instead of focusing on creating an organization." She looked at network theories to understand how innovations are developed. "We realized that there was good work happening across sectors and communities and we thought about ways to connect them to each other." They wanted a way to bring together a quite diverse set of players: practitioners, researchers, policymakers, across the public, nonprofit, and private sectors, as well as parents and families served by the field. A network, Mosle concluded, could "attract, engage, harvest, and co-create models and strategies and share them back out with others." It would be "a space that allows people to talk about what's working. To say, 'We need to think radically differently. What if we tried a 2Gen approach?'"

In 2014 Ascend used a Request for Proposals and the promise of small-grant funding for projects to attract 58 organizations into a network startup. Eight years later Ascend's national network contains more than 460 public, nonprofit, private, and philanthropic organizations serving 10 million children and families in all 50 states, the District of Columbia, and Puerto Rico. "Organizations are coming together," Mosle says, "because they see the value in the 2Gen approach and being a part of the network."

Other social innovators work in emerging, rather than established, fields, such as Health Care Without Harm in the environmental health field and the networks of practitioners and policymakers who developed the asset-building field driven by community-development financing, Individual Development Accounts, and other innovations.

An emerging field unexpectedly caught the attention of philanthropist George Soros beginning in the 1990s. Soros was investing in launching a university in former communist nations in East and Central Europe to develop the region's next generation of leaders. "I devoted myself to talking with everyone I could find who had ideas to contribute," he recalls. His conversations with Dr. Fraser Mustard, a Canadian cardiologist who was studying the impact of early childhood on human development and health, introduced Soros to a new idea. "He cited new research on the unprecedented development of the brain in the first few years, and then told me I had to start younger. Instead of focusing on university students, I should look at pregnancy and the critical first six years of childhood."

Early childhood development (ECD) is a field of practice built on science, especially neuroscience and behavioral research, that connects early experiences from birth and even before birth to future learning capacity, behaviors, and physical and mental health. The field's bottom line, described by the Harvard University Center on the Developing Child: "healthy development in the early years provides the building blocks for educational achievement, economic productivity, responsible citizenship, lifelong health, strong communities, and successful parenting of the next generation."

In 1994, Soros's Open Society Foundations started to invest in preschools in Central Eastern Europe and Eurasia, helping to restore a once robust capacity that was falling apart in the midst of financial, political, and economic crises that followed the fall of the Berlin Wall. Open Society's flagship Step by Step program focused on introducing a paradigm of early childhood development that embraced child-centered practices, parent and community involvement, and fostered creativity, responsibility, inclusivity, and critical thinking. This focus, Soros says, "evolved into a broad, holistic approach to early childhood development—an approach that included looking at health care access and social support policies."

Enter Sarah Klaus. With degrees in Russian studies and developmental psychology, she helped launch the foundation's first steps in early childhood development. "I was working in the Soviet Union in my early 20s in cultural exchange programs before starting at Open Society where I eventually focused on programs for children and

Sarah Klaus

youth. My boss was running a number of programs that all developed networks. I was interested in how that worked." At Open Society Klaus directed the Step by Step program and led the creation of a regional network to support ECD professionals in Europe and Central Asia, the International Step by Step Association (ISSA). She served as ISSA's executive director from 1999 to 2006, and as director of the foundation's Early Childhood Program until 2020. "At the time ISSA was established there wasn't a robust global field of early childhood development with interconnected networks at national, regional, and global levels," Klaus recalls. "Even informal networks did not exist in all regions, and those that existed were under-staffed and unsustainable. UNICEF brought together NGOs to support its initiatives, but it wasn't a network owned by the people in the network."

The ISSA network's initial role was to support ECD nonprofit organizations that were part of the earlier Open Society program and to strengthen the voice of ECD professionals in the region. ISSA started to link the organizations and stakeholders across Europe and Central Asia. It promoted knowledge creation and sharing to boost professional practices. It hosts a network advocating improvement of services for young Roma children and facilitates the implementation of innovative projects in home visiting, local government policy development, and the inclusion of marginalized children. The network is "all about the people," Klaus says. "You have to foster human relationships. The Belgian academic I work with couldn't believe how well people are collaborating. Anyone from this network can call anyone else in the network. There are lots of languages in the network, so especially in the early years we did everything dually in Russian and English." To help with communications, Klaus learned to speak Serbo-Croatian.

ISSA began to expand its membership and broadened its focus beyond early education to other areas of ECD. "Different people were getting involved in the network," notes Klaus. Open Society staff "was going to meetings, advising the network—but not trying to influence what it did. We supported what they wanted to do." Networking, she adds, "is most successful when the members are sharing resources. They become hotbeds of innovation, information sharing, and inspiration."

Today ISSA contains 92 member organizations in 42 countries. The members come from civil society, academia, government, and business. The network's capacities, says Klaus, "make it easier for new ideas to come in, to be tested. Once you have a network, scaling is much easier." A 2020 evaluation backs her up, noting that the network had leveraged best practices within the network to produce a framework for quality early education and care. ISSA members piloted and refined practices to implement the framework in their different contexts. They used the framework to get their countries to support early childhood development, with training modules and peer exchange processes. In 2019, the European Commission adopted a quality framework that drew extensively from expertise developed by ISSA and its members. Meanwhile, ISSA's member organization in Romania influenced a law on education to integrate, for the first time, early education and care of children under the age of three into the Ministry of Education. A network of business partners in Romania that ISSA supported successfully promoted policy changes to increase access to and quality of early education. ISSA also organizes peer learning among members, paired with capacity building and technical assistance to catalyze change. This, the 2020 assessment reported, "makes it possible for ISSA to support significant in-country change . . . as well as to take new models to scale." At the same time, ISSA is working with another ECD regional network to create tools both can use to assess the capacity of the ECD workforce.

Open Society has invested in three additional regional ECD networks, in Africa, Asia, and the Middle East; since 1999 it has granted $20 million to catalyze and support the networks. In all, between 1994 and 2020, it provided a total of $175 million to support the early childhood field. The regional networks, the 2020 assessment found, are "well-established, highly visible and influential across a variety of targets, often including regional governing bodies. This level of maturity in structure and strategy enables them to facilitate and drive change, as well as serve as the connective tissue, infrastructure and collective voice for the sector." The networks "are high-performing, with initiatives that have set the stage for advancing ECD work." They have "contributed to outcomes and impacts that have advanced the field. Notably, these impacts are not one-time results but rather a foundation for the overall capacity of the ECD sector."

The experiences of the ECD regional networks and other innovation networks provide insights into how to scale innovations in existing or emerging fields:

Define and map the field. Quite a few social innovators declare the intention to transform a field but they don't know much about the field, don't have an understanding of how fields are constructed and evolve, or how innovations can influence fields. This vagueness makes it unlikely that they will have much impact; their aspirations remain aspirational.

Innovators should precisely define the field they have targeted for change or emergence, starting with its basic conceptual frameworks and existing practices. They have to describe the boundaries of the field they target, what is "in" and what is "out" and where the field intersects with other fields. They have to know who the main players in the field are—individuals, organizations, and networks—and what ideas they champion. They should note the extent of the field's diversity and inclusion of voices, and how power is organized in the field. The US Water Alliance, says CEO Mami Hara, is greatly expanding the concept of who is in the water management field: "Water management concerns all of us. We aim to make everybody feel they can participate, from any community across the US. The Alliance centers the issues that we all contend with, like access and affordability, and creates a sense of community and commonality of purpose. We show how people from seemingly divergent perspectives can come together to develop meaningful solutions for seemingly intractable water problems."

When it comes to innovation, field-changers should scan for innovations under development in the field, as well as innovations in other fields that might be imported into the targeted field. They should answer these questions:

- What drivers of change are supporting innovation in the field?

- What are the mental models and hypotheses underlying attempts at innovation in the field?

- Are certain types of innovation being promoted more than others?

- What are the field's standards for evidence that innovations will have to meet to gain acceptance?

Innovators who develop a deep understanding of a field and its opportunities for change can produce roadmaps for how they will influence the field over the long term.

Build networks for learning and adopting innovations. Innovations tend to spread through a field through frameworks and learning communities. The frameworks establish new concepts and make visible the examples of new practices. They provide ideas and language that practitioners can use and share. This enables learning communities of practitioners to develop or apply innovations for their various contexts.

The US Water Alliance's water equity initiative "started with naming and framing, putting out a report that connected all the different aspects of how equity shows up in the water space," explains Emily Simonson, the Alliance director of strategic initiatives. "The process of creating that framework, with lots of interviews, was intense. It gave us a sense of who is doing what, what the bright spots are, and the potential appetite to do more. Then we pulled together utility leaders who wanted to do more, and formed the task force. They confronted a lot of painful history as a part of their norming and forming with equity leaders in their city, and getting to a collective set of values to move forward and make progress together. As an alliance we want to make applying an equity lens to everything utilities do a standard practice in the water sector. That would be a coup! We decided to create a larger network that is all about equity."

The Alliance made sure that its equity framework contained concrete examples of what water utilities around the US were doing. "This creates a network of referents that other people—inside and outside of the network—can look to, and that promotes another wave of growth in use of the innovative practices," says Hara.

There's an important consideration in spreading practical knowledge: most people learn by doing with others—in practice communities—not by just passively reviewing information. "The people who design knowledge management systems," says Hargadon, "originally thought that lists of best practices, reports, and PowerPoint presentations would be sufficient." They assumed that you could solve problems by reading databases. He continues, but found that these "are most useful as annotated Yellow Pages, helping them find out who to talk to about how the knowledge was really used and might be used again." So, they linked people together rather than just refer them to stored information.

Spread innovations through networked entities in the field. Even as the US Water Alliance is building its own community of practice for water equity, it maintains relationships with professional associations in the water sector—a potential distribution channel that can reach numerous actors in the field. It produced a 2021 report, "Water Equity Task Force: Insights for the Water Sector," to "document the strategic insights and lessons learned from this journey so they can be of service to the entire water sector." After laying out key insights and principles that were put into practice, the Alliance urges water leaders from utilities, community-based organizations, environmental groups, and philanthropy to "consciously choose to lead organizations in ways that put the principles of equity, community, and collaboration at the center of every plan, policy, program, and investment."

The Ascend Network engages what it calls "platforms for scale"— community colleges, United Ways, community action agencies, Head Start programs, workforce development boards, women's philanthropic funds—to spread and implement 2Gen practice and policy innovations. These national umbrella organizations and associations "are well-suited to drive rapid innovation, assess new models and practices, and scale them so that they continue to work well," explain Ascend's Executive Director Mosle and Marjorie Sims, its managing director.

The potential reach of these platforms is extraordinary. Community action agencies, for instance, cover nearly 100 percent of US counties and directly serve 15 million people. The nation's 1,200 community colleges serve more than 12 million students. United Way has 1,300 independent organizations throughout the US. No wonder Mosle and Sims conclude that "greater investment in platforms implementing a 2Gen approach is a vital step toward creating more equitable systems that enable all families to thrive."

Use the network as a culture-change carrier in the field. Fields have cultures—values, mindsets, assumptions about who should have power, and so on--and innovators often explicitly target the culture for change.

OpenNews, for example, works as a persistent advocate for racial diversity in newsroom personnel—in part by building itself into a large, diverse network of journalists. Sisi Wei, co-executive director of Open-News, recalls the unsatisfying situation she faced as a person of color in a mostly white professional field. "I wanted to experience working for an organization in which I did not feel I had to be the person who made sure we were making the right moral decisions about diversity. Where I was not the expert in the area and I could learn more about it from colleagues. I quickly realized that there was almost no newsroom that could provide me with that environment." She found what she was looking for at OpenNews.

"We feature unsung leaders, make space for them to find community with each other, and affirm that their insights are tremendously valuable," notes co-executive director Erika Owens. "We are producing inspiration—a way of demonstrating how you can walk the talk of your values." This approach has time on its side, says Sandhya Kambhampati. "OpenNews is about culture change in journalism."

The US Water Alliance is also pursuing culture change in its field. "Changing culture is much more impactful than any possible sum of efforts. We continually aim to influence and create culture beyond our membership. We push several interrelated fronts, such as the value of water, water equity, holistic and community-centered water management, and climate action," says Hara. "We're developing a culture that helps to influence the wider culture of the water sector and validates the ethos and approach the network is building. It helps to move people and organizations that are outside of the network. At a certain scale a network takes on a power and a gravity that exceeds what may be initially envisioned."

The Open Society Foundation provided substantial financial and technical support to grassroots nonprofit organizations in the early childhood development field, a way of building bottom-up empowerment that would ensure strong advocacy for young children and accountability for government policies and services, even as it also invested in top-down approaches through national government agencies.

Ascend also pursues an empowerment approach in the health and human services fields. It engages parents—beneficiaries of the system—to design and implement innovative practices and policies. "Engaging with families as equals has changed the mindset that drives the way agencies operate," Ascend says in a report on its field-changing efforts. "We are seeing a long overdue shift from a culture of blaming parents to one of respecting them."

Advance the performance of innovations. "You have to stay at the cutting edge of the field," says Karen Weigert, noting the continuous evolution of LEED products. ""Not only did LEED create something new, now the most innovative players are LEED-Zero, not just LEED-Platinum. You never can rest on your laurels."

Persuading Governments to Adopt Policies

Getting governments to approve new or revised policies is familiar work for many social innovators. They try to persuade policymakers to change government's own pervasive systems, such as human services (as Ascend does), public higher education finance, and building codes. The Campaign for Free College Tuition urges state governments to revise their higher ed funding schemes. Backers of LEED pursue government policies to incentivize and/or mandate green building standards on new construction. Innovators also try to get public entities to invest substantially in a particular social innovation, as we saw in the case of Individual Development Accounts in chapter 3.

Public policy is contested terrain, of course. Skoll Foundation CEO Don Gips observes: "You need to think through, in all cases, who's going to be opposed to this? Who are you taking power from, because much of this often will be shifting power? Or is it a win-win solution where everybody is better off and then you just need to be able to demonstrate that and get access to the right decision makers in the government?" Innovations face uphill climbs when they try to displace existing policies that likely have the substantial support of self-interested parties. "All innovations represent some break from the past," notes Hargadon. Their newness means they will not be well understood by policymakers, and they probably won't have large, important constituencies backing them.

At the same time, policymaking often occurs in contexts that may impede or spur the adoption of innovations. Lisa Mensah recalls that advocacy for federal support for IDAs coincided with a push by the George W. Bush administration to privatize Social Security. In that context, support for IDAs came to be viewed by some as enabling the administration's controversial efforts.

Even when there is a political opening to advance innovative policies, it doesn't last forever; windows of opportunity close down as well as open up. In early 2021, for instance, President Biden pushed for free community college in his Build Back Better legislation, but just a few months later dropped the policy during congressional negotiations. "Looks like we will be going back to our state-focused strategy for the time being—until the stars align again to try it at the federal level," says Morley Winograd, president of the Campaign for Free College Tuition.

In light of these factors, innovation networks do what anyone else trying to influence policy would do:

- **Provide evidence.** They provide policymakers with compelling evidence of the innovation's superior performance. Bob Friedman and allies created the American Dream Demonstration to show that people with low incomes would save money when given financial incentives and coaching. The Campaign for Free College Tuition provides lawmakers with extensive analyses that show

how they can eliminate college tuition without having to spend enormous amounts of public money.

- **Build coalitions and networks.** Policy innovators build coalitions of the like-minded to demand policy change. Support for IDA incentives and other asset-building policies has been bipartisan. Advocacy campaigns for free college have showcased polling that finds big majorities of the public support the policy change. Often, innovators can leverage existing networks of elected officials—governor to governor, for instance—and policy experts to advance new approaches.

- **Change the narrative.** Policy entrepreneurs initiate communications campaigns to build public support for changes, knowing that legislators can be moved by public opinion. They work to "shift the narrative," using messaging and communications methods to change long standing public mindsets. IDA advocates, for example, pressed for a shift from a deficit approach, which views low-income families as lacking certain attributes, to an asset approach, which focuses instead on the families' strengths and capabilities. In targeting mindsets, narrative shift can be a system-changing effort, not just a narrow campaign to win one-time acceptance of a particular innovation.

All of these efforts to influence policy may take many years to have impact. As Mensah notes about the policy window for IDAs and asset-building approaches: "When I open the newspaper in 2021 and see all these people calling for baby bonds, down payment assistance, and closing the racial wealth gap, I feel like, yeah, we were 20 years early!"

Lessons learned by policy-oriented social innovation networks include:

Build demand constituencies and alliances, not just innovations. Innovative policies don't advocate for themselves; their backers have to do the heavy lifting of persuading policymakers. This means undertaking education and advocacy and lobbying campaigns to communicate the potential of the innovation and the support it has. Messaging should make the innovative policy as easy to understand as possible.

Target specific policy makers. Government has many levels—local, county, regional, state, and federal—and many silos—education, health, housing, and more. So, a campaign for an innovation has to be clear about which decision makers it is targeting and what the messaging and constituency strategies are. The Campaign for Free College Tuition first targeted state elected officials. "There were two reasons for this," explains Winograd. "The first was the difference in constituency strength at the state/local level versus at the federal level. The second was that states were the places we could execute a bipartisan strategy the easiest."

LEED has targeted local government decision makers. As of April 2021, 120 local governments in the US have adopted a LEED framework for addressing energy, water, waste, and pollution—a flexible approach that can be applied by small and large cities, counties, business improvement districts, and neighborhoods. And a set of 15 other local governments—including Houston, West Palm Beach, Florida, and Billings, Montana—was working to join this LEED-certified cohort.

Elections and government appointments matter, too. When innovators can't win the support of elected officials, their efforts may turn to changing who the officials are and electing more supportive candidates. In addition to weighing in on election campaigns—with endorsements, campaign contributions, and other resources—they may find and cultivate candidates for office. Likewise, when innovators are focused on regulatory policies, they may try to influence who is appointed to regulatory bodies, such as public utility commissions, as well as educating and training potential appointees.

Innovation Adoption

Whichever scaling pathway an innovation takes, it's likely to be subject to what's called the "innovation diffusion curve"—the sequential adoption of an innovation by five different categories of people and organizations, depending on their motivations, risk tolerance, and capabilities. The curve was conceptualized decades ago by communications professor Everett Rogers to explain the diffusion of innovations through consumer markets. It applies well to social innovations.

Rogers described five types of adopters: innovators, early adopters, early majority, late majority, and laggards. Innovators and early adopters are the smallest groups by far, with early and late majorities making up two-thirds of a market. "Different adopter categories have different needs and attitudes toward the programs and services created for their benefit," note the Bridgespan Group's Taz Hussein and Matt Plummer. "Targeting all potential beneficiaries at once is inefficient and often ineffective."

INNOVATION ADOPTION CURVE

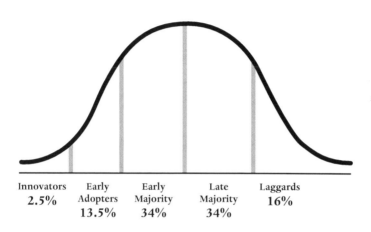

| Innovators 2.5% | Early Adopters 13.5% | Early Majority 34% | Late Majority 34% | Laggards 16% |

Innovators, in our experience, are deeply motivated by a vision for creating something that solves a problem or seizes an opportunity that matters to them. They embrace a new mental model and embed it within innovations. They are passionate about making change happen and accept the risk of failure, including the financial costs that might occur. And they have or can obtain the resources to absorb the cost and potential failure of developing innovations. Many of the innovation network leaders we've described in previous chapters fit this description. But innovators must depend crucially on early adopters to spur the process of innovation diffusion.

Early adopters typically have a problem to solve or an opportunity to seize but are wary of taking on the open-ended experimentation and risks that innovators embrace. They tend to be less visionary and more pragmatic. They look for innovations that have already made it through the proof-of-concept stage, which they are willing to apply within their contexts.

Many social innovations spread to early adopters only to have adoption stall out. This is because the next category for adoption, the *early majority* group, has much narrower criteria and capacity for what they are willing to adopt. They may face the same problem or opportunity as innovators and early adopters, but they are reluctant to take much risk at all and may be especially concerned with the potential disruption an innovation may cause and the economic costs and benefits it creates. The growing use of green infrastructure for water management has been stimulated by the potential to save money or accrue more benefits than using grey infrastructure, says the US Water Alliance's Hara. "We had to figure out how to do more with the money we had. That has been the wedge that allows green infrastructure and other innovative approaches to rise to the surface."

Often, innovation adoption can be fostered by using incentives, especially financial ones, or by creating requirements such as government regulations or corporate standards for suppliers. When Weigert started to notice LEED buildings in Chicago, she says, the product had moved out of the early adopter stage. "There were too many LEED buildings for it to just be about early adopters. The early adopters gave LEED cachet so others saw a way to get into green buildings."

The *late majority* category poses additional challenges to an innovation's spread. People in this category are habitually skeptical about innovation and have little financial capacity for adoption. They are unmotivated and, like the early majority, they may not have financial and other resources needed for adoption.

Laggards are by definition the last to adopt a change, if they do at all. They tend to focus on traditions and have little contact with innovators and early adopters. They may ignore or resist change, or change only when they have no choice due, for example, to government regulations.

Whichever adopter category you're targeting, its adoption of an innovation tends to follow a sequence: Potential adopters become aware of the innovation. They learn more about the innovation—how it works, what it costs, what impact it has, how long it takes to have impact, and so on. They assess the pros and cons of adoption, based on what matters most to them and how it fits with their capacities. Sometimes they try out the innovation without fully committing to use it. Finally, they decide whether or not to fully embrace the innovation.

Morphing Networks

As social innovation networks advance their innovations along the innovation curve and through the scaling stage, they grow much, much bigger and their underlying relationships change. We see this pattern—a natural shift from Hargadon's tight collective to a broad community—over and over.

Eighteen years ago, Jennifer Tescher started out to help people with low incomes who were "unbanked" to obtain financial services. She had been trained as a journalist but decided, she says, "not just to write about issues, but to do something about them. I never imagined that financial services would be my entry point to social change."

Jennifer Tescher

She was working as a consultant in community-development banking at Shorebank Advisory Services when the Ford Foundation paid her to research a promising development. "They said, hey, there's this new thing called the Internet and we think it's a huge opportunity to reach and serve low-income people with financial services." Tescher researched and then presented recommendations, and the foundation provided a $3 million grant. "They said, here's a check—get started."

At the outset, there was just a small team. Tescher set up shop within the consulting company because there wasn't yet a separate legal entity. She created an Innovators Roundtable with a half-dozen financial service companies. "They wanted to come together to find opportunities to collaborate on this challenge," she says. "It was a problem that required collective action." Then she convened a second roundtable of smaller banks and credit unions, and also assembled groups of companies to hash out a set of principles and best practice guides for the financial services industry. "We articulated principles about what it would look like for financial services to be a force for good," recalls Tescher. "We created best practice guides based on the principles."

By 2022 these efforts have grown into the Financial Health Network with 163 members that serve more than 80 million Americans with low-to-moderate incomes. The network has 80 employees and a $20-million-a-year budget.

The growth of this and other social innovation networks is not just due to a gradual expansion of membership over time or the filling out of membership to achieve a national presence. It's driven in large part by the natural evolution of a network's innovation process, as we mentioned at the opening of this chapter.

In *How Breakthroughs Happen* Hargadon describes this progression after studying numerous major technological innovations—including automobiles, biotechnologies, computers, lightbulbs, the telegraph, and the Xbox. He recognizes that most innovators initially draw ideas from other sources and then combine them into potential innovations—a process of "recombinant innovation" in which "combinations of people, ideas, and objects are disassembled and reassembled." To do this, innovators build bridges into multiple sources, the "small worlds" of deep technical knowledge.

This happened with social innovations described in previous chapters. OpenNews bridges the worlds of digital technology and journalism. Health Care Without Harm links the knowledge of environmental science with the practices of health care institutions. The Individual Development Account innovation emerges when Michael Sherraden combines what he learns about his own retirement account with what he hears from welfare recipients during his research.

But bridging to recombine is just the first step Hargadon identifies. When innovators have conceptualized and designed an emerging innovation, they have to build a "new world" around it to take it to scale. "The pursuit of innovation requires patiently and humbly building a new network of people, ideas, and objects around the original innovation," he explains. "Once the new venture crystallizes and acquires legitimacy, the need for the collective gives way to the advantages that only an established community can bring."

Bridging multiple worlds to develop innovations and building new worlds to take them to scale are different tasks for innovation networks.

Innovators link to multiple small worlds to find and bring back value for their own work. They are visitors, not settlers, in these other worlds. "This not only ensures that they are the first to see new opportunities," notes Hargadon, "but also that they are usually the last to be caught in the webs of established practices and embedded interests" of each small world. This is the work of a small, tightly aligned group of people who connect to other worlds and defy the skepticism and hostility that new ideas often encounter. "Groups are critical to the innovation process because they can convince themselves of the value of their ideas, the rightness of their cause, and the possibilities of their success," Hargadon says.

In contrast, when innovators move their innovations into use they expand the web of people who are involved in the work. In the shift from a tight collective to a community, Hargadon explains, "people's roles become clear and interdependent [and] ideas become shared organizing principles." The network's collective morphs as it reshapes its innovation activities and capacities and grows its web. As Hargadon sums up: constructing these different "webs of innovation . . . is a central part of the innovation process."

Networks & Pathways to Scale

Scaling changes an innovation network's web of relationships. Whatever pathway the network follows to scale, it must make new connections to reach deeply into a market, field, or government.

Each pathway presents innovators with similar types of hurdles as they try to move innovations from margins to mainstream. How should they distribute the innovation? What evidence should they provide of its effectiveness? How will they measure the performance and value of the innovation? How can they make the economics of the innovation work? How will they continuously improve the innovation? And others.

As social innovation networks consider their approach to scaling innovations, whichever pathway they follow, there is guidance from experience:

Advice for Networks on Scaling Pathways

- Be realistic about what level of scale to seek.

- Don't prematurely try to scale innovations.

- Don't assume there will be demand for an innovation; you have to build it.

- Don't count too much on philanthropy for scaling resources.

- Prepare for cross-sector engagement.

Be realistic about what level of scale to seek. Innovators may inflate the level they can reach so they can attract investment and partners. But not every innovation should or can achieve national or global scale. At least not without starting at smaller levels. As we've mentioned, TalNet started with national-level ambitions, but decided to focus on a regional level—west Michigan—and then possibly expand from there. The US Water Alliance wants to spread its equity framework throughout the water sector, but its initial scaling approach begins with 28 cities around the US. LEED's product line initially focused on individual buildings, but expanded to community level. This laddering approach—mounting one level at a time to get to bigger scale—may not seem as impressive as announcing that an innovation will capture a national market or influence a global field of practice. But it is far more realistic, can be planned for in detail, and its progress can be monitored.

Don't prematurely try to scale innovations. Many innovators and their investors push too quickly for scaling. Impatience leads them to want to scale attempts at innovation before they have actually demonstrated the innovation's capacity to reliably achieve system improvements. They push before they have developed standardized operating systems and before the sustainability of the business model has been demonstrated. This impatience actually slows down, rather than accelerating, the innovation process. It is like a private company releasing a product into the market before it is actually ready; the product failures, warranty recalls, and general bad publicity create more damage than a slower, more careful launch would have.

The TalNet team has made this mistake: assuming it was done with prototyping and ready for the scaling phase, only to find out that the solution wasn't ready for prime time. When the team pushed the innovation design to its limits, some key components just weren't finished.

Don't assume there will be demand for an innovation; you have to build it. Nonprofits and funders must "reject the notion that need equals demand," observe Taz Hussein and Matt Plummer of the Bridgespan Group. "Rather, they must be prepared to actively generate demand for social change." The authors draw insights from Rogers' innovation-diffusion theory, including the value of going beyond identifying a broad group of potential beneficiaries and focusing first on a subgroup most likely to use the innovation.

Don't count too much on philanthropy for scaling resources. A scaling plan that depends heavily on obtaining money from foundations may work. But scaling is not the "sweet spot" that most philanthropies find most attractive for investment, so they may not prove to be a reliable long-term investor. What's best is a mix of revenue sources for scaling capital—from customers, partners, government agencies, network members.

Prepare for cross-sector engagement. It's likely that in the long run your systems change effort will require taking different kinds of social innovations to scale on different pathways. This means engaging with a diverse array of people and organizations and, often, bringing them together to collaborate. This is why Deiglmeier and Greco advise that social innovators should anticipate the need for cross-sector collaborations to get to scale. Social innovators, they say, should build relationships in the private, nonprofit, and public sectors and support leaders and staff in developing "cross-sector fluency" so they can serve as "bridgers" who knit together systems and collaborations.

Scaling up moves innovations into new and tricky tasks: going into markets, growing in fields, influencing governments. It puts innovation networks into evolutionary motion; they change their capabilities, functions, and relationships to solve the puzzle of scaling up.

But that's not the end of the changes that social innovation networks make so they can achieve system-scale impact.

CHAPTER 5

Designing Networks of Networks

We live in a world which is constantly exploring what's possible,
finding new combinations—not struggling to survive, but playing,
tinkering, to find what's possible.

Margaret Wheatley

L et's pause the storyline and recap where we are.

Chapter by chapter, the complexities of scaling up social innovations to change systems have been mounting. There are different types of systems, different system-changing approaches, and different ways to find a system's leverage points. Different system-disrupting mindset shifts to embed in social innovations, different types of social innovations to develop, and different stages in the process of developing innovations. There are different pathways to get to different types of scales, with different barriers to overcome. It takes multiple years and even decades to sustain the effort. Along the way, innovation networks morph.

Taken together, these frameworks offer a map of the challenging terrain through which your network and others are journeying. The social innovation networks we've known had some of this landscape figured out as they ventured forward. But not nearly all of it. Often, they just put one foot ahead of the other, acting on instinct and perhaps some advice, stepping into uncharted space.

You can use these frameworks to anticipate what may lie ahead for your network: necessities you'll likely have to deal with, pitfalls to avoid, opportunities to look for. Or you can reflect on what's behind: what you've done well, what else you should have considered, what could be improved when you do it next time. Or you can test how you're thinking about systems change, innovation development, and scaling up. The frameworks also provide a set of ideas and a vocabulary for conversations and further learning about these topics.

The logic of the way we've laid out the frameworks—from systems to social innovations to scaling pathways—takes us to two more topics before the book concludes. In this chapter we deal with additional demands of systems changing that lead social innovation networks to evolve into more complex structures. And in the next chapter we lay out the unique roles that leaders of innovation networks play.

So, there's more to take in—yes, more frameworks! But you don't have to master the array of possibilities in all of these intersecting frameworks. There is no perfect, fool-proof way to proceed. There's the journey that you're taking and what you can learn and use from others who have trekked through the territory, whose experiences and insights inform our account.

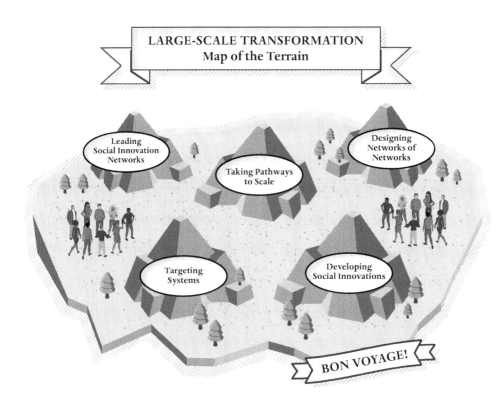

Networks of Networks

The morphing of social innovation networks that we described in the previous chapter doesn't tell the whole story of what happens to these networks as they mature and succeed. Many successful system-changing innovation networks are actually networks of networks. Their founders begin with a system-disrupting idea and an instinct for organizing collaborations to create innovations. They establish innovation development processes, but at some point they also start to conduct other functions that are not just about creating innovations.

When the High Line Network started about five years ago, it was a small group of people interested in learning how to repurpose underused urban infrastructure into parks, public squares, open-air museums, botanical gardens, and other spaces that generate social, environmental, and economic benefits for communities. The innovative work was inspired by the development in New York City of the High Line, a public park built on a 1.45-mile elevated freight rail line that neighborhood residents and the city had saved from demolition. The linear park, which opened in 2009, attracts millions of visitors annually and spurred real estate development in adjacent neighborhoods. Its well-publicized success inspired other cities to begin redeveloping their obsolete infrastructure as public space—and to come together as a learning-and-projects network guided by the High Line innovators.

"We are a strategic hub with three arms of activity: peer learning, technical assistance/advocacy, and tools/innovation," says Asima Jansveld, the network's managing director, a former urban planning consultant and vice president of the New York City Economic Development Corporation. The child of immigrant professionals from India,

Asima Jansveld

Jansveld grew up in suburban New Jersey and studied architecture. But, she says, "I learned I was not interested in designing one building. I wanted to design collections of buildings, the public realm. Most of my career has focused on what it takes to create inclusive, resilient space in cities, with an equity lens. I've been fascinated by infrastructure reuse.

Much urban infrastructure has been used to tear communities apart. Reuse is reconnecting communities."

At the beginning, the High Line Network had about 20 members, leaders of nonprofits working with cities, Jansveld says. "It was very clear that the big value was in the personal relationships and the trust to share lessons learned." When more communities asked to join the network, membership was expanded to and capped at 40. "Getting any bigger meant people would lose the intimacy they wanted," says Jansveld.

But the network doesn't just exist to serve its individual members. Its collective ambition is to scale up infrastructure reuse innovations within the field of urban design, especially to establish more and better green, public space. To have impact beyond its members, the High Line Network developed a toolkit with tested processes and downloadable tools that can be used to help reuse projects result in equitable, rather than gentrifying and dislocating, impacts on neighborhoods. To make the toolkit, the network partnered with the Urban Institute and Harvard graduate researchers, who worked with subsets of members. "This is how we can create change in the field," Jansveld explains.

Now the network also provides technical assistance to communities that are shut out from becoming members. It is considering launching a fellowship program to increase the number of leaders of color in its ranks and in the field. A subgroup of members is developing a federal policy advocacy agenda; another cohort is engaging in racial equity training so they can develop diversity, inclusion, and equity plans for their organizations.

What began as an innovation network to refine and spread knowledge of new practices in infrastructure reuse is adding functions to its innovation-development activities. These new functions are implemented by their own small cohorts of members, non-members, and staff, with some overlap across functions.

In moving beyond innovation development and scaling and embracing a broader system-change approach, the network is making a shift that other social innovation networks also use. Networks that have been around much longer than the High Line Network have added yet other types of functions to their systems-change portfolios. They have already become what the High Line Network is becoming: a network of networks, a growing web of relationships and collaborations that engage in system change.

The Ascend Network, for instance, provides consulting services, leadership development, narrative shift, movement building, measurement development, and research to system-changers in human service fields. That's on top of developing practice and policy innovations.

The Financial Health Network, introduced in the previous chapter, provides capital investment in "fintech" enterprises that use digital technologies to support financial services, as we saw in its investment in Attune. It also conducts consulting services, measurement development, narrative shift, and research.

The Nebraska Community Foundation, a network we'll describe in more detail later in this chapter, provides consulting services, leadership development, research, narrative shift, and movement building to community-based system changers—in addition to developing an impressive innovation in community-based philanthropy that is scaling up.

We've identified at least eight functions that systems-changing networks of networks may perform while also doing innovation development. These tasks support a network's growth and evolution, but that's not their primary purpose. Instead, they are part of a wide-ranging, emergent approach to systems change that contains multiple functions and networks. The functions, in alphabetical order, are:

- Capital investment

- Celebrations

- Consulting/technical assistance

- Leadership development

- Measurement development

- Movement building

- Narrative shifting

- Research

Below we briefly describe each function and provide examples from networks in this book.

Capital Investment

Some networks provide their members with much-needed capital.

The Opportunity Finance Network, with more than 350 members that are community development financial institutions (CDFIs), manages more than $980 million that it lends to members to help them lend, invest, and change markets underserved by banks. "We are a major lender to our field," says CEO Lisa Mensah. "It's an unusual role for an intermediary." The network also launched a program of $8.5 million in grants and $170 million of debt funded by Google so that OFN member CDFIs can offer low-cost, more flexible loans to small businesses, led by Black, Latino, and Native entrepreneurs, and to those located in under-served communities.

Ascend develops initiatives, funded by philanthropies, in which it regrants some money to participating organizations. For instance, 26 nonprofit organizations in its Family Prosperity Innovation Community (phases I and II) received more than $4 million to support their projects. Ascend also surveyed the Phase II partners to gather their ideas and votes about how to spend about $240,000 that remained in its grantmaking pool.

The Financial Health Network operates an innovation fund that has invested in more than 40 financial services companies and products. "It's a huge way in which we seed and promote innovations that then either scale up on their own or by adoption by others," network CEO Jennifer Tescher explains.

Celebrations

The networks regularly acknowledge and praise the efforts and successes of their members and other change agents.

The US Water Alliance celebrates innovations in water management on World Water Day, Earth Day, and A Day Without Water. It annually awards prizes—to non-members as well as members—for achievements in advancing sustainable, integrated, and inclusive solutions to water challenges. Its 2021 Water Prize for Outstanding Artist went to Salmon Speakers, a team of Indigenous people in southeast Alaska and British Columbia facilitating gatherings, story circles, and interviews to explore Indigenous sovereignty, sustainability, and food security.

Salmon Nation launched an annual, virtual "Festival of What Works" in 2020. The days-long festival, celebrating community-led approaches to living well in the bioregion, attracts thousands of residents for discussions, workshops, film screenings, and panels with Indigenous leaders, activists, scientists, authors, and entrepreneurs.

In 2021, Health Care Without Harm gave out four awards for Emerging Physician Leaders, which recognize medical students, residents, and fellows who demonstrated a passion for sustainable health care.

Consulting/Technical Assistance

Providing advice and technical assistance to organizations in a targeted system can help an innovation network build its presence in the system, learn more about how the system works, and anticipate some of the ways that scaling up in the system might be pursued.

The Ascend Network, Financial Health Network, High Line Network, Nebraska Community Foundation, and other networks provide this kind of support, usually on an informal basis rather than as a program, to some member organizations as well as non-members. They typically target organizations that are undertaking significant internal changes in strategy and practice.

Leadership Development

Cultivating the values, vision, and strategies of leaders in a system helps them become more effective as system change agents. It can instill new mental models that become the basis for thought and action.

Ascend operates a fellowship program to connect and develop diverse cohorts of leaders who are positioned to build the political will and policy agendas for systems change. During 18 months, 20 selected fellows participate in peer-to-peer forums and create and carry out action plans in their organizations.

The US Water Alliance published a guide to change leadership for water utilities, "Six Essential Capacities," and initiated a mentorship program that connected up-and-coming utility leaders—rising professionals—with changemaking veteran utility CEOs. Each mentee did virtual coaching calls with the CEO with whom they were matched, and participated in three peer learning exchanges on different leadership topics. The mentees also formed their own peer-to-peer network. "The network building among their cohort became really important in their growth as 'One Water' leaders—the opportunity to troubleshoot, adapt, and innovate with their peers," says Katy Lackey, director of climate action at the Alliance. Some of the CEOs found a welcome

Katy Lackey

benefit in their 1:1 relationship with a mentee, she adds. "Many ended up feeling they were in this to learn from rising professionals just as much as vise versa. After all, leadership is a continuous action in which one learns and adapts along the way." Network members could participate as mentors and could have a mentee from their organization in the program.

In March 2022 the Alliance published lessons from the first year of its Mentoring Connections Program and began accepting applications for the second cohort of rising professionals. The program occurs annually, with intermittent activities connecting cohorts from different years to help expand their peer networks.

Measurement

Social innovation networks that are scaling innovations based on new mental models can't rely on existing systems to collect and analyze data that will inform their efforts. The systems don't usually have the indicators and information that are relevant to the innovations. So, the networks create and use new measurement models.

The Financial Health Network, for instance, created the FinHealth Score® Toolkit to track improvements in financial health of financial institutions' customers and employees. "Measurement is the first step to improving financial health for all," it says, "with data to foster success for your business and those you serve." The network measures the financial health of banked consumers, to gain a deeper understanding of the health needs of financial institutions' customers. Its 2021 report concluded that two-thirds of Americans were not financially healthy.

Ascend created a 2Gen Outcomes Bank, a database with indicators that it crowdsources from the field to capture and organize outcomes and evidence for two-generation innovations in human services.

Movement Building

Many systems change-agents say they are in the movement building business. What they usually mean is they work to inspire large numbers of people inside and outside of a system to demand transformation of the system. The demand may be general, as in the adoption of a new mental model, or it may be specific, as in the application of certain innovations. Strong demand can influence—even overwhelm—the thinking and actions of a system's leaders, disrupting the status quo. And a growing movement can be a seedbed from which new innovators emerge.

The US Water Alliance calls itself "the hub of the One Water movement" and its website is "a gateway to connect with resources and fellow One Water leaders."

Ascend's executive director Anne Mosle uses similar language: "We are a bit of a movement," she says, noting the network regularly communicates directly with 12,000 people and works with human-service field leaders and organizations that collectively serve 10 million families.

A hallmark of movement building is the summit, a regular gathering of movement members who connect with each other, often across historical dividing lines that have kept them apart. They learn together, plan collaborations, and energize each other. All of this also sends signals to decision makers within the system. The US Water Alliance runs an annual "One Water Summit," gathering water system leaders, practitioners, activists, artists, and stakeholders to share ideas, learn, and work together. Its 2019 summit in Austin, Texas drew more than 1,000 participants—most of them not Alliance members—for site visits, networking, and speakers.

Narrative Shifting

Influencing prevailing public narratives—widely held mental models—is another strategic function of these networks. They use communications methods to replace narratives that impede adoption of their social innovations.

Ascend partners with a communications firm, Spitfire Strategies, and others to help reframe narratives about families and communities to more accurately and positively reflect the realities and lived experiences of people with low incomes. Spitfire reports that it works with Ascend "to develop ways to shift the narrative on family prosperity from one of personal responsibility toward societal support and collective engagement. This messaging allows decisionmakers and leaders in the field to make the case for scaling up innovative approaches, through local, state, and federal efforts with the goal of creating more fair and equitable conditions for children and their families to thrive."

The Salmon Nation website declares "Welcome aboard the Magic Canoe. Welcome home." The Magic Canoe is a digital space in which people tell and share each other's stories about the bioregion. Through these stories, the site explains, "we paint an increasingly vivid picture across a palette of possibility in our bioregion." Many of the narratives there are short videos in which people tell personal "Salmon Stories," answering questions: What do wild salmon mean to you? To your community? The stories are told by Indigenous leaders, fishing professionals, scientists, journalists, mothers, bankers, loggers, teachers, children, and others. This is a way to grow a new narrative, to "support the understanding that the fight for wild salmon is about much more than fish; it's about culture, community, livelihood, sustainability, life."

Ian Gill, journalist and co-founder of Salmon Nation, says the Magic Canoe name came from Cecil Paul, Wa'xaid, of the Killer Whale Clan of the Xenaksiala people of the Kitlope Valley. Some three decades ago, Paul was working to protect the valley from industrial logging. Gill recounts Paul's words: "'I was alone in a canoe,' he once famously said. 'But it was a Magic Canoe. It was magic because it could make room for everyone who wanted to come on board, to come in and paddle together. The currents against us were very strong. But I believed we could reach our destination. And that we had to for our survival.'" Gill adds, "And lo, the Kitlope was saved, in 1994, and today it is known as Huschduwaschdu Nuyem Jees, the land of milky blue waters and all the stories it contains."

Research

Innovation networks conduct various types of research to inform system-changing efforts of others in the fields, markets, and governments they have targeted.

The Nebraska Community Foundation surveyed 1,000 youth from 25 communities to understand why young Nebraskans choose to remain in, return to, or leave their hometowns. "Well over half told us their dream communities look a lot like where they live now, small towns, a reason to believe our future is bright," says foundation CEO Jeff Yost. "When asked whether a stigma accompanied staying in or returning to their community, 76 percent said no. The old narrative about rural communities is changing and young people are telling a very different story from those who came before them." The foundation also conducts a periodic study of the intergenerational transfer of wealth that will occur from generation to generation in Nebraska—with an eye on ensuring some of the wealth stays in the state. Its 2021 report found that during the next 10 years in Nebraska more than $100 billion will transfer from one generation to the next.

Ascend works with pollsters for both the Democratic and Republican Parties to gauge public opinion about 2Gen innovations and related social service and family prosperity issues and possible policy changes. It also conducts focus groups of recipients of public benefits to understand their experiences in the systems and gather their ideas for change.

System-changing innovation networks are not obligated to add these or other functions. They establish them in response to needs and opportunities they perceive, and they may go with just a few or many of the functions, as the table below shows.

"These are not simply stand-alone functions," notes Tescher. "The intersections and interconnections among them are critical. For instance, one of the reasons for deploying capital to drive innovation may be to drive narrative change. That's one of the reasons that networks of networks are complicated beasts: it's not just about running multiple functions; it's about how they leverage each other to achieve the ultimate goal."

Other systems-changing functions may emerge. Some networks, for instance, have become active in ensuring their members become more knowledgeable about how to incorporate racial equity into their work.

Once networks start to add functions and the means to implement them, the overall design of the network's structure changes too.

Multiple Functions of Networks of Networks	
Ascend Network	Celebrations, Consulting/TA, Leadership Development, Measurement, Movement Building, Narrative Shift, Research
Financial Health Network	Capital Investment, Consulting/TA, Measurement, Narrative Shift, Research
Health Care Without Harm	Celebrations, Leadership Development, Movement Building, Narrative Shift, Research
High Line Network	Consulting/TA, Leadership Development
Nebraska Community Foundation	Celebrations, Consulting/TA, Narrative Shift, Research
Opportunity Finance Network	Capital Investment, Measurement, Narrative Shift
Salmon Nation	Capital Investment, Celebrations, Narrative Shift
US Water Alliance	Celebrations, Leadership Development, Movement Building, Narrative Shift, Research

Network Structures

By *network structure* we mean two things that are entwined.

First, it's the pattern of connections and relationships among network members or nodes, which we detailed in *Connecting to Change the World* (pages 109-117). A network's pattern of connectivity is crucial to the network's success. When network participants become confident that they can rely on each other's intentions, integrity, judgment, and abilities they will act in new ways toward each other—sharing secrets, making commitments, providing support, taking care, being accountable. The trust that is built supports the quality of information exchanged and the efficiency of transactions that flow between participants. It also activates what we call the "connect-to-align-to-produce" (C-A-P) sequence, a crucial evolution of a network's capability to have impact. In the connection phase, members exchange information and built trust. They capitalize on their connections to align, discovering, exploring, and defining shared goals, strategies, and points of view. Alignment sets the stage for the production phase in which members organize to take joint action. (More on C-A-P in *Connecting to Change the World*, pages 104-109.)

Perhaps the most familiar connectivity structure in networks is the Hub-and-Spoke, in which one node in the network (an individual, organization, or group) connects to many other nodes that are mostly unconnected to each other. The hub becomes the network's "connectivity center," through which information and resources flow to the other nodes. This is a typical structure for early-stage networks.

Elements of Network Design

A network's connectivity structure is one element of design. In *Connecting to Change the World* (pages 39-74) we described eight other elements:

- *Purpose*—What is the network's reason for being?
- *Value Propositions*—What will be the compelling benefits of membership—for individuals and collectively?
- *Membership*—Who is eligible to become a member? What are the membership benefits and requirements? How many members will there be?
- *Coordination, Facilitation, and Communication*—How will network members link and work with each other?
- *Resources*—What is the network's funding model?
- *Governance*—Who decides what the network will do, and how do they decide?
- *Assessment*—How will the network monitor its condition and performance?
- *Operating Principles*—What rules guide the network's culture?

Other, quite different connectivity structures arise in networks, including:

- Clusters, in which every node is connected to every other node; cluster members usually converge around a common purpose or project.

- Multiple-Hubs, in which two or more hubs (with their many spokes) are connected to each other as well as to their nodes.

- Many-Channels, in which many nodes connect directly with each other, in addition to their links with hubs and within clusters.

A network's connectivity structure may change over time as members connect, align, and produce together. Valdis Krebs, an expert network analyst, and June Holley, an avid social network builder, depict a multi-stage, ideal evolution of a network's connectivity structure. It starts with unconnected, scattered nodes that begin to connect and form a hub-and-spoke structure around the founders of the network. It evolves into a network with multiple clusters and multiple hubs, and then on to an end state that Krebs and Holley call "core/periphery." "The periphery," they write, "allows us to reach ideas and information not currently prevalent in the network." The core, they continue, "allows us to act on those ideas and information." This core-periphery structure recalls Hargadon's model of an innovation network in which a core of innovators reaches out for ideas and then carries its innovations into the markets, fields, or governments at its periphery.

The second type of network structure is the arrangement of power over the network's decisions and resources. This is the governance of the network. In evolved social innovation networks, governance tends to be more centralized, with a core of well-connected network leaders exercising power while consulting members about their perspectives and priorities.

Strategic Hubs

An innovation network's leaders establish its mix of functions. This leadership is usually comprised of a blend of some staff and members, advisors, outside experts, investors, and partner organizations. The leaders serve as a *strategic* hub for the system-changing effort. They consult with network members and resonate to their views, interests, and feedback. But they do not simply follow the membership; they exercise informed but independent judgment about the network's goals, strategies, and activities. And they shepherd resources to what makes strategic sense to them, depending on situations and opportunities.

Ascend's strategic hub is made up of its staff, working in consultation with a large number of network members, experts, and others. "We are the hub in the spokes," says executive director Mosle. "The Ascend network is activated in different ways at different times" from the hub. But, she adds, hub decisions are guided by the network's shared purpose of advancing Ascend's 2Gen approach. "We have a clear North Star that people can see themselves in. A North Star with core values."

The network's vision is also the connective tissue at Salmon Nation, the bioregional system-changing initiative that we described in chapter 2. Its strategic hub consists of four founding partners and a set of trustees. "There are no operations at the trustee level," notes cofounder Spencer Beebe. "Just bioregional vision alignment and a small group of people aggregating a modest amount of capital for allocation to a very few bioregional experiments."

The Opportunity Finance Network "is a hub institution" for community development financial institutions, says CEO Lisa Mensah. "We have over 350 members, some of them are networks, so it's an even bigger network than it looks like. We exist to build a field—a sector that can reach into communities in a way that is fair and just."

The US Water Alliance functions as a strategic hub network that manages multiple innovations and a set of other functions. It is guided by a core of strategic leaders, including members of the Alliance's board of directors, staff, and participants in its One Water Council. The council, says its chair, Kishia Powell, COO of DC Water, "brings together people from different parts of the water sector—it's not just public or private, it's not just utilities or consultants, it's anyone who has a passion for effectively managing water," Powell says. "I consider it a brain trust; all that power of thought working together."

Strategic hubs operate as Hub-and-Spoke structures. The central hub makes decisions, usually without subjecting the decision to explicit membership approval. "One of the benefits of having a network like ours, in which there's no real governance by the members, is it gives me more ability and freedom to push the network," says Tescher of the Financial Health Network.

Although strategic hubs centralize control, they are not a top-down, command-driven apparatus, the way organizations' top executives would usually function. Instead, network hub leaders have to build strong trust with network members or they risk losing the shared understanding, commitment, and voluntary collaboration on which the network's essential connectivity structure is based. Strategic hub leaders have to blend the centralized structure of power with the non-hierarchical structure of network relationships. This is an extraordinarily challenging task.

NETWORK OF NETWORKS STRUCTURE

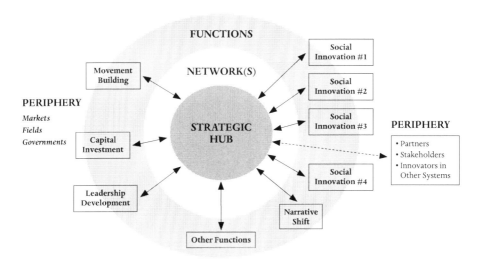

Some of the most prominent pitfalls in operating a strategic hub include:

- **Low connectivity in the network.** A hub may not invest sufficiently in weaving relationships among participants across the various functions the network conducts. Instead, it begins to operate more like an organization, with decisions at the top and implementation by distinct and specialized units that are mostly unlinked to each other. The network's identity as a collective will fade. The risk of low connectivity can be mitigated by increasing opportunities for network members to connect with each other and by supporting network members who are natural "boundary spanners," nodes who build connections across the network's divides.

- **Weak or failed feedback loops.** The hub needs a regular flow of reliable information from the network's functions. Or else it cannot understand enough about what is working well and what is not and must be improved. Strong flows from many sources help the hub to develop new strategic insights. But feedback loops need to be developed and managed; they require continuing investment. Hubs may not do this well, often because they do not recognize it as a priority. Another source of feedback weakness can be a lack of membership trust in the network's leadership, perhaps because members don't feel heard in decision- making processes.

- **Insufficient central direction.** When the hub tries to please everyone—members, stakeholders, partners—rather than choosing which strategies to pursue and which not to pursue, it essentially defaults decision making to the network's flat relationship structure. But the relationships are not designed to make collective strategic choices, and the network will flounder. The core leadership has to find a way to become more decisive or the leadership has to be changed, by network members or perhaps by investors in the network.

- **Excessive central control.** When the hub overrides or ignores what network members care about, it disempowers the relationship structure. Why would members try to connect, align, and produce together when the center's decision makers totally go their own way? Dana Bourland, senior vice president at the JPB Foundation, recognized that a network of dozens of organizations that she was funding had this problem with its hub: "You could see the struggle of organizations in a top-down system: being told what resources they can have but not how the decisions were made. There was no effort to allocate resources in a transparent way. We needed a network that was much more supportive of and accountable to the needs of the organizations." With this problem, too, a solution may be to change the leadership's behavior or change who the leaders are. But there's an additional possibility: a strategic hub can develop a system of "distributed control" throughout the network, a different power structure.

Distributed Control

Jeff Yost, president and CEO of the Nebraska
Community Foundation (NCF), has toiled more
than a decade to scale up a promising innovation
in community philanthropy, in which local donors
fund local projects to improve a community's
well-being. At the heart of his effort has been the
issue of control: who decides how philanthropic

Jeff Yost

funds will be used—the statewide community foundation or the local
communities themselves? Should control be centralized or distributed?

Yost is passionate about the answer: "The only people who can build
and sustain a community are the people who live and work in the
community. Our foundation's mission is community building from the
ground up. We unleash abundant local assets, inspire charitable giving
and connect ambitious people to build stronger communities."

A lifelong Nebraskan, graduate of the state university, and former
policy and budget advisor to a Nebraska governor, Yost grew up in Red
Cloud, one of the many small towns that characterize the mostly rural
state of nearly 2 million residents. Since 2003 he's been running the foundation and, along with the NCF board of directors and thousands of
people in towns, honing a set of principles for reinvigorating declining
communities by helping each of them to build a collective vision for their
future, civic leadership, discretionary capital, and citizen engagement.
"You have to make this as locally owned and controlled as possible," he
says, "and support people over many, many years."

Today, 270 communities in Nebraska—nearly all of them small
towns—have their own philanthropic funds, supported by the NCF.
These and additional community-focused funds contain a total of $164
million in philanthropic endowments, held in perpetuity, fueled by more
than 46,500 donations in just the past five years. Roughly 1,500 volunteers in these communities guide the convening, fundraising, and grantmaking of their funds. Much of the donated money—about $70 million
in total—is "unrestricted," meaning its use is at the discretion of the
community funds, not the donors. In the last three fiscal years roughly
4,000 grants have been made per year, a total of $86.2 million to support
community projects.

Two examples were highlighted at NCF's March 2022 board meeting. Keith County in western Nebraska, population 8,335, has amassed $13.5 million in unrestricted endowment, and its grants have supported the public library, early childhood education, renovation of a community center, rescue equipment for the fire department, a pocket park, youth entrepreneurs, and more. A future priority is to increase housing in the county. McCook, a city with fewer than 7,500 residents, has built an affiliated fund with $6.8 million in endowed assets, and has a pipeline of future donations of nearly $1.5 million.

All of the locally driven philanthropy, Yost says, adds up to more connections, collaborations, and trust among residents in communities, which are crucial for giving people compelling reasons to move back, move to, or remain in Nebraska's towns. "People are attracted to being invited to be productive together and share their gifts and dreams with their neighbors. If you want to have a community-based fund, you and your neighbors have to figure out what community means to you. The way the money gets raised is leaders of the funds go to their friends and neighbors saying, 'Will you do what I did?'" Yost adds that "deployment of these new philanthropic resources is helping to fuel a growing number of young families moving to Greater Nebraska. In 53 counties the number of people in their 30s and 40s is on the rise." The wave of local philanthropic engagement, he says, is building "distributed leadership—a network of leader-full communities" throughout the state.

In effect, the statewide foundation at the "center" has created a network of hundreds of locally controlled, "distributed" foundations. "We have always been about giving away power to the communities," says Yost. It's an approach he first embraced as a college freshman. "In a leadership development course, I learned that the most important thing to understand about power is that if you want to make something different, give it away."

This is not the norm for the hundreds of community foundations across the US. If the NCF was a more typical community foundation, its board and staff would be directing the grantmaking, perhaps with some advice from local people. But it would not have delegated decision making to local entities, known as "affiliate funds," to do the bulk of the fundraising and to guide *all* of the grantmaking. "When I first got involved in the community foundation world," recalls Yost, "when people talked about their work, *community* was in lower case in a little font and *foundation* was in capital letters and a great big font. It didn't make sense to me that the foundation was the tool and the community was a junior partner. Here we're putting first things first: we are a community builder." Breaking the mold to grow empowered affiliates wasn't simple, he adds: "A part of the design has involved figuring out the balance of power between the affiliates and the 'mother ship.' I had to spend a lot of time for a lot of years trying to figure out how much power and decision-making authority we can give away. If you give it away, you damned well should not try to take it back or tell the affiliates their decisions were wrong."

The NCF approach, Yost says, makes it "the most decentralized and most community-centric of the community foundations" in the US. And it's a flexible approach; affiliates can change their structure over time. "We have funds that started as one town in a county and now are county-wide and have changed their name. We have lots of differences in what communities want."

The NCF model still has a strategic hub, the statewide community foundation, but its role has changed. It's still the hub in a hub-and-spoke relationship structure and it's the developer of the strategy of community building through empowered community-based affiliates, the network's North Star. But instead of controlling local affiliate decisions, the hub provides them with decision-making power. In this distributed arrangement, the statewide community foundation has two main roles: (1) establish a standard set of rules for affiliates to comply with the law and national standards in the community philanthropy field and (2) provide affiliates with capacity building and support to do their work. The combination, says Yost, "creates a 'floor' whereby no affiliate falls to a depth if they screw up."

NCF's rules come in the form of written policies that all affiliates review annually—covering conflict of interest, acceptance of donations, investment of funds, inclusiveness and diversity guidelines, confidentiality, and more. "They agree to take on these responsibilities," Yost notes. The agreements are not legally binding, but they create "moral authority" that guides affiliates' actions.

NCF's support is broad and adaptive. It provides workshops about grantmaking and cultural competence, and training for affiliates' treasurers. It helps affiliates determine their priorities and market themselves to donors. It supports peer learning among the affiliates, with 90 community volunteer leaders serving as peer mentors. In the past 18 months, more than 300 peer mentor activities have occurred. "We are constantly trying to figure out what smaller innovations we can make to help communities," Yost notes. More recently, NCF is sponsoring arts and culture asset-mapping in six communities to test its potential value for the affiliates. "It has helped us to identify, name, and mediate longstanding local conflicts," Yost says. "People are discovering longstanding commonalities they never knew they had: music, woodworking, photography. The community takes a learning journey together."

NCF's peer learning processes connect many affiliate members to each other. In the last decade, probably 300 affiliate leaders have engaged in intensive peer-learning processes focused on raising money and engaging their communities, Yost says. Once a year as many as 250 people from affiliates convene for a day-and-a-half of peer learning. NCF holds regional meetings that bring together as many as a dozen funds in a region of the state.

Some affiliates have begun to work with each other. "Families" of affiliate funds, usually in geographic proximity to each other, have been meeting to work on housing and health care concerns, Yost reports. Developing a more robust relationship structure among the affiliates is becoming an overriding objective for NCF. Yost envisions this as yet another major shift in the network's structure—webs of linked affiliates supported by the statewide foundation. It would be a network with many-channels connecting the nodes with each other, rather than the current hub-and-spoke model. He uses a nature-system metaphor to describe the next stage: "I want the Nebraska Community Foundation to be the wetland in the system: creating tons of nutrients for many different species, cleaning and filtering the water. That is my grandest hope within this broad ecosystem."

The potential evolution of NCF into a connected ecosystem has been made possible by the distribution of power to the affiliates.

Toward An Ecosystem

In a system-changing social innovation *ecosystem* the power and relationship structures are in a dynamic balance. Centralize the power too much and you reduce the autonomy of the network's many players. Without sufficient autonomy, they will simply wait for commands from the center/top and, eventually, rebel or exit from the network. Distribute the power too much and the players will each go their own ways, and the network loses the alignment, coherence, and collective identity that support collaborations that would make it productive. It becomes chaotic.

A crucial move for achieving balance is the creation of guiding rules that don't disempower members of the network and help them to align around the network's North Star. For example, Project ECHO, the global "telementoring" network for training health care clinicians that we described in chapter 2, imposes little governance and minimal legal requirements on its implementation partners. But it does require them to agree to operational standards and to fund their own costs. And it supports them with training materials, access to research, and ways to engage with other partners. Shared vision, distributed control from the center, standards for participation, and support for members' capacities: these ingredients are similar to those NCF uses. Together, they enable the local actors—the Nebraska affiliates, ECHO's implementing partners—to make their own decisions in response to local conditions, but in ways that are consistent with their shared guiding vision and overarching rules.

This is not a "cookie cutter" approach in which the members are expected to replicate a received model (usually developed by experts). Instead, it champions diversity and variation, within a shared framework. Yost stresses this point: "My colleagues ask me, what should the communities do? My answer is, it depends. It drives my colleagues crazy, but that's my answer. It depends on the specific community, on the people, on the relationships. We have to be smart enough to listen to them and build their confidence, efficacy, and skill. That's how we help people help themselves."

Project ECHO has a similar perspective toward local autonomy. "Individual adopters in each localized platform" apply the model "as they see fit for their context," note Tamara Kay and Jason Spicer, authors of the ECHO case study.

In a social ecosystem of this sort, autonomous local players don't just take independent action; they also collaborate with each other. Tescher, who embraces an ecosystem vision for the Financial Health Network, sees it bringing together multiple sectors—finance, health, and others—to "surround people with opportunities to improve their financial health." The ecosystem will contain different sectors and actors, "and ultimately, it's about the ways these companies and organizations will collaborate." This approach echoes a point made by the Open Society Foundations, which invested in development of the ISSA network for early childhood, described in chapter 4: "In a healthy ecosystem, civil society, government, academic and training institutions, and businesses are fluent in early childhood development. Together they flexibly design, implement, and monitor services and address challenges on their own without donor intervention. . . . When all parts of the system are engaged and capable, it can self-correct."

Togetherness—relationship building—is key. "In an emerging ecosystem," says the JPB Foundation's Bourland, "everybody changes as a result of being in relationship through the loose organizing structure."

The design of an ecosystem model of a social innovation network may seem highly conceptual, but it boils down to just a few basic characteristics:

- **Autonomous members.** These are people and organizations who make choices about how to act based on information in their local environment. The decisions these agents make influence the actions of other agents with whom they are linked in the network.

- **Networked structure.** The autonomous agents share decision-making "rules" about how they decide what to do next. As we've seen, it's the strategic hub that establishes, at least initially, these networkwide rules—standards, specifications, rights, for example. The rules serve to align the agents and allow a coherence to emerge among them. The rules may evolve as they are used, depending on how successful they are in fostering innovation and network outcomes.

- **Profuse experimentation.** The network is full of experimentation by the agents, who react to small changes, communicate almost instantly with each other, experiment with dozens of possible responses if they encounter barriers, and rapidly exploit solutions they find.

These characteristics allow the ecosystem to avoid control from the center that would lock members into a rigid order that cannot evolve, while also providing enough order so that the whole network doesn't fall into chaos.

"It's pretty straightforward in a lot of ways," says Spencer Beebe, cofounder of Salmon Nation, the bioregional network described in chapter 2. "You get the right people with the right social architecture. You find these people, connect them, and support them."

Networks & Structural Design

As a system-changing network develops multiple innovations and additional functions, it becomes more complex and needs more coordination of its many moving parts. It may change, by design or not, into an organization or an association with a top-down decision-making structure and hierarchical, siloed relationships organized to execute commands. Or, instead, it can continue to evolve as a network, either as a strategic hub or as a distributed ecosystem.

In light of the structural inflection points that can be anticipated, here's some advice for social innovation networks as they design for the complex challenges and opportunities they face.

Advice for Networks on Structural Design

- An innovation network's structure must be flexible, able to change to meet shifting necessities and emerging opportunities.

- Networks of networks may eventually need to create tiers of membership.

- Investors in system-change networks must recognize the dynamic, fluid nature of the work.

An innovation network's structure must be flexible, able to change to meet shifting necessities and emerging opportunities. "Disequilibrium and creativity, that's how healthy systems really work," says Beebe. Never locked in, always evolving.

A network's purpose, strategies, innovations, functions, and design—all may shift. OpenNews morphed from a network concentrating on digital technologists in journalism to a network also focusing on racial inclusion in the news media. The US Water Alliance shifted from a small, exclusive network of water-management professionals into a large, inclusive network of water-sector change agents. During the innovation development process, a network shifts from a tight collective for ideation and testing into a broad community for scaling. As a network continues to engage with a system, it adds new functions to enhance its innovation strategy. A strategic hub may emerge to guide the network through the growing complexity it faces. And out of a strategic hub, perhaps an ecosystem of connected but autonomous actors will emerge.

These shifts may present networks with fundamental tensions to manage. "The paradox inherent in the innovation process is that innovators need wide-ranging ties in the first place," notes Andrew Hargadon, "yet they also need strong, focused ties to build communities around emerging innovations." Similarly, the tension between a network's power and relationship structures has to be managed.

In short, a successful innovation network is often in the process of changing; it maintains a dynamic stability. This is a natural strength to build on, not a flaw to be corrected.

Networks of networks may eventually need to create tiers of membership. The growing complexity of system-changing innovation networks makes it likely that a one-size-fits-all membership model won't work for evolved networks. Some participants may be active in developing innovations, others in scaling them, still others in different system-changing functions. Since network membership defines the benefits, opportunities, and responsibilities of members, it may become important to differentiate types of members with differing roles and value propositions for being in the network.

Investors in systems-change networks must recognize the dynamic, fluid nature of the work. Yes, funders, innovation networks are different from what you may usually invest in. Changing systems is not like funding a program or service; it's a long game of many parts: multiple and continuous innovation making, as well as other functions. Developing and scaling innovations is not like making widgets; it entails a lot of uncertainty and a changing mix of capabilities. Building and sustaining networks is not like funding organizations; it doesn't lend itself to a static "logic model" that identifies precisely what the processes, outputs, and outcomes will be.

Some funders are attracted to the efficiency and apparent efficacy of funding intermediary organizations to start, service, and even lead social-change networks. While intermediaries can catalyze innovation among network members, investing with them to build innovation networks requires attention to the power and agency of members. "Intermediaries seem to be convenient," says Chrystie Hill, a deputy director at the Gates Foundation. "You can make one big grant to them and they do all the sub-grants." But funders should recognize that an intermediary may unbalance a network's relationship-to-power structures if, for instance, it takes on too much decision-making power or builds too little connectivity among network members. In addition, Hill says, "it's problematic not to listen to and directly support the people who are at or most proximate to the point of need. Intermediaries are so far up the chain from that point. The money is too far away from the solution."

Funders should also realize that supporting a network is not the same as also supporting members of a network. JPB's Bourland has learned this lesson: "As a funder you have to make sure that the organizations that belong to the network have enough bandwidth to show up on their own. They have to have some autonomy and be able to drive the network to be what they need it to be." She began, through the Fund to Build Grassroots Power, to provide capacity-building financial support directly to organization-members of networks in addition to investing in the network.

Designing and nurturing networks that develop social innovations and take them to system-changing scale doesn't happen by chance. Nor is it simply a technical follow-the-steps process. At the heart of the work that we've described—targeting and engaging a system; articulating a profound mental model change; developing social innovation products, know-how, or policies that embody the mental model; choosing a scale to achieve; designing a fluid, collaborative capacity, and implementing and changing it—are individual people and groups of people who choose to lead in the midst of great complexity.

They lead in a way that is quite unlike leading in the top-down, command-driven hierarchies of organizations. Given the intricate realities of engaging in networked social innovation, leaders take on challenging roles that are as complex and dynamic as the networks themselves.

CHAPTER 6

Leading Social Innovation Networks

*Our work to revolutionize systems requires a dedication to experimentation
and fearlessness. We will make mistakes and will learn and grow from them.*
Native Women Lead

The courage to innovate is a prerequisite for successfully leading a social innovation network. Innovation-network entrepreneurs must have a bias for innovation. They must "actively desire to change the status quo," as *The Innovator's DNA* puts it—to "steer entirely clear of a common cognitive trap called the status quo bias—the tendency to prefer an existing state of affairs to alternate ones."

But the drive to innovate is not enough. Innovators, The Innovator's DNA continues, must "regularly take smart risks to make that change happen." They must "spend a significant portion of time trying to discover how to change the world." In other words, they must know how networks can be used to develop and advance innovations that transform systems. Some of that know-how is contained in our previous chapters on systems thinking, the innovation development process, pathways to scale, and network design.

Yet another critical aspect of social innovation network leadership is the recognition that leaders play several key roles as they shape the network's structures, practices, and culture. By leaders we mean founders, members, managers, and investors who step up to guide the network.

You can see some of the leadership roles articulated when networks need to replace leaders and have to draft position descriptions. In early 2021, for instance, Johanna Partin was writing a job description for the search for her successor as director of the Carbon Neutral Cities Alliance (CNCA), an international network of 22 cities working aggressively to achieve big reductions in greenhouse gas emissions. Partin had become the network's founding director six years earlier and spearheaded its formation, fundraising, growth, and strategic direction, but she was moving on. "In my opinion, there were several non-negotiable characteristics for CNCA's new leadership," she recalls. "Number one was someone who has been in the same settings as our members—working for a city on climate change." This is another way of saying someone with innovation know-how: lived expertise in what needs to be done to lower carbon emissions in cities and how city governments get it done.

"Number two," Partin continues, "was listening to our members. They are the experts. Our guidance comes from the members." This is a bottom line for leadership of any network: an ability to respond to the members as they connect and interact, and to support a network culture. "CNCA has a close-knit culture that places a high priority on member-led decision-making, open communication, and active genial collaboration," the final version of the job description states. "The Director advances this culture in all professional duties and activities."

From our conversations and collaborations with network leaders like Partin, and our scan of what experts say, we identified four distinct roles for leadership of social innovation networks:

- **Innovation Broker**

- **Community Weaver**

- **Trusted Strategist**

- **Story Teller**

You'll notice that playing each of these roles effectively depends—not surprisingly—on establishing the basic glue of networks: strong relationships among people so they can collaborate successfully. "You can't do it without building trust," says Maggie Ullman, cofounder of the Southeast Sustainability Directors Network and a consultant for many social-change networks.

Maggie Ullman

Few network leaders are fully experienced in or otherwise prepared for every aspect of these different roles. For most, leading has involved learning on the job and, often, adapting their approach. As Jennifer Tescher puts it after 18 years leading the Financial Health Network: "The world changes. Our purpose evolves. The funders are fickle. The pace is relentless. If I weren't someone who's extremely comfortable with change, we would be dead by now."

Innovation Network Leadership Roles – Checklist

Innovation Brokers...

- Put into place best practices for innovation development.
- Help networks develop a culture of innovation.
- Protect innovators from resistance and interference.
- Insist on disciplined innovation development and improvement of the network's innovation processes.

Community Weavers...

- Never stop weaving.
- Attend to the diversity of ideas and experiences in the network.
- Look outside the network core, not just inside.
- Value and respect others who are doing related innovation work.
- Regularly assess the network's connectivity—a key indicator of health—and work to improve it.

Trusted Strategists...

- Blend multiple inputs to formulate strategies.
- Use strategy making to make choices and set priorities for the network.
- "Listen" to the outside world to spot opportunities and risks for the network, and maintain nimbleness to shift strategies accordingly.
- Evaluate the network's performance to find ways to improve.

Story Tellers...

- Help to craft a compelling narrative about the network's work.
- Shift the story as the network evolves.
- Identify the most effective communications tools to use.
- Use stories to build productive relationships with investors.

Innovation Broker

Leaders of social innovation networks serve as brokers of innovations, not as the masterminds. It's an organizing role neatly summed up by Leslie Crutchfield, author of *How Change Happens*, who says that change leaders "enable the parts of the system around them to succeed, rather than trying to shore up resources and do all the work themselves—and soak up the credit, media limelight, or other valuable assets."

Brokers put into place best practices for innovation development. As enablers, brokers hold high standards for the network's innovation processes and outputs. They help to implement the practices that ensure that networks capture good ideas that arise, keep ideas alive in the face of resistance or disinterest, and put promising ideas to the test. They build the members' trust in the processes. "For a process to work effectively," note scholars Joanna Cea and Jess Rimington, "it requires a mindset among participants that the process is to be trusted and that it is worth the effort—even if it means pushing one's comfort limits." Brokers also manage potential pitfalls of innovation processes. Cea and Rimington offer an example: "Prototyping too often can cause creative decision fatigue among participants, ask too much of people's time, or stymie an intuitive flow of work." Because innovation prototyping can result in outright failure or the need for numerous revisions, networks have to learn to get comfortable with prototyping.

Brokers help networks develop a culture of innovation. They support the formulation of shared rules, behaviors, and experiences for network members, investors, and partners, the overall culture of the network. "Culture," notes Andrew Hargadon in How Breakthroughs Happen, "has a profound effect on innovation via the value it places on tradition versus change, the stigma that is associated with ignorance and failure, the role of competition versus collaboration, and the value placed on invention versus using old ideas." CNCA's job description for a director said that the position is responsible for "fostering a collaborative, transparent, equitable, and inclusive culture."

Supporting experiments is a key part of culture-making. "I don't want to waste money," says Jeff Yost, CEO of the Nebraska Community Foundation, "but I'm happy to spend money on experiments. That's how we learn. Some should fail, or we're not thinking expansively enough. You're constantly in the process of not letting conventional wisdom eat you up."

Another culture-building effort focuses on the network's diversity—a key to supporting the creativity that innovation processes need: "You can have all the beer-busts, staff meetings, communities-of-practice leaders, intranets, knowledge data-bases, and free sodas you can afford," Hargadon says, "but if the variety of experiences isn't there, all these management techniques won't make people creative."

Brokers foster "possibility thinking," creating spaces in which network participants challenge assumptions, reframe issues, question, and brainstorm. They also encourage the discovery of relevant ideas outside of the network. You have to avoid creating a "not invented here" culture, notes Hargadon.

Another element of an innovation network's culture: brokers have to acknowledge mistakes and turn failures into lessons learned. Mistakes are nothing to be ashamed of.

Brokers protect innovators from resistance and interference. They have to clear the path for innovators. "There are times you need to go for it," explains Tescher. "To build the Attune innovation [see chapter 4], we put it on an island. People knew what was going on and we got internal buy-in. But we walled off things during the product development process. If I had put it into the organizational mix entirely, we'd still be building it."

Brokers protect new ideas by exploring their potential value before subjecting them to critical debate. "As new ideas arise," says Norma Camacho, former CEO of Valley Water in California, in a leadership report by the US Water Alliance, "we have to stop focusing on the things that will kill it, why it's not good. Create a culture open to brainstorming before you start talking about the pros and cons."

Brokers insist on disciplined innovation development and improvement of the network's innovation processes. They demand that innovations show results before pushing them to scaling. Their mantra could well be: invent, field test, scale, and then continuously improve.

They debrief the innovation process "to solidify emerging knowledge and spell out implications for future innovation efforts," report Christian Seelos and Johanna Mair in "When Innovation Goes Wrong." They ask probing questions: "Which pathologies occurred during your innovation process? . . . Which assumptions turned out to be faulty enough to require a thorough redesign of your project? . . . What are you learning about the resource requirements for successful scaling?"

Organizing quick feedback loops is a critical part of the improvement process. "Market and systems change take a long time," notes Tescher. "If you wait years for the feedback loop to deliver, it's too late." But, she adds, a continuous stream of feedback can be difficult to manage. "To be constantly tweaking [an innovation] is an impossible task for a lot of people. It creates a level of instability for staff that doesn't feel good."

Network Weaver

All networks live—or die—based on connectivity: the links among members and links with partners, stakeholders, and other entities at the network's periphery. After members and others connect, they can align around ideas and opportunities, and then they can collaborate on innovations and other outputs.

Some connecting occurs naturally. People meet, talk, hang out, get to know each other, and decide to stay in touch, work together. But that's not enough connectivity for building and sustaining an innovation network seeking impact. Sooner or later, it matters to bring new people into the collective or community, but connecting with them won't happen automatically. That's where weaving comes in.

Weaving is the art of introducing people to each other in ways that stick. Relationships stick when there is trust between the participants. There's more to weaving than hosting, as we noted in *Connecting to Change the World*. Weavers serve as the "on-the-ground eyes and ears" of the network, picking up information as they connect with people. They help network members to develop new knowledge and skills that allow *them* to connect with others more easily. They model an approach to relationships that is positive, appreciative, and focused on strengths and gifts. They encourage people to listen deeply to each other and practice reciprocity, exchanging information, resources, advice for mutual bene-fit. Sisi Wei, of OpenNews, notes in a blog that "organizing conversations are about listening to people, identifying what they care about, present-ing a vision of what is possible, and moving people to action." And, she adds: "It's a two-way street. The relational 1-1 includes me, too, and many times I give my own answers to the questions I'm asking, share my experiences, and talk about all the things that resonate with me." (For more on weaving, see *Connecting to Change the World*, pages 89–101.)

Weavers face challenges specific to being in an *innovation* network. They are not just trying to connect people to each other. Instead, they are connecting people with the aim of developing innovations. This requires collective alignment and collaborative production of outputs, for which linking is just a first step.

The network's morphing from a tight collective to a large community, described in chapter 4, means that network membership and participation grow and change over time. Gaining many new and diverse members can overwhelm a network unless new and old participants become well connected. In some cases, this disruption is what network leaders are looking for. For instance, back in chapter 1 we discussed the way the US Water Alliance is expanding membership and participation to include community-based groups, environmentalists, and other entities that are not water utilities. The inclusion effort depends on trust, says OJ McFoy, the Alliance board vice president. As he noted in chapter 1: "The rebuilding of the Alliance that was performed over the last few years will be integral for the Alliance continuing to have the trust of community organizations and philanthropic organizations and the water utilities. If that continues, we will be able to make some great changes going forward."

In other cases, an influx of players can stall the network's momentum as newcomers and veterans try to develop their relationships and alignment so they can work well together. Many of these people may come from different small worlds, with their own mental models about the targeted system, experiences of innovation and change, and expectations, values, skills, and practices for collaboration. When it comes to identifying and cultivating common ground, these differences pose a trust-and relationship-building challenge.

Weavers never stop weaving. The bottom line for network building: weaving and trust building never end in a network. "I always have our community's wellbeing in mind," says Bill Guest, cofounder and facilitator of TalNet. "To be a part of what we are doing together, it feels really good. We have good people who together are getting something done."

Weavers attend to the diversity of ideas and experiences in the network. "Diverse perspectives—including strong representation of voices that are often excluded or silenced—are needed to generate innovative insights," note Cea and Rimington. But, they add, "heterogeneity leads to better outcomes only when it is thoughtfully engaged."

Diversity doesn't usually emerge naturally in a network since members tend to recruit and attract people like themselves. It has to be intentionally woven into the network, by engaging with people with different backgrounds and points of view. But engaging diverse people so they can become collaborators requires facilitation processes to help them find shared language and common ground.

Weavers also feed a network's diversity through the network's range of activities, not just the variety of its membership. "Which colleagues we talk to, which events we notice, which articles we read, which phone calls we return, and countless other daily activities all shape how we think," notes Hargadon. "Breakthrough innovations require seeing many of those same things but thinking about them differently."

Weavers look outside the network core, not just inside. An innovation network's weaving work goes beyond its own internal community of members. As a network matures and turns to scaling up innovations, it may need to build relationships with stakeholders and other individuals and entities who can be partners for scaling. A weaver's outside work may start long before that—establishing relationships that can be tapped down the road when needed. "Those managing systems change work need to pay extra attention to helping stakeholders to remain motivated and committed, to suppressing pathological behavior, and to improving stakeholders' capacity to accumulate relevant knowledge and other resources that increase the number of options for productive action," say Seelos and Mair.

Weavers value and respect others who are doing related innovation work. "There are a number of networks in west Michigan working on talent," notes Guest. "Hundreds of people are contributing to improving the talent system and if you want to be successful, you have to be patient enough to get to know people and refrain from judgment."

CNCA recognized that limiting access to its funds for innovation projects to its 22 member cities was creating the perception that it was an elitist group, a club. In 2021, recalls Partin, "We asked ourselves, what could we do to support the many more cities around the world that were demonstrating leadership but didn't meet our membership criteria, without throwing out our criteria, which is a key differentiator for CNCA? How could we broaden the tent? We recognized that we were not the only innovative cities in the world. Others may not have our targets but were doing some groundbreaking work. How could we benefit from their expertise? We had a real need to figure out what we were doing in the Global South especially." So, CNCA decided to open up its Game Changer Fund to non-member cities and also to Indigenous nation's governments.

Weavers regularly assess the network's connectivity—a key indicator of health—and work to improve it. We made this point in Connecting to Change the World: take the network's pulse. We presented a framework for network assessment that examined connectivity, health, and impact. We noted that to assess a network you have to look closely at its members' multiple value propositions and web of relationships, their decision-making processes, and the stage of the network's evolution. (See *Connecting*'s chapter 6.)

Trusted Strategist

Network leaders live in the tension between decision making by the members and decision making by the leadership, especially staff. "I talk about this with every network client," says network consultant Ullman. "They have to balance a member-driven and a staff-driven approach. Members are not the experts in network building or field building; staff are. So, there's a push and pull. Especially if the network has to make a strategic pivot."

Members must be a big part of strategy making, of course. But the aggregation of members' insights and preferences does not automatically lead to a well-honed strategy that doesn't just default to "all of the above," everything that members want. "Full-fledged experiments in consensus have gone wrong when organizations interpret power sharing to mean a free-for-all in which everyone has equal say," observe Cea and Rimington. "Without thoughtfully designed roles and processes, sharing power can lead to confusion, delays, and even injustice, as those most impacted by a decision may not have commensurate say to influence it."

Strategists blend multiple inputs to formulate strategies. What's ideal is a situation in which the membership trusts the leadership to (a) hear its concerns and ideas, (b) develop a strategic approach for moving forward that incorporates other information, such as funder preferences or factors external to the network, then (c) submit a plan to the membership for feedback, and finally (d) adopt a plan. This balances the top-down and bottom-up approaches, but it depends heavily on the members' trust in leadership.

"I had a good sense of what the members were prioritizing," notes CNCA's Partin. "But I could also say, 'Here's a strategy I think would benefit the network most effectively.' And I could gently guide the network's conversation in that direction. You have to listen to the members, but at some point, you have to be a leader who can make a strategic decision. It's a nuanced balance." As an example, she offers the network's Game Changer Fund, launched in 2021 to mobilize the development, adoption, and implementation of game-changing climate policies in cities around the world. "It wasn't an idea that came from the members. It came my observation of what I was seeing in the landscape and what we were hearing from members that they needed. Taking all of that and swirling it around and coming up with a new directional strategy. I put it on the table and the members agreed."

Strategists use strategy making to make choices and set priorities for the network. We've seen network strategic plans that list 10-12 strategies or more—far too many for the membership to understand and remember or for the leaders to focus on for effective implementation. The strategists have thrown in everything, usually to make sure there's something for everyone, to please the members, funders, stakeholders, partners. This tends to happen when either the network leadership doesn't have a clear vision for the network's future impact and/or when leadership has simply defaulted to "what the members want" rather than making difficult choices.

Even when a network members' priorities are all over the map, it's up to leaders to help align and focus strategy. Ullman recalls working with a national network that had more than 300 organization members, some of whom were in conflict with each other. "The leader needed to reset the trust between members before they could talk about strategy.

Fortunately, they all trusted her and believed in her." After rebuilding those relationships, she laid out several non-negotiable elements for the network's strategic plan based on members' input, such as embedding racial justice at the core of the plan. A first cut at the strategy yielded 8-10 strategic priorities, designed to ensure many members could see their interests in the plan. But it wasn't feasible to split up the network's resources over that many efforts. Over time, the leader helped the network align around just 3-4 priorities that could be revisited and changed every few years.

Strategists "listen" to the outside world to spot opportunities and risks for the network, and maintain nimbleness to shift strategies accordingly. "If you're not paying attention to what's going on in the world and where the world is going, you will have a problem," Tescher explains. "The network's purpose evolves because the world evolves. It's easy to get captured or to be too internally focused, so focused on the network that it's hard to see how it might need to evolve."

One advantage of networks is their flexibility. In theory, they don't get locked into a strategy forever; they remain nimble. The more locked in they have gotten, the riskier it may seem to change strategy. "You never want to be so deep into something that you can't come back out of it and make a different move," says Ullman. When a network's membership participation and revenues are down, or members are in conflict, she continues, "leaders have to say, 'Nope, this is not working. We have to pivot.' But it can take a ton of effort to get people back on board. That's why you have to catch these trends early. You should be constantly assessing and preparing to pivot, because it's hard to build back trust in leadership."

Big changes are part of most innovation networks' lives, if only because they morph from tight collectives into broad communities and become networks of networks, as described in chapters 4 and 5. "Part and parcel of building collectives and communities," reports Hargadon, "is knowing their limits: when they can become too insulated and when they should be dismantled."

Strategists evaluate the network's performance to find ways to improve. "The ideal candidate" for leading CNCA, according to the job description, "will be confident in evaluating and prioritizing new opportunities, comfortable balancing the need for focus and flexibility, and secure in taking strong, courageous public stands on climate issues." Yet, evaluation can often be a forgotten tool for improvement or, worse, can be regarded as just a compliance exercise dictated by a funder. Rarely is it built into the fabric of network operations.

Network leaders can use probing evaluation processes to assess fundamentals of the network, from purpose to performance, to "smell the smoke" that tells you something is going wrong and has to be fixed, and to generate insights about what to do next and what to change.

Network Evaluation Helps Set Strategic Direction

Today, OpenNews is a sprawling network of technologists and other journalism professionals whose activities far exceed the scope of what was first imagined as a program to place technically skilled Fellows in newsrooms. (See chapter 1 for OpenNews details.) The decision to develop OpenNews as an open and inclusive network that is introducing more diverse voices into journalism benefitted from an external evaluation that documented how "news nerds" engage with OpenNews, what they value most, and how they are connecting.

The Knight-Mozilla Fellowship program, conceived as a way to accelerate a shift from traditional to digital journalism, in its first five years placed more than 30 open source-oriented technologists across 19 news organizations in the US and internationally. In 2016, Knight Foundation commissioned an evaluation of the Fellowship and hired Network Impact to lead the assessment. The foundation's primary goal was to understand the impact that the Program was having on direct participants—Fellows and news organizations—but the scope of the evaluation was expanded to consider the role that Fellows were playing within a wider community of OpenNews-connected technologists that was emerging at the time. According to Erika Owens, co-executive director of OpenNews, soon after the Fellowship launched, its leaders organized to find "other small pots of money" to support activities that engaged more people. "We realized," says Owens, "that having an impact on the field was not just about bringing in new people. It was about engaging the people who are already here."

At the time of the evaluation, OpenNews had "touched" upwards of 2,000 people through the Fellowship or by other means including an OpenNews website, a highly attended annual ON conference, and a variety of smaller "code convenings" and community calls.

Network Impact developed a survey that was distributed to Open-News direct participants as well as to "non-OpenNews" technologists across the world. The survey was segmented to include questions targeted to Fellows, newsroom partners, other OpenNews participants as well as "non-OpenNews" others. In addition to answering questions about their experience as technologists working in journalism and with OpenNews in particular, all respondents were asked to name their top five connections in the journalism tech community, people with whom they shared information or advice on a regular basis. In all, 514 people responded: 250 OpenNews participants and 264 journalism tech professionals who had not connected with OpenNews.

One of the most powerful results of the assessment was the network maps showing new nerds' top five connections (sample below). The most named connections were ties to journalists in leading newsrooms that had hosted Fellows. The maps also showed that Fellows were connecting with peers in other newsrooms, serving as avenues for information exchange. "One of the headlines for us from the network maps," remembers Owens, was that Fellows "were serving as bridges in a wider network. This helped us to engage them more intentionally as network weavers."

Most compelling for the development of an OpenNews network strategy were two additional findings. First, Fellows and other Open-News participants reported that the support and camaraderie fostered through the OpenNews activities was a differentiator compared to other opportunities for professional development and skills building.

"The pattern of making every event a) welcoming b) accessible c) diverse, EVERY TIME, really left a mark on me about OpenNews," noted one respondent. "It both makes me want to connect the whole world to OpenNews so others can benefit from the same as well as help me think about my own events in a more thoughtful manner."

The second finding: among all journalism tech survey respondents, diversity/inclusivity was the number one response to the open-ended question: "What does the journo tech community need now?" "That was really exciting to see," says Owens, "because the question was not constructed to get that answer. It was implicit in a lot of how we work, but we weren't shouting about that kind of work at the time."

Based on analysis of costs, the evaluation ultimately concluded that "while the Fellowship produces value for individual Fellows and newsrooms, it is not a scalable way of introducing technologists to journalism or transforming newsroom culture/ practice." In contrast, the evaluation pointed to an opportunity to influence the journalism field by strengthening the OpenNews network and building technologists leadership skills through other OpenNews elements, including support for a culture of openness and a focus on equity.

"For me, the biggest takeaway was permission to really push into that direction even more," says Owens. "Knowing that social justice, equity orientation, is something that is core has given us permission to ask, what are the ways we could be most effective in making those kinds of changes in journalism?"

Access Network Impact's OpenNews evaluation at https://tinyurl.com/OpenNewsReport

Story Teller

Every network has stories to tell. The stories provide the network's members with a shared identity. They inform people and organizations with whom the network engages, setting expectations of the network. They offer thought leadership to other innovators and entire fields, markets, and other scaling structures. And some stories help to make rain, bringing in revenue for the network.

Story tellers help to craft a compelling narrative about the network's work. Network leaders are constantly trying to figure out what the network's best story is, how to tell it, and how to use it to "seed" funder clouds. It's not easy. "We were not doing a good enough job of telling our story, and it's critical," Partin says of CNCA. "We were dated, in an old mindset about how to tell the story: writing case studies and best practice documents, and organizing webinars. That's not a good way to tell a story about innovations and lessons learned."

Story tellers shift the story as the network evolves. Early on the story that matters is the network's aspiration, development of its innovation capacities, and the potential of its innovations and other activities. You're selling informed hope. Down the road, though, the story has to change to one of impacts—the way the world is changing due to network activities. You're selling hope realized. The shift to an impact story is particularly important to maintain and attract investment.

The story that innovation networks tell potential investors also evolves. Typically, it starts as a tale of aspiration—a "what could happen" story. It progresses into a story about building the capacity to innovate—usually, the network's emerging collective, developed through weaving and aligning the participants. Then the focus shifts to innovation activities—ideation, prototyping, and so on. And on to a plan for scaling the innovation(s) and finally to implementation of a scaling pathway.

Having a clear strategic focus matters for storytelling. "Selling a network is selling a tool," observes Ullman. "You buy tools to build something, not just to have them. But when you have no strategic focus, you only have a loose, unimpressive story to tell."

Story tellers identify the most effective communications tools to use. At CNCA, Partin says, "Storytelling for the members and the network had not evolved in a way that was useful for scaling innovations." CNCA concluded that the network should use short videos featuring the practitioners, not an intermediary, telling what they'd done and learned. "Think of TED talks—you see a good one and it'll change your world view. But we had to enable our members to do that well. Most of our cities were not good at telling short video stories. Too often in the nonprofit space we say, 'That's expensive, that's marketing. We don't do that.'"

Story tellers use stories to build productive relationships with investors. A great deal has been written about the challenges that social innovators face when seeking philanthropic funding, usually a core resource for social innovation. There's a lot that networks cannot control about funders, and it's often difficult for them to decode the intentions and language of foundations. Ultimately, though, what's key for obtaining investment is to build deep, sustained relationships with investors who value your efforts. Without begging for money. "Most not-for-profits have a subservient relationship with foundations," notes Phillip Jackson, founder of the Black Star Project in Chicago. "That's not something we were willing to be. When we were coming to the foundation, we were saying, 'Hey, you need us as much as we need you.' . . . We have solutions, you have dollars to fund the solutions. Let's work together."

Tell the network's story in a way that invites foundations to be partners, not just grant makers, and to recognize the demands of the system-changing work you (and they) have taken on. Build a relationship based on candor, mutual respect, and learning that can evolve. Offer to set impact goals together and commit to being a long-term partner with the funder. (See sidebar, "Advice to Funders.")

Recognize, too, that investors can provide much more than money: they have insights, expertise, and connections, and they can also be inspiring.

Advice to Funders

A growing chorus of experts advises foundations to invest differently in innovation and networks. For instance:

- "Rather than the traditional funder-recipient relationship, which can feel like a transaction of funds for results, funders and innovators should set an impact goal together and commit to being long-term partners in the journey to crack very tough problems." — Kriss Deiglmeier and Amanda Greco
- "To make lasting progress in addressing issues like inequality, organizations need robust, sustainable, predictable support, giving them the capacity to seize opportunities and create greater impact, and the stability it takes to drive change over the long term." — Ford Foundation
- "The traditional 'go-it-alone' foundation approach, often driven by a board's need for attribution, conflicts with what is truly needed to move systems. . . . They need to become matchmakers and collaborators, not just grantmakers." — Srik Gopal and John Kania
- "It's critical for foundations to clarify their orientation to power because how a foundation approaches power affects its role as a change agent." — John Kania, Mark Kramer, Peter Senge

Connecting to Change the World contains a section (pages 75-82) of advice for foundations investing in networks for social impact, including:

- Don't dictate the network's purpose; co-create it with potential start-up partners.

- Don't dictate the network's purpose; co-create it with potential start-up partners.

- Let network membership expand naturally through members' connections, not through funder dictates.

- Entice other funders into the game.

Leaders as Learners

Leading an innovation network is a journey, a work in progress, not a destination. Innovation network leaders constantly adapt their approaches, identify what they know and are good at, and what else they need to know how to do. Their self-awareness makes it easier to accept critical feedback from others.

"God gave me *two* ears and just one mouth for a reason," says Jeff Yost of the Nebraska Community Foundation. "I have needed to become a much better active listener. Not seeking to promote my ideas, but seeking to understand what people are sharing with me. This was hard for me."

"I am generally a pleaser and hard on myself," says Financial Health Network CEO Jennifer Tescher. "The speed and pace at which I like to operate doesn't work for most people. I've needed to recognize that and grow as a leader. Mostly I have tried to mitigate my worst impulses and invest a lot in building a leadership team that can run the network day-to-day."

In addition to learning to do things differently, networks leaders have to be ready and willing to learn from others, not think they have all the answers. "The most refreshing thing for me," says Kishia Powell, chair of the US Water Alliance's One Water Council, and chief operating officer of DC Water, "the most freeing thing, is being able to say, 'I don't know. What do you think?'"

These longtime innovation leaders acknowledge their shortcomings—and how they are working to improve their abilities. They make a personal priority out of learning how to be better leaders. This requires great awareness and flexibility, as well as feedback loops and receptivity to feedback.

Leaders may have much to *unlearn*. Cea and Rimington say that the leadership unlearning that their research uncovered "included having to get comfortable with different ways of distributing decision-making authority, embracing uncertainty, and collectively imagining and creating a different way to be in community." They provide an example: unlearning assumptions about the superiority of professional expertise as a type of knowledge. "It can be challenging for many people to accept that all types of knowledge are legitimate," explain the scholars. "Because most innovation processes heavily privilege knowledge that reflects academic or technical training, it is important to actively source knowledge in other ways. This often requires people to unlearn what we refer to as 'expert bias.'"

Networks & Balanced Leadership

At heart, leadership of social innovation networks is a balancing act.

You have to balance exhilarating aspiration with meticulous performance. A tolerance for risk taking with a bias for action. The time-consuming weaving of trusting relationships with the urgency of making impact. Changes in strategy with continuity. The interests of members with the insights of leaders. The requirements of investors with the necessities of system-change processes. Knowing what to do with the need to experiment, improvise, and unlearn.

If that's not tricky enough, you have to do this for years, engaging with a great many people who move in and out of your innovation world. It's not an impossible job, and the personal rewards can be deeply fulfilling. But it's not the usual sort of change leadership work that happens in organizations.

Here's some final advice about leading innovation networks:

Get comfortable with discomfort. Social innovation work is often uncomfortable. Finding your balance means being out of balance at times. "Find your discomfort zone," advises Andrew Hargadon. It's the price for being able to free yourself from binding and blinding ties that impede innovative thinking.

Advice for Network Leaders

- Get comfortable with discomfort.

- Pay attention to your blind spots and figure out how to eliminate them.

- Don't let things become about you.

- Don't become an obstacle to innovation.

- Be flexible—anticipate the network's needs.

Pay attention to your blind spots and figure out how to eliminate them. Network leaders can't know everything they need to know, but it's important that they recognize what they don't know and do something about it. For instance, we've emphasized that you have to know a lot about the system you're trying to change so you can find leverage points for change. But social change innovators are often naïve about what they really know about how a system works and how it will respond to attempts to disrupt the status quo. This is especially true with nonprofits trying to change private for-profit systems. Health Care Without Harm's experience with the Greenhealth Exchange, covered in chapter 4, is a good example. The network leaders' assumptions and strategies didn't take into account the way the market works and what it would take, at least financially, to directly compete in the market.

Don't let things become about you. Network leadership requires humility. "If you're a skilled network leader," says Partin, "you're not talking about how amazing you are. You're talking about how amazing your members are." And this, she notes, leads to yet another balancing act: "You need to find a balance between putting your individual members forward and putting the network forward."

You have to be aware of the risk of dominating the network. Tescher says innovation brokers have to solve this leadership problem: "How do you grow your own brand in a way that is benefitting the broader cause but at the same time not become a cult of personality? So that the network's there even without you." As JPB Foundation's Dana Bourland explains, "Some networks burn out if they have a strong, charismatic leader and are not able to evolve."

Jeff Yost frames the egocentric approach as antithetical to a network approach: "It's really about understanding the dynamics of distributed leadership versus the 'great man' leadership model that is still embraced in many places."

Don't become an obstacle to innovation. It can happen. Innovation brokers can become barriers. Sometimes, says Hargadon, they "will fight hard to maintain their unique advantages and keep the networked landscape exactly as it is. . . . When ideas come along that threaten the flow of resources through the central broker, the broker will use every possible advantage to prevent those ideas from taking hold."

Be flexible—anticipate the network's needs. "I have become a more versatile leader—so I can do what the network needs from me," says Tescher. This can only happen if you anticipate what the network needs before it needs it, or if you can change your approach very quickly when you recognize what the network needs right away.

We started *Connect > Innovate > Scale Up* with stories of four networks seeking large scale impact. Those networks' leaders told the stories of their networks—from origin and growth to morphing and initial scaling success. They described their own motivations and work as leaders. In subsequent pages, we introduced many more network leaders—founders, managers, members, investors—to describe how they approach systems change, social innovation development, scaling up, and network design.

Building and operating innovation networks is hard, hard work. No one can know everything they need to know for this labor of love. No one can move perfectly through years of network and innovation building without making mistakes, becoming frustrated, and having to learn and unlearn how to make things work. Sometimes, improvisation is the only way to go.

Nearly everything we've written about comes directly from the experiences of social innovation networks. The frameworks we've offered cover a large and complex territory, and map many routes taken. They provide navigational insights and tools that may inspire, inform, and energize you and other readers.

Hopefully the know-how from the field in the previous pages is already becoming a useful resource for the system-changing journey you are on, with the ideas resonating in your mind and heart and shared with your colleagues.

The Long Arc of Systems Change

Don't stop dreaming, don't stop believing
'Cause you know our time is coming up
So with all you've got, don't stop
Jon Batiste ("Don't Stop")

Many people decide to spend much of their lives changing systems. They may grow up in a family, community, or broad movement that is driven to change the world, especially its injustices. They may discover they have a burning passion for upending a particular system and setting it right; a flame that rarely goes out. Or they may embrace a specific idea for a change and start to work on it, only to discover that there is much more they can do to achieve their goals, and they keep at it.

Whatever their motivation, social innovators may learn a great deal from elders who have their own experiences, their own stories about pushing for change. And they may mentor the next generation of change agents, with advice and support and by example.

"I just finished reading *The Future of Wealth Building*, which contains 63 essays from 100 authors," says Bob Friedman, whose decades-long efforts for people-centered, asset-based approaches to human welfare were described in chapter 3. "None of the essays were from me or Prosperity Now [the organization he created]. That made me wonder about my contribution. And then I thought that the real contribution of my work was recruiting more, smarter, younger, and more diverse people to the cause. Prosperity Now's greatest contribution may well be its diaspora of alumni—staff, board, partners—and friends. It is younger, smarter, Black and brown, Native, and immigrant leaders that give me hope."

When leaders of social innovation networks look back at their efforts, they often smile and say they didn't know what they were doing at certain points. They had to improvise. That led them to other people to help figure things out in new ways, to find new ideas, energy, and inspiration. And to innovate together—to form tight collectives and loose communities that shape the dream of change into powerful social innovations.

Social innovation is not all forward movement at the same speed. Often progress is slow, painstaking. It can collapse in an instant or rush ahead on an insight. It passes through tension points, in which contradictions have to be managed. "I refer to my work as a combination of patience and tenacity," says Jeff Yost, two-decade leader of the Nebraska Community Foundation. "I am patiently tenacious."

In 1989, Gary Cohen joined with Bhopal survivors to organize a protest at the Union Carbide shareholders meeting in Houston, Texas. It was part of the extended aftermath of the world's worst industrial disaster—in which thousands of people died overnight when a pesticide factory exploded and thousands more were dying from the acute chemical poisoning. The 1984 incident had triggered the uprise of a movement for planetary health and Cohen, deeply stirred by the calamity, was on his way to founding Health Care Without Harm, the global systems-changing network we described in chapter 2.

A few years later, Cohen worked with survivors' organizations to arrange for an international medical commission to visit Bhopal and assess the long-term health impacts on survivors. He returned to Bhopal many times, including to support the launch of a free medical clinic to address the health impacts of the disaster. On one of these trips, he

Shweta Narayan

met a young woman, Shweta Narayan, who was part of a community support group providing solidarity for the campaign against chemical violation.

Some 20 years later Cohen became reacquainted with Narayan. Trained as a social worker, she had led Health Care Without Harm's advocacy work in India to help build Doctors for Clean Air. In 2021, she was hired by the network as a global campaigner to connect its work with the climate justice movement. "At around the same time," Cohen says, "the TED organization was planning its first climate conference in Edinburgh, Scotland. I suggested to the conference organizers they invite Shweta as a speaker."

Narayan's TED talk in October 2021 took 9 minutes and has been viewed more than 1.2 million times. Listen and you, too, will conclude that she is a persuasive advocate for the disruptive mental model that Cohen and the Health Care Without Harm network have helped bring into the world at scale.

Standing alone on a stage in a darkened venue, Narayan starts with her childhood in Bokaro, India, an industrial community surrounded by power plants and steel smelters. "One of my fondest memories as a child was to stare in the evenings at the beautiful orange skies and flaring chimneys of the steel plant. Little did I know at that time that these were all classic signs of severe air pollution." Then she moves to the present. "I now work at the intersection of environment, health, and justice. I've been in this space for nearly two decades and my experience tells that the negative impacts of industrialization have outweighed the good."

And on to her main theme: "The doctrine of 'do no harm' forms the basis of the Hippocratic Oath, one of the oldest and most widely known codes of ethics." Narayan urges listeners to place "the philosophy of 'first, do no harm' at the heart of all decisions, beyond health, including those taken by our CEOs and politicians." Applause erupts from the darkness.

There's more going on here than a compelling speech. "I felt incredibly proud," Cohen says about watching the video. "But more than proud. I felt reassured the candles the Bhopal survivors continue to light have now joined with so many lights of resistance and healing around the world. I feel relieved to know that these lights will carry on the work long after I am gone, that the traumas we are living now will be healed as more and more people are awakened into our essential connection with all of life."

This is the beautiful, long arc of systems change: from Gary Cohen in America to Shweta Narayan in India, from the 1980s to the 2020s. Made possible by the immense, enduring power of social innovation networks, of hopeful people linking across distant places and successive generations, uniting in cause and action, tenacious and patient, scaling to a better world.

Gratitude

In times such as these, it is no failure to fall short of realizing
all that we might dream—
the failure is to fall short of dreaming all that we might realize.
Dee Hock

W e have dreamed with our many partners and clients of a world that might be, and have used social innovation networks to try to bring that dream into being.

Connect > Innovate > Scale Up ties together several strands of our collective lived experiences, thinking, and work, some of which began more than two decades ago. Our gratitude starts with a prequel for friends and colleagues who influenced and supported us long before this book was in mind.

Betsy Campbell, Melvin Oliver, and Mil Duncan at the Ford Foundation in the 1990s, stimulated Pete's first thinking about pathways to scale.

John's work with the Manufacturing Council in Grand Rapids, Michigan, prompted especially by Fred Keller of Cascade Engineering, led to our initial understanding of innovation processes. Joann Neuroth partnered with John and Pete, forming the nonprofit On Purpose Associates, to develop an understanding of systems thinking and complex adaptive systems, coauthoring *Welcome to the Edge of Chaos: Where Change is a Way of Life*. We worked together with Doug Ross, Nan Gill, Paul Dimond, and many others to create University Preparatory Academy, a K-12 charter school district in Detroit.

Our focus on social innovation emerged more fully thanks to work supported by Gail McClure, Ted Chen, and Sterling Speirn when they were at the Kellogg Foundation. The foundation's grant enabled John and Pete to start the nonprofit Innovation Network for Communities

209

(INC) with Richard Anderson in 2007.

Marion Kane, then-president of the Barr Foundation, first alerted us to the untapped potential of networks to generate social change. Marion introduced Pete and Madeleine to each other, a collaboration that led to our 2014 book about generative social-impact networks, *Connecting to Change the World*. Then Madeleine started Network Impact with Anne Whatley.

INC's network-building activities have been enthusiastically supported by its board of directors: Richard Anderson, Keith Cooley, Alvaro Lima, Juan Olivarez, Chinwe Onyeagoro, Janet Topolsky, and Margaret Trimer.

We learned a great deal early on about networks from Jennie Curtis, Heather Grant, Chrystie Hill, June Holley, Julia Parzen, Graham Richard, Janet Topolsky, and Bill Traynor. Warren Cook supported our earliest efforts to write about networks. Lois DeBacker and Jessica Boehland at the Kresge Foundation, Darryl Young at the Summit Foundation, and Chrystie Hill at the Gates Foundation were instrumental in supporting research-and-development projects that expanded our work with and understanding of social innovation networks.

These many strands emerged in non-linear fashion, giving no inkling that they could one day be bundled into a whole. But in that wonderful way that life sometimes has, they prepared us for the many engagements and relationships that were around the corner waiting to meet us. In 2020, as the COVID pandemic spread, we decided to write *Connect > Innovate > Scale Up*—and another round of gratitude unfolded.

For crucial support of this effort, we especially thank The JPB Foundation and Dana Bourland, senior vice president of the environment program, for providing financial backing that accelerated our research and writing.

For extensive conversations about their experiences and insights, as well as feedback about various sections of the manuscript, we thank Spencer Beebe, Scott Bernstein, Dana Bourland, Rachel Cleveland-Holton, Gary Cohen, Jennie Curtis, Bob Friedman, Bill Guest, Mami Hara, Chrystie Hill, Asima Jansveld, Sandhya Kambhampati, Sarah Klaus, Katy Lackey, Luis Lugo, Oluwole A. (OJ) McFoy, Lisa Mensah, Anne Mosle, Erika Owens, Johanna Partin, Graham Richard, Olivia Roanhorse,

Doug Ross, Chuck Savitt, Emily Simonson, Marjorie Sims, Jennifer Tescher, Maggie Ullman, Sisi Wei, Karen Weigert, Ben Welsh, Morley Winograd, and Jeff Yost.

Our experiments with self-publishing—begun with two earlier books, *In Harm's Way: How Communities Are Addressing Key Challenges of Building Climate Resilience* and *Welcome to the Edge of Chaos: Where Change is a Way of Life*, and continuing with this book—depend on the superb book design and graphic illustration work of Carol Maglitta. Thank you also to Steven Plastrik for proof reading the manuscript with a lawyerly eye for clarity.

We acknowledge the tremendous value that *Stanford Social Innovation Review* has provided over the years as a window onto the world of social innovation. A large amount of the material we cite in the previous pages came from articles and reports in SSIR.

We are also grateful to Island Press, and especially to its president, David Miller, for publishing *Connecting to Change the World*, sales of which revealed to us that there are thousands of network entrepreneurs who are hungry for practical knowledge about how to boost their impact. Connecting brought many of them to our in-boxes with questions and insights.

It's said that one of the most important things in life is your network—the people with whom you travel as you make your way. We are fortunate to have an extensive and enduring web of caring and thoughtful people sharing our dreams and work.

Notes

All quotations in *Connect > Innovate > Scale Up* are from interviews and presentations unless otherwise noted below.

Epigraph

Wheatley quote: https://conversational-leadership.net/quotation/world-doesnt-change-one-person-at-a-time/.

Bailey quote: http://chqdaily.com/2019/08/jennifer-bailey-lennon-flowers-join-krista-tippett-to-discuss-grace-in-grief-and-social-change/.

Mazzucato quote: Alisha Haridasani Gupta, "An 'Electrifying' Economist's Guide to the Recovery," *New York Times*, November 19, 2020, https://www.nytimes.com/2020/11/19/us/economist-covid-recovery-mariana-mazzucato.html?referringSource=articleShare

Introduction

Harari quote: David Marchese, "Yuval Noah Harari Believes This Simple Story Can Save the Planet," *New York Times*, November 7, 2021, https://www.nytimes.com/interactive/2021/11/08/magazine/yuval-noah-harari-interview.html.

Sherraden quote: Michael Sherraden, Richard P. Barth, John Brekke, Mark w> Fraser, Ron Manderscheid, and Deborah Padgett, "Social Is Fundamental: Introduction and Context for Grand Challenges in Social Work," working paper, Grand Challenges for Social Work Initiative, 2015.

Definition of social innovation: James Phills Jr., Kriss Deiglmeier, and Dale Miller, "Rediscovering Social Innovation," *Stanford Social Innovation Review*, Fall 2008, https://ssir.org/articles/entry/rediscovering_social_innovation#

Hargadon quotes on Edison: Andrew Hargadon, *How Breakthroughs Happen: The Surprising Truth About How Companies Innovate* (Boston, Massachusetts: Harvard Business Press, 2003), xii, 12, 13, 28, https://www.amazon.com/How-Breakthroughs-Happen-Surprising-Companies/dp/1578519047.

The Innovator's DNA quote: Jeff Dyer, Hal Gregersen, Clayton M. Christensen, *The Innovator's DNA: Mastering the Five Skills of Disruptive Innovators* (Boston: Harvard Business Review Press, 2011), see chapter 5.

Schindler quote: Anamarie Schindler, "Letter from Ashoka," Ashoka Leading Social Entrepreneurs 2019, vi, https://www.ashoka.org/en-us/files/2019lsewebpdf.

Frameworks Institute quote: Frameworks Institute, "Mindset Shifts: What Are They? Why Do They Matter? How Do They Happen?" June 2020, 34, https://www.frameworksinstitute.org/wp-content/uploads/2021/02/FRAJ8064-Mindset-Shifts-200612-WEB.pdf.

Deiglmeier and Greco quote: Kriss Deiglmeier and Amanda Greco, "Why Proven Solutions Struggle to Scale Up," *Stanford Social Innovation Review*, August 10, 2018, https://ssir.org/articles/entry/why_proven_solutions_struggle_to_scale_up.

Crutchfield and Grant quote: Leslie R. Crutchfield and Heather McLeod Grant, *Forces for Good: The Six Practices of High-Impact Nonprofits*, rev. ed. (San Francisco: Wiley & Sons, 2012), 6, https://www.amazon.com/Forces-Good-Practices-High-Impact-Nonprofits/dp/1118118804/ref=sr_1_1?crid=106PN3ZH2C438&dchild=1&keywords=forces+for+good+the+six+practices+of+high-impact+nonprofits&qid=1602088284&sprefix=forces+for+good%2Caps%2C1521&sr=8-1.

Aviv quote: Diana Aviv, foreword for Tine Hansen-Turton and Nicholas D. Torres, eds., *Social Innovation and Impact in Nonprofit Leadership* (New York: Springer Publishing, 2014), xxvii.

Bridgespan Group quote: Taz Hussein, Matt Plummer and Bill Breen, "How Field Catalysts Galvanize Social Change," *Stanford Social Innovation Review*, Winter 2018, https://ssir.org/articles/entry/field_catalysts.

Picower quote: Barbara Picower, "Doing More With Big Bets," *Stanford Social Innovation Review*, Spring 2019, https://ssir.org/articles/entry/doing_more_with_big_bets. As of 2017, the JPB Foundation's assets totaled more than $4 billion.

Kania, Kramer, Senge quote: John Kania, Mark Kramer, Peter Senge, "The Water of Systems Change," *Stanford Social Innovation Review*, June 2018, https://www.fsg.org/publications/water_of_systems_change.

Villanueva quote: Edgar Villanueva, *Decolonizing Wealth: Indigenous Wisdom to Heal Divides and Restore Balance* (Oakland, California: Berrett-Koehler, 2018), 6.

Horowitz quote: Sara Horowitz, *Mutualism: Building the Next Economy From the Ground Up* (New York: Random House, 2021, 15.

GoodSAM app: Alicia Clegg, "Smartphone Samaritans," *Stanford Social Innovation Review*, Spring 2019, 15, https://ssir.org/articles/entry/smartphone_samaritans.

Fisher quote: Dana R. Fisher, *American Resistance: From the Women's March to the Blue Wave* (New York: Columbia University Press, 2019), 16-17.

Suarez and Bingham quote: Kiko Suarez and Alph Bingham, "Seeking and Solving," *Stanford Social Innovation Review*, Winter 2017, https://ssir.org/articles/entry/seeking_and_solving.

#WirVsVirus: Johanna Mair and Thomas Gegenhuber, "Open Social Innovation," *Stanford Social Innovation Review*, Fall 2021, https://pacscenter.stanford.edu/wp-content/uploads/2021/08/Mair-Gegenhuber-Fall-2021-SSIR-Open-Social-Innovation.pdf.

Brooks quote: David Brooks, "America is Having a Moral Convulsion," *The Atlantic*, October 5, 2020, https://www.theatlantic.com/ideas/archive/2020/10/collapsing-levels-trust-are-devastating-america/616581/.

Klein quote: Ezra Klein, "Four Ways of Looking at the Radicalism of Joe Biden," *The New York Times*, April 8, 2021, https://www.nytimes.com/2021/04/08/opinion/biden-jobs-infra-structure-economy.html?referringSource=articleShare.

A majority of young foundation staff...: Louise Lief, "Philanthropy Can't Solve the Toughest Problems Unless it Breaks Out of Silos," *The Chronicle of Philanthropy*, December 17, 2018, https://www.philanthropy.com/article/philanthropy-cant-solve-the-toughest-prob-lems-unless-it-breaks-out-of-silos/.

Lazu quote: Thomas B. Edsall, "The Marriage Between Republicans and Big Business is On the Rocks," *The New York Times*, April 14, 2021, https://www.nytimes.com/2021/04/14/opinion/woke-capitalism-democratic-party-us.html?action=click&module=Opinion&pg-type=Homepage.

Coussa quote: Greg Coussa, "To Impact Millions, the Social Sector Needs to Scale Scaling Up," *Stanford Social Innovation Review*, January 24, 2019, https://ssir.org/articles/entry/to_impact_millions_the_social_sector_needs_to_scale_scaling_up.

IDEO leaders quote: Jocelyn Wyatt, Tim Brown & Shauna Carey, "The Next Chapter in Design for Social Innovation," *Stanford Social Innovation Review*, Winter 2021, 45, https://www.ideo.com/journal/its-taken-decades-for-social innovation-to-become-mainstream.

Cea and Rimington quote: Joanna Levitt Cea and Jess Rimington, "Creating Breakout Innovation," *Stanford Social Innovation Review*, Summer 2017, 32, https://ssir.org/articles/entry/creating_breakout_innovation#.

Deiglmeier and Greco 'stagnation chasm' quote: Deiglmeier and Greco, "Why Proven Solutions Struggle to Scale Up."

Grant quote: Heather McLeod Grant, "Creating a Cross Sector Leadership Team," *Stanford Social Innovation Review*, Winter 2018, https://ssir.org/articles/entry/creating_a_cross_sector_leadership_network#.

Young Foundation quote: Geoff Mulgan, et al., "Social Silicon Valleys," The Young Foundation, Spring 2006, 5 - https://youngfoundation.org/wp-content/uploads/2013/04/Social-Silicon-Valleys-March-2006.pdf.

Seelos and Mair quote: Christian Seelos and Johanna Mair, *Innovation and Scaling for Impact: How Effective Social Enterprises Do It* (Stanford, California: Stanford University Press, 2017), 4.

Details on coauthors' relationships with networks discussed in the book: one or more coauthors provided consulting and/or evaluation services to Ascend (Plastrik), Biophilic Cities Network (Plastrik), Carbon Neutral Cities Alliance (Cleveland, Plastrik), Energy Efficiency for All (Plastrik), Financial Health Network (Cleveland, Plastrik), Health Care Without Harm (Cleveland), International Step By Step Association (Taylor), Nebraska Community Foundation (Cleveland, Plastrik), OpenNews (Taylor), RE-AMP (Plastrik), Salmon Nation (Plastrik), US Water Alliance (Plastrik). The Campaign for Free College Tuition used the Innovation Network for Communities, cofounded by Cleveland and Plastrik, as a fiscal sponsor for several years. Cleveland is a founder of the Talent Innovation Network of West Michigan (TalNet) and serves as a network facilitator; he is also part-owner of Metrics Reporting, Inc., which provides services to TalNet. John also serves on the board of directors of Health Care Without Harm.

Chapter 1

Hargadon quote: Hargadon, *How Breakthroughs Happen*,11.

IDEO authors quote: Wyatt, Brown & Carey, "The Next Chapter in Design for Social Innovation, 47.

Mucha quote: US Water Alliance, "One Water Delegations," http://uswateralliance.org/sites/uswateralliance.org/files/One%20Water%20Summit%202017_Delegations%20Overview_2%201%2017%20(002).pdf.

US Water Alliance website quote: US Water Alliance website, "Vision and Mission," accessed February 4, 2021, http://uswateralliance.org/about-us.

The report identifies new practices...: Zoë Roller and Danielle Mayorga, "An Equitable Water Future: A National Briefing Paper," US Water Alliance, 11, http://uswateralliance.org/sites/uswateralliance.org/files/publications/uswa_waterequity_FINAL.pdf

Seven learning teams in cities: Atlanta, Buffalo, Camden, Cleveland, Louisville, Milwaukee, and Pittsburgh.

Buffalo's roadmap: "An Equitable Water Future: Buffalo," US Water Alliance, 4, http://uswateralliance.org/sites/uswateralliance.org/files/publications/uswa_equity_buffalo_040219_a.pdf.

The initial 17 cities and counties: Atlanta, Austin, Baltimore, Buffalo, Camden, Cincinnati, Cleveland, Detroit, Houston, Louisville, Milwaukee, Montgomery County, Pittsburgh, Prince George's County, San Francisco, Seattle, Washington, DC. The 17 include the original seven learning teams. For details, see http://uswateralliance.org/waterequitynetwork. The 25 million residents was communicated in a February 25, 2022 e-mail to the authors from Letitia Carpenter, senior program manager, US Water Alliance.

Tennessee Promise had enrolled: "TN Promise Annual Report: 2020," https://www.tn.gov/thec/research/tn-promise-annual-report.html.

Network's website quote: Campaign for Free College Tuition, "Who We Are," accessed December 21, 2020, https://www.freecollegenow.org/who-we-are.

Mercy Health doubled its number: data from Shana Welch, "Health Care Industry Briefing NAWB," presentation at National Association of Workforce Boards, March 27, 2017. Welch was regional director of talent acquisition at Mercy Health. The doubling occurred between 2010 and 2017, while employment at the system also increased substantially.

90,000 employees: per e-mail to authors from Rachel Cleveland-Holton of HireReach, March 2, 2020.

TalNet quote: TalNet, "Talent Innovations," accessed February 11, 2021, http://talnet.org.

West Michigan region data: from The Right Place; complete dataset available at https://www.rightplace.org/why-west-michigan

TalNet: For detailed information about TalNet's innovation and activities, see these websites: TalNet www.talnet.org, HireReach www.hirereach.org, Metrics Reporting http://www.metricsreporting.com/talnet.html, and The Brookings Institution, https://www.brookings.edu/research/an-evidence-based-selection-process-for-equitable-hiring-in-west-michigan/.

More information about TalNet's other innovations in development: see TalNet, "TalNet Innovations," http://talnet.org.

More than 1,100 journalism technologists: a finding from a 2016 evaluation of OpenNews, not publicly available.

Vision25 quote: Sisi Wei, "Vision25: Building racial equity in newsrooms," OpenNews, October 1, 2020, https://opennews.org/blog/vision25-building-racial-equity-in-newsrooms/.

NY Times diversity report quote: Katie Robertson, "New York Times Calls for Workplace Changes in Diversity Report," *New York Times*, February 24, 2021, https://www.nytimes.com/2021/02/24/business/media/new-york-times-workplace-diversity.html?referringSource=articleShare.

Wei blog quote: Sisi Wei, "New Beginnings, Sisi Wei Joins OpenNews," OpenNews, February 25, 2020, https://opennews.org/blog/sisi-wei-joins-opennews/.

Social-impact networks arise in different ways for different reasons:
see chapter 1 of *Connecting to Change the World: Harnessing the Power of Networks for Social Impact* (Washington, DC: Island Press, 2014).

Chapter 2

Scharmer quote: C. Otto Scharmer, *The Essentials of Theory U: Core Principles and Applications* (Oakland, CA: Berrett-Koehler, 2018), 3.

Cohen quotes: Gary Cohen, "The Power of Collective Healing to Support Healthy People on a Thriving Planet," Health Care Without Harm, 2020, https://skoll.org/2020/12/07/the-power-of-collective-healing-to-support-healthy-people-on-a-thriving-planet/.

Meadows quotes: Donella H. Meadows, ed. Diana Wright, *Thinking in Systems: A Primer* (White River Junction, Vermont: Chelsea Green Publishing, 2008), 145, 167, 166, 168, 161-164.

Attalla quote: "What We Mean When We Say 'Systems Change," Garfield Foundation, May 13, 2021, https://garfield-foundation.medium.com/what-we-mean-when-we-say-systems-change-8d8b8cbf2d32.

Kania, Kramer, Senge quote: Kania, Kramer, Senge, "The Water of Systems Change."

2021 Alliance report quote: US Water Alliance, "Water Equity Taskforce: Insights for the Water Sector," 13, https://waterfdn.org/wp-content/uploads/2021/08/USWA-Water-Equity-Taskforce-Insights-for-the-Water-Sector-June-2021.pdf.

FrameWorks Institute report quote: FrameWorks Institute, "Mindset Shifts: What Are They? Why Do They Matter? How Do They Happen?"

Meadows quote, "It's one thing…": Meadows, *Thinking in Systems*, 167.

Mercury Awareness Day: Health Care Without Harm, "2020 Annual Report," 8, https://noharm-uscanada.org/documents/2020-annual-report.

Cohen quote, "We no longer need…": Health Care Without Harm, "2020 Annual Report," 31, https://noharm-uscanada.org/documents/2020-annual-report.

Silbert and Mukamal quote: Rebecca Silbert and Debbie Mukamal, "How Philanthropy Can Create Public Systems Change," *Stanford Social Innovation Review*, Spring 2020, 30, https://philanthropynewsdigest.org/columns/ssir-pnd/how-philanthropy-can-create-public-systems-change.

Waddell "warrior" quote: Steve Waddell, "Four Strategies for Large Systems Change," *Stanford Social Innovation Review*, Spring 2018, 42, https://philanthropynewsdigest.org/columns/ssir-pnd/four-strategies-for-large-systems-change.

Mensah quote: "Lisa Mensah, President and CEO, Opportunity Finance Network," *PND*, February 1, 2021, https://philanthropynewsdigest.org/5-questions-for/lisa-mensah-president-and-ceo-opportunity-finance-network.

FSG: For more about FSG and collective impact design, see https://www.collectiveimpact-forum.org.

Waddell "as a transformation" quote: Waddell, "Four Strategies for Large Systems Change," 42.

Meadows quote: Meadows, *Thinking in Systems*.

Seelos and Mair quote: Christian Seelos and Johanna Mair, "Mastering System Change," *Stanford Social Innovation Review*, Fall 2018, http://www.christianseelos.com/Fall_2018_Mastering_System_Change.pdf. https://ssir.org/articles/entry/mastering_system_change.

Beebe, Brookfield, Gill essay quotes: Spencer B. Beebe, Christopher Brookfield, Ian Gill, Salmon Nation, 2019, 15, 37, https://salmonnation.net/wp-content/uploads/2020/09/Salmon-Nation-Thesis-v2-Pages-Web-v2-91520.pdf.

Project ECHO: An excellent case study, on which this description of ECHO is based, was published in early 2021: Tamara Kay and Jason Spicer, "A Nonprofit Networked Platform for Global Health," *Stanford Social Innovation Review*, Winter 2021, https://ssir.org/articles/entry/a_nonprofit_networked_platform_for_global_health.

Kay and Spicer quotes on ECHO: Tamara Kay and Jason Spicer, "A Nonprofit Networked Platform for Global Health," *Stanford Social Innovation Review*, Winter 2021, https://ssir.org/articles/entry/a_nonprofit_networked_platform_for_global_health.

Waddell "those who are…" quote: Steve Waddell, "Four Strategies for Large Systems Change," *Stanford Social Innovation Review*, Spring 2018, 42, https://philanthropynewsdigest.org/columns/ssir-pnd/four-strategies-for-large-systems-change.

Kania and Kramer quote: cited in Eric Nee, "Beyond Collective Impact," *Stanford Social Innovation Review*, Winter 2020, https://ssir.org/articles/entry/a_flexible_framework_for_going_beyond_collective_impact.

Blatz, White, and Joseph quote: Byron P. White, Jennifer Blatz, and Mark L. Joseph, "Elevating Community Authority in Collective Impact," *Stanford Social Innovation Review*, Winter 2019, https://www.strivetogether.org/wp-content/uploads/2019/02/F_Elevating-Community_FINAL.pdf.

Seelos and Mair quote: Seelos and Mair, "Mastering System Change."

Sawyer and Ehrlichman quote: David Sawyer and David Ehrlichman, "The Tactics of Trust," *Stanford Social Innovation Review*, Winter 2016, 61, https://ssir.org/articles/entry/the_tactics_of_trust#.

Kania, Kramer, Senge quote: Kania, Kramer, Senge, "The Water of Systems Change."

Curtis quote: Jennie Curtis, "Digging Out of Philanthropy's Entrenched Practices," The Garfield Foundation, July 29, 2019, https://garfield-foundation.medium.com/digging-out-of-philanthropys-entrenched-practices-b7be9bd9c999.

RE-AMP information: "About," RE-AMP website, https://www.reamp.org/about/.

OpenNews initiated research: https://opennews.org/blog/vision25-building-racial-equity-in-newsrooms/

Bourland experiences: Dana L. Bourland, *Gray to Green Communities: A Call to Action on the House and Climate Crises* (Washington, DC: Island Press, 2021), see "Preface."

Bourland quote, "Much to my horror…": Bourland, *Gray to Green Communities*, xviii-xix.

EEFA $454 million: "About Energy Efficiency for All," EEFA, accessed May 10, 2021, https://www.energyefficiencyforall.org/about/.

Herman quotes: Melissa Herman, "The Critical Role of Traditional Knowledge in Social Innovation," *Stanford Social Innovation Review*, Winter 2018, https://ssir.org/articles/entry/the_critical_role_of_traditional_knowledge_in_social_innovation.

Berman quote: Jennifer Berman, et al., "What We Mean When We Say 'Systems Change,'" Bioneers, https://bioneers.org/what-mean-when-we-say-systems-change-zp0z2107/

Sibbet quote: David Sibbet, *Visual Teams: Graphic Tools for Commitment, Innovation, and High Performance* (Hoboken, New Jersey: Wiley & Sons, 2011), see https://books.google.com/books?id=j-RQTtRngjAC&pg=PT385&lpg=PT385&dq=jennie+curtis+garfield+%22image%22&source=bl&ots=ks4k48vbfx&sig=ACfU3U3Nf03VFrLhtRmRum-JiF1MIVm0eLQ&hl=en&sa=X&ved=2ahUKEwiepvnAjKnwAhXtHDQIHc9XA_AQ6AEwEnoECA8QAw#v=onepage&q=RE-AMP&f=false

Seelos and Mair quote, "because of the complexity…": Seelos and Mair, "Mastering System Change."

Meadows quote: Donella Meadows, "Leverage Points: Places to Intervene in a System," Academy for Systems Change, Donella Meadows Archives, http://donellameadows.org/archives/leverage-points-places-to-intervene-in-a-system/.

Seelos quotes: Christian Seelos, "Changing Systems? Welcome to the Slow Movement," *Stanford Social Innovation Review*, Winter 2020, 40, http://www.christianseelos.com/SSIR%20Winter2020-Feature-Seelos-Changing-Systems.pdf.

Seelos and Mair "experienced professionals" quote: Seelos and Mair, "Mastering System Change."

Sotos quote: Eleni Sotos, "Transcending Business as Usual by Funding Collaborative Processes," The Garfield Foundation, October 27, 2020, https://garfield-foundation.medium.com/transcending-business-as-usual-by-funding-collaborative-processes-1bcd-c1d2871b

Attalla quote: "What We Mean When We Say 'Systems Change,'" Garfield Foundation.

Kania, Kramer, Senge quote: Kania, Kramer, Senge, "The Water of Systems Change."

Scharmer quote: C. Otto Scharmer, *The Essentials of Theory U*, xi.

Splash in China: Eric Stowe, "Managing Risk to Scale Impact," *Stanford Social Innovation Review*, summer 2017, https://ssir.org/articles/entry/case_study_managing_risk_to_scale_impact.

RE-AMP quote: "The Framework," RE-AMP website, accessed May 10, 2021, https://www.reamp.org/the-network-approach/edd/.

Chapter 3

Musa & Rodin quote: Muhammad Musa and Judith Rodin, "Scaling Up Social Innovation," *Stanford Social Innovation Review*, Spring 2016, https://ssir.org/articles/entry/scaling_up_social_innovation.

Sherraden quotes: Michael Sherraden, *Assets and the Poor: A New American Welfare Policy* (Armonck, New York: M.E. Sharpe, 1991), xv, 148, 181-182, 231.

Friedman "accidental inheritor … I was given" quotes: Robert E. Friedman, *A Few Thousand Dollars: Sparking Prosperity for Everyone* (New York: The New Press, 2018), 7-8, 4.

Game changers report: Coauthors Cleveland and Plastrik were principal authors of the Carbon Neutral Cities Alliance report.

Health Care Without Harm climate impact checkup: https://www.greenhospitals.net/checkup/?mc_cid=3deeb0c2f0&mc_eid=abb6cbd5ae.

Biophilic Cities Network: For more about the network see https://www.biophiliccities.org/our-vision.

Seattle "democracy vouchers": see https://www.seattle.gov/democracyvoucher/about-the-program.

Authors of "The Many Roads to Revenue Generation" quote: Marya Besharov, Jean-Baptiste Litrico, and Susanna Kislenko, "The Many Roads to Revenue Generation," *Stanford Social Innovation Review*, Fall 2019, https://givingcompass.org/article/nonprofits-many-roads-to-revenue-generation/.

A 2019 analysis of "big bets" quotes: William Foster, Gail Perreault, and Bradley Seeman, "Becoming Big Bettable," *Stanford Social Innovation Review*, Spring 2019, https://ssir.org/articles/entry/becoming_big_bettable.

Bridgespan leaders quote: William Foster, Gail Perreault, and Bradley Seeman, "Becoming Big Bettable," *Stanford Social Innovation Review*, Spring 2019, https://ssir.org/articles/entry/becoming_big_bettable.

Khan quote: Khan was interviewed in "Creating a Funding Environment for Scaling Up Social Impact," *Stanford Social Innovation Review*, Spring 2016, https://ssir.org/articles/entry/creating_a_funding_environment_for_scaling_up_social_impact.

Starr quote: Kevin Starr, "We're Beating Systems Change to Death," *Stanford Social Innovation Review*, April 8, 2021, https://ssir.org/articles/entry/were_beating_systems_change_to_death.

Nayar, Saleh, and Minj quote: Rahul Nayar, Asif Saleh, and Anna Minj, "Scaling Up Innovations with Government," *Stanford Social Innovation Review*, Spring 2016, https://ssir. org/articles/entry/scaling_up_innovations_with_government#.

#WirVsVirus: Mair and Gegenhuber, "Open Social Innovation."

Deiglmeier and Greco quote: Deiglmeier and Greco, "Why Proven Solutions Struggle to Scale Up."

IDEO leaders quote: Wyatt, Brown & Carey, "The Next Chapter in Design for Social Innovation," 44

Seelos and Mair quote: Christian Seelos and Johanna Mair, "When Innovation Goes Wrong," *Stanford Social Innovation Review*, Fall 2016, https://ssir.org/articles/entry/when_ innovation_goes_wrong.

Sherraden had never had much savings: Friedman, A Few Thousand Dollars, 33-34.

The Innovator's DNA **quotes:** Dyer, Gregersen, Christensen, *The Innovator's DNA*, 18-21.

IDEO leaders quote: Wyatt, Brown & Carey, "The Next Chapter in Design for Social Innovation," 46.

Cea and Rimington quote: Cea and Rimington, "Creating Breakout Innovation."

Silbert and Mukamal "a network of philanthropies" quote: Silbert and Mukamal, "How Philanthropy Can Create Public Systems Change," 30.

American Dream Demonstration: Friedman, *A Few Thousand Dollars*, 34-36. For the ADD evaluation report see https://openscholarship.wustl.edu/cgi/viewcontent.cgi?arti- cle=1263&context=csd_research.

GoodSAM app: Clegg, "Smartphone Samaritans," 15.

When the US Water Alliance worked with water utilities and community organizations: US Water Alliance, "Water Equity Taskforce: Insights for the Water Sector," 19.

Tantia quote: Piyush Tantia, "The New Science of Designing for Humans," *Stanford Social Innovation Review*, Spring 2017, 29, https://ssir.org/articles/entry/the_new_science_of_ designing_for_humans.

DIVA Centres in Zambia: Wyatt, Brown & Carey, "The Next Chapter in Design for Social Innovation," 47.

The US Water Alliance's water equity network of 25 cities: US Water Alliance, "Water Equity Taskforce: Insights for the Water Sector," 21, 23.

Friedman quote: Friedman, *A Few Thousand Dollars*, 46.

565 million acres: see Forestry Stewardship Council, https://fsc.org/en/facts-figures, accessed September 23, 2021.

Forestry Stewardship Council: Ford Foundation, "Asset Building for Social Change: Pathways to Large-Scale Impact," 37, https://www.fordfoundation.org/work/learning/ research-reports/asset-building-for-social-change-pathways-to-large-scale-impact/.

US Department of Housing and Urban Development: Friedman, *A Few Thousand Dollars*, 45.

600 programs in all 50 states: Melvin Oliver and Thomas Shapiro, *Black Wealth/White Wealth: A New Perspective on Racial Inequality* (New York: Routledge, 2006), 258.

Oliver and Shapiro quote: Oliver and Shapiro, *Black Wealth/White Wealth*, 259.

Hamilton quote: Annie Lowrey, "A Cheap, Race-Neutral Way to Close the Racial Wealth Gap," The Atlantic, June 19, 2020 https://www.theatlantic.com/ideas/archive/2020/06/close-racial-wealth-gap-baby-bonds/613525/.

Oklahoma, Maine, and Pennsylvania IDAs: Patricia Cohen, "College Accounts at Birth: State Efforts Raise New Hopes," *The New York Times*, April 27, 2021, https://www.nytimes.com/2021/04/27/business/economy/child-education-accounts.html?referringSource=articleShare.

New York City...: Tara Siegel Bernard, "Seeding Accounts for Kindergarten and Hoping to Grow College Graduates," *New York Times*, October 112, 2021, https://www.nytimes.com/2021/10/11/your-money/529-savings-plans-baby-bonds.html.

Universal Savings Accounts: For more details about the design of USAs see Friedman, *A Few Thousand Dollars*, 53-58.

Chapter 4

Gargani & McLean "We can't chart..." quote: John Gargani and Robert McLean, "Scaling Science," *Stanford Social Innovation Review*, Fall 2017, https://ssir.org/articles/entry/scaling_science#.

Gargani and McLean "innovators must develop..." quote: Gargani and McLean, "Scaling Science."

LEED: For more about LEED, see https://www.usgbc.org/articles/green-building-101-what-leed.

Architecture 2030 quote: Architecture 2030, "Why The Building Sector," accessed October 10, 2021, https://architecture2030.org/why-the-building-sector/.

More than 69,000 buildings: https://www.statista.com/statistics/323383/leed-registered-projects-in-the-united-states/.

Texas has the most LEED-certified residential projects: https://www.builderonline.com/building/safety-healthfulness/the-top-us-cities-for-leed-certified-construction_o.

Saved more than $2.1 billion: https://www.usgbc.org/leed/why-leed

120 US cities: https://www.usgbc.org/articles/usgbc-announces-15-cities-and-counties-selected-2021-leed-cities-local-government.

First LEED business improvement district: Ingrid Tunberg, "DC Business District Named World's First LEED-Certified Community," October 7, 2019, https://www.globest.com/2019/10/07/dc-business-district-named-worlds-first-leed-certified-community/?slreturn=20220202134202.

1,100 LEED-certified buildings: https://wtop.com/business-finance/2021/02/dc-led-green-building-in-2020/.

USGBC data: email from Taryn Holowka to authors, April 19. 2022.

Deiglmeier and Greco quote: Deiglmeier and Greco, "Why Proven Solutions Struggle to Scale Up."

Seelos and Mair quote: Seelos and Mair, "When Innovation Goes Wrong."

Gargani & McLean quote: Gargani and McLean, "Scaling Science."

2021 Criterion Institute report: Joy Anderson, "Disrupting Fields: Addressing Power Dynamics in the Fields of Climate Finance and Gender Lens Investing," Criterion Institute, January 2021, https://criterioninstitute.org/resources/disrupting-fields-addressing-power-dynamics-in-the-fields-of-climate-finance-and-gender-lens-investing.

USGBC quote: USGBC, "Engaging with state and local governments on LEED," accessed October 11, 2021, https://www.usgbc.org/articles/engaging-state-and-local-governments-leed.

New Mexico: USGBC, "Engaging with state and local governments on LEED," accessed October 11, 2021.

A global treaty: for more information see Josh Karliner, Gary Cohen, and Peter Orris, "Lessons in Global Change," *Stanford Social Innovation Review*, Winter 2014, https://ssir.org/articles/entry/lessons_in_forging_global_change.

Field of microfinance: Deiglmeier and Greco, "Why Proven Solutions Struggle to Scale Up."

Blatz and Canada quote: Jennifer Blatz and Geoffrey Canada, "The Importance of Place," *Stanford Social Innovation Review*, Spring 2022, 61-62,

Gargani and McLean quote: Gargani and McLean, "Scaling Science."

Rockefeller Philanthropy Advisors quote: Rockefeller Philanthropy Advisors, "Seeing, Facilitating, and Assessing Systems Change: Learnings from the Scaling Solutions Toward Shifting Solutions Initiative," July 2020, https://www.rockpa.org/wp-content/uploads/2020/11/11-17-RockPA-Scaling-Solutions-03-Report-LowRes.pdf.

iPhones sales and users: see https://appleinsider.com/articles/21/09/22/at-2-billion-iphones-sold-apple-continues-to-redefine-what-customers-want.

2021 article in *Stanford Social Innovation Review* quote: Greg Starbird, Fiona Wilson, and E. Hachemi Aliouche, "The Promise of Social Sector Franchising," *Stanford Social Innovation Review*, Spring 2021, https://ssir.org/articles/entry/the_promise_of_social_sector_franchising#.

Deiglmeier and Greco quote: Deiglmeier and Greco, "Why Proven Solutions Struggle to Scale Up."

Goodwill placed more than 126,000: Goodwill Industries, "Impact," accessed December 12, 2021, https://www.goodwill.org/annual-report/.

"Promise of Social Sector Franchising" quote: Starbird, Wilson, and Aliouche, "The Promise of Social Sector Franchising."

LEED variations: "LEED rating system," https://www.usgbc.org/leed.

Ascend National network: Anne Mosle and Marjorie Sims, "State of the Field: Two-Generation Approaches to Family Well-Being," June 2021, https://ascend-resources.aspeninstitute.org/resources/state-of-the-field-two-generation-approaches-to-family-well-being/.

Harvard University Center on the Developing Child quote: Center on the Developing Child, "Three Core Concepts in Early Development," https://developingchild.harvard.edu/resources/three-core-concepts-in-early-development/.

Soros quotes: Open Society Foundations, "Early Childhood and Open Society: Creating Equitable and Inclusive Societies," December 2020, 2, https://www.opensocietyfoundations.org/publications/early-childhood-and-open-society.

ISSA contains 92 member-organizations: Network Impact, "How Regional Networks Catalyze Impact in Early Childhood Development," December 2020, 13-14, https://www.networkimpact.org/wp-content/uploads/2020/12/Network-Impact_How-Regional-Networks-Catalyze-Impact-in-Early-Childhood-Development_Final_December-20201.pdf.

$20 million: Open Society Foundations, "Early Childhood and Open Society," 31.

2020 assessment of regional ECD networks: Network Impact, "How Regional Networks Catalyze Impact in Early Childhood Development," 2, 7, 9.

Hargadon quote: Hargadon, *How Breakthroughs Happen*, 149.

Water Equity Task Force quote: US Water Alliance, "Water Equity Task Force: Insights for the Water Sector," June 2021, 43.

Mosle and Sims quotes: Ascend at the Aspen Institute, "2Gen Platforms for Scale: Whole-Family Approaches Rooted in Community with National Reach," October 2020, 29, https://ascend-resources.aspeninstitute.org/resources/2gen-platforms-for-scale-whole-family-approaches-rooted-in-community-with-national-reach/.

Ascend quote: Anne Mosle and Marjorie Sims, "State of the Field: Two-Generation Approaches to Family Well-Being," 26, 29.

Gips quote: Skoll Foundation, "Working with Governments Toward Scalable Solutions: A Conversation with Don Gips," February 16, 2022, https://skoll.org/2022/02/16/working-with-governments-towards-scalable-solutions-a-conversation-with-don-gips/.

Hargadon quote: Hargadon, *How Breakthroughs Happen*: 32.

15 other local governments: USGBC, "USGBC Announces 15 Cities and Counties Selected for 2021 LEED for Cities Local Government Leadership Program," https://www.usgbc.org/articles/usgbc-announces-15-cities-and-counties-selected-2021-leed-cities-local-government.

Everett Rogers: see https://en.wikipedia.org/wiki/Diffusion_of_innovations.

Hussein & Plummer quote: Taz Hussein and Matt Plummer, "Selling Social Change," *Stanford Social Innovation Review*, Winter 2017, https://ssir.org/articles/entry/selling_social_change.

Hargadon quotes: Hargadon, *How Breakthroughs Happen*, 25-28, 103, 108.

Hussein and Plummer quote: Hussein & Plummer, "Selling Social Change."

Deiglmeier and Greco advise: Deiglmeier and Greco, "Why Proven Solutions Struggle to Scale Up."

Chapter 5

Wheatley quote: Margaret J. Wheatley, "The Unplanned Organization: Learning From Nature's Emergent Creativity," Noetic Sciences Review, #37, Spring 1996, https://www.margaretwheatley.com/articles/unplannedorganization.html.

Opportunity Finance Network $8.5 million: Opportunity Finance Network, "About," accessed November 29, 2021, https://ofn.org/about.

Salmon Speakers: US Water Alliance, "US Water Prize for Outstanding Artist: Salmon Speakers," http://uswateralliance.org/resources/blog/us-water-prize-outstanding-artist-salmon-speakers.

Festival of What Works: https://www.festivalofwhat.works/about-us/.

Health Care Without Harm awards: Health Care Without Harm, "Celebrating the 2021 Emerging Physician Leader Award recipients," https://noharm-uscanada.org/articles/news/us-canada/celebrating-2021-emerging-physician-leader-award-recipients.

Ascend fellowship program: Ascend, "Ascend Fellows," accessed November 29, 2021, https://ascend.aspeninstitute.org/fellowship/

"Six Essential Capacities": Peter Plastrik was principal researcher and writer of this report, available at http://uswateralliance.org/sites/uswateralliance.org/files/publications/uswa_leadership_report_FINAL_0.pdf.

Lackey quote: Katy Lackey e-mail to the authors, March 17, 2022.

FinHealth Score Toolkit: Toolkit can be downloaded at https://finhealthnetwork.org/tools/financial-health-score/#toolkit.

2Gen Outcomes Bank: the data can be accessed at https://outcomes.ascend.aspeninstitute.org.

US Water Alliance quote: http://uswateralliance.org/one-water.

Spitfire reports: Spitfire, "Family Prosperity movement," accessed November 29, 2021, https://www.spitfirestrategies.com/work/family-prosperity-movement.

Salmon Nation/Magic Canoe quote: https://salmonnation.net/stories.

Gill quote: Ian Gill, "'I Was Alone in a Canoe. But It Was a Magic Canoe,'" *The Tyee*, December 4, 2020, https://thetyee.ca/Culture/2020/12/04/Magic-Canoe-Waxaid/.

Yost quote: Jeff Yost, "Youth Are Changing the Greater Nebraska Narrative," Nebraska Community Foundation, https://www.nebcommfound.org/news/youth-are-changing-the-greater-nebraska-narrative/.

Nebraska transfer of wealth: report available at https://www.nebcommfound.org/wp-content/uploads/2022/02/2021-TOW-State-report-brochure-pages.pdf.

Krebs and Holley quotes: Valdis Krebs and June Holley, "Building Sustainable Communities Through Social Networks," *Nonprofit Quarterly*, Spring 2004, 46-53.

Beebe quote: Spencer Beebe e-mail to the authors, undated.

Powell quote: http://uswateralliance.org/one-water/one-water-insight-interview-kishia-powell.

Yost quote: Jeff Yost, "Communities built with capital, trust," *Kearney Hub*, December 19, 2019.

270 communities … $70 million: from Nebraska Community Foundation, "NCF At A Glance, as of 12/31/21."

Keith County and McCook: Progress reports provided by Nebraska Community Foundation, April 2, 2022.

Yost quote: Jeff Yost, "Communities built with capital, trust."

NCF supports: Nebraska Community Foundation website, "Nebraska Community Foundation Education & Training," accessed March 18, 2022, https://www.nebcommfound.org/wp-content/uploads/2021/04/Education-and-Training-UPDATE.pdf.

Kay and Spicer quote: Kay and Spicer, "A Nonprofit Networked Platform for Global Health."

Open Society Foundation quote: Open Society Foundations, "Early Childhood and Open Society," 27.

Hargadon quote: Hargadon, *How Breakthroughs Happen*, 89.

Chapter 6

Native Women Lead quote: Native Women Lead, "Community Working Agreement," accessed April 23, 2021 https://www.nativewomenlead.org/blog/2020/6/2/blacklivesmatter.

Innovator's DNA **quote**: Dyer, Gregersen, Christensen, *The Innovator's DNA*, 21.

CNCA Director job description: Koya Partners, "Director: Carbon Neutral Cities Alliance," June 8, 2021.

Crutchfield quote: Leslie R. Crutchfield, *How Change Happens: Why Some Social Movements Succeed While Others Don't* (Hoboken, New Jersey: Wiley & Sons, 2018), 59.

Cea and Rimington "for a process…" quote: Cea and Rimington, "Creating Breakthrough Innovation," 37-38.

Cea and Rimington "Prototyping too often…" quote: Cea and Rimington, "Creating Breakthrough Innovation," 37.

Hargadon "culture has…" quote: Hargadon, *How Breakthroughs Happen*.

CNCA Director job description: Koya Partners, "Director: Carbon Neutral Cities Alliance."

Hargadon "You can have all…" quote: Hargadon, *How Breakthroughs Happen*, 157.

Comacho quote: US Water Alliance, "Six Essential Capacities: One Water Change Leadership, 24, http://uswateralliance.org/sites/uswateralliance.org/files/publications/uswa_leadership_report_FINAL_0.pdf.

Seelos and Mair quote: Seelos and Mair, "When Innovation Goes Wrong," 33.

Wei quote: Sisi Wei, "Journalists: If you've worked with others to change your newsroom, you're probably an organizer," January 13, 2022, https://rjionline.org/news/journalists-if-youve-worked-with-others-to-change-your-newsroom-youre-probably-an-organizer/.

Cea and Rimington "Diverse perspectives…" quote: Cea and Rimington, "Creating Breakthrough Innovation," 36.

Hargadon quote: Hargadon, *How Breakthroughs Happen*, 27.

Seelos and Mair quote: Seelos and Mair, "Mastering System Change."

Cea and Rimington "Full-fledged experiments" quote: Cea and Rimington, "Creating Breakthrough Innovation,"35.

Hargadon "part and parcel" quote: Hargadon, *How Breakthroughs Happen*, 117.

Jackson quote: Jackson quoted in Edgar Villanueva, *Decolonizing Wealth* (Oakland: Berrett-Koehler, 2018), 149.

Deiglmeier and Greco quote: Deiglmeier and Greco, "Why Proven Solutions Struggle to Scale Up."

Ford Foundation quote: Ford Foundation BUILD program, https://www.fordfoundation.org/work/our-grants/building-institutions-andnetworks/.

Gopal and Kania quote: Srik Gopal and John Kania, "Fostering Systems Change," *Stanford Social Innovation Review*, November 20, 2015, https://ssir.org/articles/entry/fostering_systems_change.

Kania, Kramer, and Senge quote: Kania, Kramer, Senge, "The Water of Systems Change," 14, 16..

Powell quote: US Water Alliance, "One Water Change Leadership for Utilities: Six Essential Capacities."

Cea and Rimington "having to get comfortable" quote: Cea and Rimington, "Creating Breakthrough Innovation," 39.

Cea and Rimington "It can be challenging" quote: Cia and Rimington, "Creating Breakthrough Innovation," 36.

Hargadon "Find your discomfort" quote: Hargadon, *How Breakthroughs Happen*, 209.

Hargardon "will fight hard" quote: Hargadon, *How Breakthroughs Happen*, 61.

Coda

Batiste quote: https://genius.com/Jon-batiste-dont-stop-lyrics.

Narayan's TED talk: go.ted.com/shwetanarayan, accessed December 31, 2021.

Cohen quote: Gary Cohen, "A Winter Solstice Reflection," e-mail from Gary Cohen to John Cleveland and other board members of Health Care Without Harm, December 23, 2021.

Appendices

FrameWorks quotes: FrameWorks Institute, "Mindset Shifts," 28, 30.

Truth Initiative: Alex Daniels, "Truth Initiative Wins Award for Successful Antismoking Campaign," *The Chronicle of Philanthropy*, June 4, 2018, https://www.philanthropy.com/article/truth-initiative-wins-award-for-successful-antismoking-campaign/.

More about Albert Bandura and social learning theory: see https://www.simplypsychology.org/bandura.html.

Gratitude

Hock quote: Dee Hock, *Birth of the Chaordic Age* (San Francisco:

Berrett-Koehler, 1999), 3.

Resources

Systems Change

- Rob Abercrombie, Ellen Harries, and Rachel Warton, "Systems Change: A Guide To What It Is and How To Do It," *NPC*, June 2015, https://www.thinknpc.org/resource-hub/systems-change-a-guide-to-what-it-is-and-how-to-do-it/.

- John Cleveland, Joann Neuroth, and Peter Plastrik, *Welcome to the Edge of Chaos 2.0: Where Change is a Way of Life*, revised 2020, self-published, available at https://www.amazon.com/Welcome-Edge-Chaos-Where-Change-ebook/dp/B08JNKB72V/ref=tmm_kin_swatch_0?_encoding=UTF8&qid=1634912322&sr=8-1.

- The Collective Impact Forum: https://www.collectiveimpactforum.org/.

- FrameWorks Institute, "Mindset Shifts: What Are They? Why Do They Matter? How Do They Happen?" June 2020, https://live-frame-works-institute.pantheonsite.io/wp-content/uploads/2021/02/FRAJ8064-Mindset-Shifts-200612-WEB.pdf.

- Heather McLeod Grant and Adene Sacks, *Leading Systems Change: A Workbook for Community Practitioners and Funders* (Open Impact, 2019), download free PDF at https://www.openimpact.io/leading-sys-tems-change.

- Peggy Holman, *The Change Handbook – The Definitive Resource on Today's Best Methods for Engaging Whole Systems* (San Francisco: Berrett-Koehler, 2007).

- John Kania, Mark Kramer, Peter Senge, "The Water of Systems Change," FSG, June 2018, https://www.fsg.org/publications/water_of_systems_change.

- John Kania, Junious Williams, Paul Schmitz, Sheri Brandy, Mark Kramer, and Jennifer Splansky Juster, "Centering Equity in Collective Impact," *Stanford Social Innovation Review*, Winter 2022, https://ssir.org/articles/entry/centering_equity_in_collective_impact.

- Donella H. Meadows, *Thinking in Systems: A Primer*, ed. Diana Wright (White River Junction, Vermont: Chelsea Green Publishing, 2008).

- Geoff Mulgan, *Another World is Possible: How to Reignite Social and Political Imagination* (London: Hurst, 2022)

- Network Impact, "How Regional Networks Catalyze Impact in Early Childhood Development," https://www.networkimpact.org/wp-content/uploads/2020/12/Network-Impact_How-Regional-Networks-Catalyze-Impact-in-Early-Childhood-Development_Final_December-20201.pdf.

- C. Otto Scharmer, *The Essentials of Theory U: Core Principles and Applications* (Oakland, CA: Berrett-Koehler, 2018).

- Christian Seelos, "Changing Systems? Welcome to the Slow Movement," *Stanford Social Innovation Review*, Winter 2020, http://www.christianseelos.com/SSIR%20Winter2020-Feature-Seelos-Changing-Systems.pdf.

- Christian Seelos and Johanna Mair, "Mastering System Change," *Stanford Social Innovation Review*, Fall 2018, http://www.christianseelos.com/Fall_2018_Mastering_System_Change.pdf.

- David Peter Stroh, *Systems Thinking for Social Change: A Practical Guide to Solving Complex Problems, Avoiding Unintended Consequences, and Achieving Lasting Results* (White River Junction, Vermont: Chelsea Green Publishing, 2015).

- Systems Innovation Network: a global community of systems innovators, see the Si Toolkit, www.systemsinnovation.network.

- Tamarack Institute website and newsletter: https://www.tamarack-community.ca/.

- Edgar Villanueva, *Decolonizing Wealth: Indigenous Wisdom to Heal Divides and Restore Balance* (Oakland: Berrett-Koehler, 2018).

- Steve Waddell, "Four Strategies for Large Systems Change," *Stanford Social Innovation Review*, Spring 2018, https://philanthropynewsdigest.org/columns/ssir-pnd/four-strategies-for-large-systems-change.

Social Innovation

- Spencer Beebe, *Cache: Creating Natural Economies* (Portland, OR: Ecotrust, 2010).

- Joanna Levitt Cea and Jess Rimington, "Creating Breakthrough Innovation," *Stanford Social Innovation Review*, Summer 2017, https://ssir.org/articles/entry/creating_breakout_innovation#.

- Jeff Dyer, Hal Gregersen, Clayton M. Christensen, *The Innovator's DNA: Mastering the Five Skills of Disruptive Innovators* (Boston: Harvard Business Review Press, 2011).

- Robert E. Friedman, *A Few Thousand Dollars: Sparking Prosperity for Everyone* (New York: The New Press, 2018).

- Steve Haines, *The Product Manager's Desk Reference*, 2nd edition, (New York: McGraw Hill Education, 2009).

- Andrew Hargadon, *How Breakthroughs Happen: The Surprising Truth About How Companies Innovate* (Boston: Harvard Business Press, 2003)

- Mauricio L. Miller, *The Alternative: Most of what you believe about poverty is wrong* (Morrisville, North Carolina: Lulu Publishing, 2017).

- Anne Mosle and Marjorie Sims, "State of the Field: Two-Generation Approaches to Family Well-Being," Ascend at the Aspen Institute, June 2021, https://ascend.aspeninstitute.org/state-of-the-field-two-generation-approaches-to-family-well-being/.

- Jocelyn Wyatt, Tim Brown, Shauna Carey, "The Next Chapter in Design for Social Innovation," *Stanford Social Innovation Review*, Winter 2021, https://www.ideo.com/journal/its-taken-decades-for-social innovation-to-become-mainstream.

- US Water Alliance, "Water Equity Taskforce: Insights for the Water Sector," June 2021, http://uswateralliance.org/sites/uswateralliance.org/files/FINAL%20Water%20Equity%20Taskforce%20Insights%20for%20the%20Water%20Sector.pdf.

Scaling Up

- Jeffrey Bradach, "Scaling Impact," *Stanford Social Innovation Review*, Summer 2010, https://ssir.org/articles/entry/scaling_impact.

- Kriss Deiglmeier and Amanda Greco, "Why Proven Solutions Struggle to Scale Up," *Stanford Social Innovation Review*, August 10, 2018, https://ssir.org/articles/entry/why_proven_solutions_struggle_to_scale_up.

- Ford Foundation, "Asset Building for Social Change: Pathways to Large-Scale Impact," https://www.fordfoundation.org/work/learning/research-reports/asset-building-for-social-change-pathways-to-large-scale-impact/.

- John Gargani and Robert McLean, "Scaling Science," *Stanford Social Innovation Review*, Fall 2017, https://ssir.org/articles/entry/scaling_science#.

- Skoll Foundation Social Edge web site, "Seven Scaling Capacities," www.socialedge.org.

- The Bridgespan Group, "The Strong Field Framework: A Guide and Toolkit for Funders and Nonprofits Committed to Large-Scale Impact," June 2009, https://irvine-dot-org.s3.amazonaws.com/documents/64/attachments/strongfieldframework.pdf?1412656138.

Social Impact Networks

- David Ehrlichman, David Sawyer & Matthew Spence, "Cutting Through the Complexity: A Roadmap for Effective Collaboration," *Stanford Social Innovation Review*, March 15, 2018, https://ssir.org/articles/entry/cutting_through_the_complexity_a_roadmap_for_effective_collaboration.

- June Holley, *Network Weaver Handbook: A Guide to Transformational Networks* (2012)

- Leadership Learning Community, https://leadershiplearning.org/about-us. Leadership Learning Community is a national nonprofit organization transforming the way leadership development work is understood, practiced and promoted, primarily within the nonprofit sector.

- Netcentric Campaigns, https://netcentriccampaigns.org/about/. Netcentric Campaigns has been working to bring thought leadership, experience, skill, guidance and professionalism to the networking challenges that key movement leaders are facing.

- Network Impact website: https://www.networkimpact.org.

- Peter Plastrik, Madeleine Taylor, John Cleveland, *Connecting to Change the World: Harnessing the Power of Networks for Social Impact* (Washington DC: Island Press, 2014).

Appendices

A. Donnella Meadows' List of 12 System Leverage Points

Meadows organized her list in reverse order of her assessment of their leveraging power.

12. Constants, parameters, numbers
11. The size of buffers and other stabilizing stocks, relative to their flows
10. Structure of material stocks and flows (such as transport network, population structures)
9. Length of delays, relative to the rate of system changes
8. Strength of negative feedback loops, relative to the effect they are trying to correct against
7. Gain around driving positive feedback loops
6. Structure of information flow (who does and does not have access to what kinds of information)
5. Rules of the system (such as incentives, punishment, constraints)
4. Power to add, change, evolve, or self-organize system structure
3. Goal of the system
2. Mindset or paradigm that the system—its goals, structure, rules, delays, parameters—arises from
1. Power to transcend paradigms

Other system changers have consolidated and revised Meadows' list. See, for instance, John Kania, Mark Kramer, Peter Senge, "The Water of Systems Change," FSG, June 2018, https://www.fsg.org/publications/water_of_systems_change; David Ehrlichman, "Identifying Leverage Points in Systems," https://medium.com/converge-perspectives/identifying-leverage-points-in-a-system-3b917f70ab13; and Adam Saint, "Designing at leverage points," https://ux.shopify.com/designing-at-leverage-points-cffa42462f73.

B. Promotion – Another Type of Social Innovation

There's another type of social innovation: the promotion of new behaviors through social learning processes. Information has the power to shape the way people live their lives. "What people read, see, and hear can, over time, shift their mindsets," notes the FrameWorks Institute report on mindset shifts. Promoting social learning relies on educational processes to influence specific behaviors such as sexual practices, the purchase and use of products, and participation in community affairs. The quality of the information may not be enough to persuade people, but how the information is delivered—who communicates it and how it is communicated—can make the information irresistible. "The sources of messages shape how they are received," FrameWorks continues. "Most members of the public form their opinions, in significant part, based on what aligned opinion leaders (e.g., elites from their political party) say. Shifts in what opinion leaders say can lead to corresponding shifts in the opinions of people who trust them."

Perhaps the most cited example of this is the anti-smoking campaigns that rely of social information processes. Truth Initiative, an advocacy group that specializes in what the Chronicle of Philanthropy calls "edgy videos that pit rebellious youths against stodgy, lying corporations" is credited with dramatically reducing cigarette use by high-school students. The effort was not the usual advertising campaign, notes one of the judges for the Communications Network, which in 2021 picked the nonprofit for an award. "Instead of exposing people to what happens with smoking," says Jesse Salazar, chairman of the network, the initiative's efforts "activate youth to be ambassadors for their message." In other words, social dynamics—peer-to-peer in this case—generate the impact. "That shift of their posture from exposing to activating is really remarkable," Salazar adds. Smoking among high-school students dropped from 23 percent to 6 percent in the past two decades.

The scale of promotion innovations is audiences: large groups of people with a similar behavior—parenting young children, managing a particular disease, engaging in crime, smoking, or sexual practices, for example—that can be targeted for change. These types of behaviors are often learned by individuals in social situations. Young people and some of their specific behaviors—alcohol and tobacco use, reproductive health, for instance—are an often-targeted audience.

Scaling up promotion innovations typically involves campaigns that use social learning processes that lean on the theory that individuals learn new behaviors by observing what others do, what characters in books, films, and other media do, and by taking in instructions that describe and explain behaviors. "Most human behavior is learned observationally through modeling: from observing others one forms an idea of how new behaviors are performed, and on later occasions, this coded information serves as a guide for action," explains Albert Bandura, a leading developer of social learning theory.

C. Assessing the Potential of Social Innovations Under Development

The table below summarizes some of the questions that innovation developers ask to determine if their efforts meet basic innovation criteria.

Criteria	Questions to Ask
Systems Changing Potential	• Is there a clear hypothesis about how scaling of the innovation could contribute to a significant change in the current system? • Is this hypothesis feasible?
Significant Performance Improvements	• Is there evidence the innovation can create significant and cost-effective improvements in performance compared to the current system? • Are there indicators to measure these improvements? • Is it clear how the innovation will produce these performance improvements?

Financial Sustainability	• Are the potential users for the innovation clearly identified and is there a compelling value proposition for them to use the innovation?
	• Is there clarity about the costs of the innovation?
	• Are reliable long-term revenue sources identified and are these embedded in a rigorous financial model for sustainability?
	• Is the front-end "risk capital" investment that is needed to develop the innovation reasonable?
	• How long will it take before the innovation generates revenue?
Scalability	• Is there a feasible business design for distributing the innovation?
	• Is there a well-defined "unit of production" that gets expanded in scaling?
	• Can the innovation easily be adopted and implemented by others?
	• Are there any significant barriers to scaling, such as the need for highly specialized human talent or unique sets of relationships to implement the innovation?

D. Assessing an Innovation Hypothesis

Ask these kinds of questions at the conceptualization stage of the innovation process:

- What is the system you are trying to influence? What are the "boundaries" of that system?

- How much do you know about the system? Have you worked in it? Do you have "professional standing" in it? What are your networks within the system?

- Do you have detailed operating knowledge of the system? Do you know its economics, incentive structures, and regulatory environment?

- Are there any players in the system that share your instinct about where the opportunity is?

- Are you familiar with other efforts to change this system? Do you have a hypothesis about why they failed?

- What kind of data is there on the current performance of the system? Have you done a rigorous root cause analysis for this performance?

- Is it clear what kinds of performance improvements the innovation is trying to make?

- Is there a clear hypothesis about the leverage points in the system? Are there examples of what it takes to move these kinds of leverage points from other systems?

- Can the innovation hypothesis be expressed clearly and succinctly (two pages, not 20)?

- How much "sweat equity" have you put into your innovation hypothesis? How long have you been working on trying to solve this problem/opportunity?

- Is the design of the innovation biased by any fuzzy values that obscure your ability to see the facts clearly?

- If the innovation were to be unsuccessful, would you start working on another leverage point? How wedded are you to your perceived "solution"?

E. Prototyping Questions to Wrestle With

For most prototyping, whatever the type of innovation, there are a number of inescapable questions for the innovation network to consider:

- What is the minimum scale at which the innovation can be prototyped?

- Which design features of the innovation are most prone to "early design lock-in" that precludes easy adaptation later on? How can these be avoided or minimized?

- What are the economics of the prototyping process going to be? Are you set up to accurately understand your costs? Will they tell you anything about the economics of the finished innovation?

- Who are the "lead users" you are going to be working with? Are they representative of the broader user population? Are you structured to get honest feedback from them?

- How will you do "knowledge management" at this stage and make sure you learn as you go?

- How will you avoid premature publicity or marketing on the innovation?

- What will the transition from prototyping to the operational stage look like?

About the Authors

Peter Plastrik has been a journalist, state government official, social entrepreneur, network builder and consultant, and is coauthor of six other books. He is a cofounder of the Innovation Network for Communities. He was born in Paris, grew up in New York City, raised

Peter Plastrik

a family in Michigan, and lives alongside Puget Sound with his wife Deb, their pugs, fruit trees, and the Big Garden—near their two sons and their families.

Madeleine Beaubien Taylor is a social anthropologist and the co-founder Network Impact. She works with funders and practitioners on strategy, program development, and assessment with a primary focus on social impact networks. A native of Montreal, Madeleine spent

Madeleine Taylor

a decade as a researcher and filmmaker in Mozambique before moving to the US. She and her family divide their time between Brazil, the US, and Canada.

John Cleveland has worked as an executive in state government, a Continuous Quality Improvement leader in higher education, a strategy consultant in manufacturing, and a leader in urban climate change. He is a cofounder of the Innovation Network for Communities.

John Cleveland

Born in Virginia, he grew up in remote Alaskan villages, went to high school outside of Boston, raised a family in Michigan, and resides in the White Mountain region of New Hampshire. He enjoys skiing, hiking, and biking, and with his wife Michelle gets great pleasure from their five children and eight grandchildren.

More at www.in4c.net and www.networkimpact.org

Index

A

adoption, 33–35, 103, 121, 127, 144, 146–148, 160, 163, 192
Ascend at the Aspen Institute, 21, 77, 134

B

Batiste, Jon, 205
Beebe, Spencer, 8, 65, 169, 178
Bernstein, Scott, 8, 94, 128, 132
Biophilic Cities Network, 21, 86
Bourland, Dana, 8, 74, 171, 202
broker, 19, 132, 184–187, 201–202, 251

C

Campaign for Free College Tuition, 21, 25, 33, 46–47, 49, 64, 80, 86, 122,
    143–144, 146
Carbon Neutral Cities Alliance, 21, 86, 123–124, 183
Cohen, Gary, 8, 53, 58, 93, 130, 206–207
Community Independence Initiative, 21, 94, 96
Connecting to Change the World, 12, 49, 166–167, 188–189, 191, 199
Curtis, Jennie, 8, 71

D

Deiglmeier, Kriss and Greco, Amanda, 15, 19, 91, 108, 119, 125, 131, 153, 198
distributed control, 171–172, 176

E

ecosystems, 16, 273
Energy Efficiency for All (EEFA), 21, 75, 87

F

fields, 47, 98–99, 115, 120–123, 125–127, 134, 136, 139–140, 142–143, 153, 159, 164,
    168, 170, 196, 283
Financial Health Network, 9, 21, 128, 132, 149, 159–162, 169, 177, 185, 199
Fox, Radhika, 8, 27, 31, 73, 93
Friedman, Bob, 8, 83, 90, 97, 100, 109, 144, 205

G

Gargani, John and McLean, Robert, 115
Good SAM, 17, 21
governments, 46–47, 50, 54, 86–87, 96, 109, 111, 115, 120–123, 125–126, 143, 146, 153, 164, 168, 170, 184, 191, 292
Guest, Bill, 8, 36, 49, 55, 69, 73, 125, 189

H

Hara, Mami, 8, 25–26, 31, 139
Hargadon, Andrew, 14, 23, 116, 118, 141, 144, 149–151, 168, 179, 186–187, 190, 193, 200, 202, 295
Health Care Without Harm, 21, 59–61, 86, 93, 120–122, 130–131, 136, 150, 161, 201, 206–207
High Line Network, 8, 21, 157–158, 161, 166
Hill, Chrystie, 8, 180

I

Individual Development Accounts, 21, 85, 115, 136, 144
International Step by Step Association, 21, 137

J

Jansveld, Asima, 8, 157

K

Kambhampati, Sandhya, 8, 41, 44, 73, 142
Klaus, Sarah, 8, 137

L

Lackey, Katy, 8, 162
learner, 199, 315
Lugo, Luis, 8, 40

M

markets, 18, 37, 46–47, 66, 108, 111, 115, 120–123, 125–129, 131, 146, 153, 160, 164, 168, 170, 196, 321
McFoy, Oluwole, 9, 27, 29, 30, 189
Meadows, Donnella, 54-56, 58, 64, 79, 235
Mensah, Lisa, 9, 63, 100, 131, 144, 160, 169
Miller, Mauricio Lim, 9, 94–95
morphing networks, 149
Mosle, Anne, 9, 134, 163
Musa, Muhammad and Rodin, Judith, 83

N

Narayan, Shweta, 9, 206–207
Native Women Lead, 183
Nebraska Community Foundation, 21, 159, 161, 165, 172, 175, 186, 199, 206
network structures, 166
networks of networks, 21, 47–48, 155–157, 159, 161, 163, 165–167, 169, 171, 173, 175, 177–179, 181, 193

O

OpenNews, 8–9, 21, 25, 41–47, 50, 73, 87, 98, 121, 134, 142, 150, 179, 188, 194–196, 335
operational stage, 105
Opportunity Finance Network, 22, 63, 101, 121, 131, 160, 169
Owens, Erika, 9, 87, 98, 142, 194

P

Partin, Johanna, 9, 124, 183
practices, 15–16, 25, 29–30, 37, 40–41, 46–47, 49, 59, 67–68, 73, 77, 80–81, 86, 88, 90, 102, 105, 110–111, 120–121, 126–127, 132–134, 137–143, 150, 158, 183, 185–186, 189, 346
products, 13, 46–47, 49, 74, 80, 88, 91, 99, 103, 105–106, 108, 110–111, 119, 126–133, 143, 160, 181, 349
Project ECHO, 22, 67–68, 176
prototype, 91–92, 100, 102, 104, 350

R

RE-AMP, 22, 72–73, 78, 81, 87
Roanhorse, Olivia, 9, 76
Ross, Doug, 9, 32–33, 74, 87, 94

S

Salmon Nation, 8, 22, 65–67, 161, 164, 166, 169, 178
scale up, 8, 12, 14, 16, 18–20, 22, 24, 26, 28, 30, 32, 34, 36, 38, 40, 42, 44, 46, 48, 50, 54, 56, 58, 60, 62, 64, 66–68, 70, 72, 74, 76, 78, 80, 82, 84, 86, 88, 90, 92, 94, 96, 98, 100, 102, 104, 106, 108, 110, 112, 114, 116, 118–120, 122, 124, 126–128, 130–132, 134, 136, 138, 140, 142, 144, 146, 148, 150, 152, 156, 158, 160, 162, 164, 166, 168, 170, 172, 174, 176, 178, 180, 184, 186, 188, 190, 192, 194, 196, 198, 200, 202, 206, 244
scales, 45, 47, 50, 66, 115, 117, 119–123, 125, 127, 129, 131, 133, 135, 137, 139, 141, 143, 145, 147, 149, 151, 153, 155, 362–363
Scharmer, C. Otto, 53, 80
Seelos, Christian, 57, 79
Seelos, Christian and Mair, Johanna, 20, 65, 70, 78, 92, 119, 187, 190
Simonson, Emily, 9, 28, 140
Sims, Marjorie, 9, 77, 142

social innovation networks, 8, 11, 13, 15–16, 19–20, 22, 24–25, 45, 48–50, 78, 88, 91,
    97, 112, 115, 120, 122, 126, 145, 149–151, 153, 155–158, 162, 168, 178, 183–187,
    189, 191, 193, 195, 197, 199–201, 203, 206–207
stage gates, 91, 112
story teller, 184–185, 196–197
strategic hubs, 47, 168–169
strategist, 184–185, 191–193, 375
systems, 11–13, 15–18, 23–25, 31, 36–37, 40–41, 43, 45–51, 53–63, 65–67, 69–75,
    77–81, 84, 88–89, 106–107, 112–113, 120, 122, 125–130, 135, 141–143, 152–153,
    155–156, 158–159, 161–163, 165, 170, 179–180, 183, 188, 190, 198, 201–202,
    205–207, 378
systems change, 12, 16–17, 25, 49, 51, 55, 57, 60, 62, 65–66, 78–80, 106, 127, 153,
    155, 159, 161, 163, 188, 190, 202, 205, 207

T
Talent Innovation Network of West Michigan, 22, 25, 36
Tescher, Jennifer, 9, 128, 149, 160, 185, 199
The Innovator's DNA, 14, 98–99, 183

U
Ullman, Maggie, 9, 184
US Green Building Council, 22
US Water Alliance, 8–9, 22, 25–26, 46–47, 49–50, 57, 73, 80, 86, 93–94, 102, 106, 112,
    120–122, 134, 139–142, 148, 152, 160–161, 163, 166, 169, 179, 187, 189, 199

W
weaver, 184–185, 188–191, 195, 397
Wei, Sisi, 9, 44, 73, 142, 188
Weigert, Karen, 9, 116, 119, 143
Welsh, Ben, 9, 42
Wheatley, Margaret, 7, 155, 399
Winograd, Morley, 9, 32, 50, 64, 73, 126, 144

Y
Yost, Jeff, 9, 165, 172, 186, 199, 202, 206

Made in the USA
Middletown, DE
25 October 2022

13477884R00141